Contents

List of Tables

The New Politics of Welfare

An Agenda for the 1990s?

Edited by

Michael McCarthy

MACMILLAN

First published 1989 by
THE MACMILLAN PRESS LTD
Houndmills, Basingstoke, Hampshire RG21 2XS
and London
Companies and representatives
throughout the world

ISBN 0–333–47156–3 hardcover
ISBN 0–333–47157–1 paperback

A catalogue record for this book is available
from the British Library.

12 11 10 9 8 7 6 5 4
03 02 01 00 99 98 97 96 95

Printed in Hong Kong

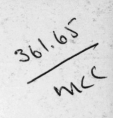
The New Politics of Welfare

List of Figures

Acknowledgements

I wish to record my thanks to a small but valued group of friends and colleagues who helped bring some long-held ideas and arguments into focus and fruition in this book. Particular thanks are due to Jo Campling, who, as ever, gave me her time and wise counsel and supported my endeavours throughout. My thanks are also due to Stephen Kennedy and Victoria Yogman at Macmillan, who not only liked the outline of the book but encouraged its path to publication. Special thanks are due to Keith Povey for his skill and help in sharpening the text and to Ann Lowe who helped with typing and progress-chasing.

Above all, I must thank my wife, Rosalind Barnes, without whose support and encouragement this endeavour could never have succeeded.

MICHAEL McCARTHY

Notes on the Contributors

Judith Allsop is a Principal Lecturer in Social Policy in the Social Sciences Department, South Bank Polytechnic. She has written a number of books and articles on health policy including *Health Policy and the NHS* and *The Emperor's New Clothes: Family Practitioner Committees in the 1980s*. She is currently a member of a District, and a Special, Health Authority in London and is researching user grievances and medical regulation.

Miriam David is Head of the Department of Social Sciences at South Bank Polytechnic. Her research interests are in educational policy and family policy. She has published widely in these areas, in both Britain and North America. Her key publications are *The State, the Family and Education* and *For the Children's Sake: Making Child Care more than Women's Business* (with Caroline New). She is currently doing research on an evaluation of the implementation of the Education Reform Act, 1988, particularly on the changing role of parents in educational decision-making. She is also writing a book on the relations between families and schools.

Martin Knapp is Deputy Director of the Personal Social Services Research Unit and Reader in the Economics of Social Policy, University of Kent at Canterbury. His current work includes evaluation of care in the community for former long-stay hospital residents, numerous studies of child welfare services and interventions for young offenders, and a study of the roles of the private and voluntary sectors in social and health care provision. He is author of *The Economics of Social Care*.

Ruth Lister is Professor of Applied Social Studies at the University of Bradford. From 1971 to 1987 she worked for the Child Poverty Action Group, from 1979 as Director. She has written and spoken extensively on the issues of poverty and income maintenance. Her publications include *Supplementary Benefit Rights* and *Welfare Benefits*. She received an honorary doctorate from the University of Manchester in 1987.

Michael McCarthy is Regional Director of Retirement Security Limited, a company specialising in the development of very sheltered private housing for elderly people. He was previously Assistant Secretary of the British Association of Social Workers and before that Head of Research of a major trade union. From 1975 to 1983 he lectured in British politics at Trent Polytechnic. He has written and contributed to a number of books and academic journals on politics and social policy and from 1985 to 1988 he wrote the social policy column of *Social Work Today*.

Molly Meacher is the Director of Action Trust and Campaign for Work and company secretary for Workforce Publications, publishers of the *Signing On* newspaper for unemployed people. She is also a Mental Health Act Commissioner and Council member of the Family Policy Studies Centre. She has served on the Executive Committee of the Child Poverty Action Group and is the author of *Scrutiny in the Welfare*, co-author of *To Him Who Hath*, and editor of *New Methods of Mental Health Care*.

Rod Morgan is Senior Lecturer in Criminology and Director of the Centre for Criminal Justice, University of Bath. He is currently doing research on the Implementation of the Police and Criminal Evidence Act 1984, and on lay visitors to police stations. His books include *The Future of the Prison System*, *Prisons and Accountability* and *Coming to Terms with Policing*.

Nick Raynsford was member of Parliament for Fulham, 1986–7. He is best known for his work and expertise in the housing field. Before becoming an MP he was Director of SHAC for ten years and played a leading role in the campaign for legislation to extend homeless people's rights. Since the 1987 General Election he has been working as a housing consultant.

Alan Walker is Professor of Social Policy and Chairperson of the Department of Sociological Studies, University of Sheffield. He has written extensively on the subject of community care, social policy, social gerontology and disability. He is editor of *Community Care*, *Ageing and Social Policy*, and author of *Social Policy* and *The Caring Relationship* (with Hazel Qureshi).

Introduction:
The Boundaries of Welfare

MICHAEL McCARTHY

'One of the most damaging aspects of the myth that the welfare state was created whole by Labour after 1945, is that it was also created perfect: the ultimate, total, flawless welfare state. So that ever afterwards suggested change of even the most necessary and obvious sort has been greeted with howls of outrage about 'dismantling and destroying'. This is a ridiculous state of affairs. 1987 is very different from 1947 ... Life has changed, needs have changed, people's expectations have changed, and it is necessary for what we call our 'welfare state' to change as well.' (John Moore, MP, Secretary of State for Social Services, 26 September 1987, in a speech to a Conservative Political Centre Conference.)

'Our country's relative decline is not inevitable. We in the Conservative Party think we can reverse it, not because we think we have all the answers but because we think we have the one that matters most. We want to work with the grain of human nature, helping people to restore that self-reliance and self-confidence which are the basis of personal responsibility and national success.' (*The Conservative Manifesto, 1979.*)

Even before she had descended from the hustings with victory in the 1979 General Election firmly in her grasp, Margaret Thatcher's impact upon the political topography of Britain at large and upon the contours of British Conservatism in particular was already passing into the folklore of her party. Divided, factionalised,

1

embittered by the failures and contradictions of the Heath years, and deeply uncertain about its prospects for government, the 'developing leadership' of Mrs Thatcher was seen as the one bright spot in 'the odium theologicum which now blights the life of the Tory party and which the party scarcely troubles to conceal from the public' (T.E. Utley in Cowling (ed.) 1978).

The habitual loyalty shown to Conservative leaders by the parliamentary party was still in doubt in the spring of 1979 (and that of the first Thatcher Cabinet for some time after that) and the Party's instinct for self-preservation remained blunted by the recent political in-fighting. But with the cloak of victory about her Mrs Thatcher could now begin to drive home something which had become deeply unfashionable in the Heath years – the unashamed case for capitalism. Utley described Margaret Thatcher in 1978 as a 'wholly English Conservative' speaking the language of liberty, with a firm belief in individual freedom and an unshakeable respect for institutions and tradition. This powerful combination of practical good sense and an unswerving belief in personal standards and a common morality was keenly displayed in a determination to press the virtues of competition and self-help upon an alleged 'divided and disillusioned people' (*The Conservative Manifesto 1979*) and to promote acceptance of the idea that freedom and responsibility were indivisible.

The means of expelling the malaise of the present lay in the past. How appropriate, therefore, that the 1979 manifesto should open with a line that neatly juxtaposed the values of the past and virtues of continuity with a vigorous belief in modernity also. 'This election is about the future of Britain – a great country which seems to have lost its way.' The part played by the new Conservatism would thus be restorative, almost medicinal. The remedial and curative metaphor was quickly exhausted. The sick man of Europe would be rapidly restored to a rude Victorian health; the British disease would be cured; an ailing economy would be revived; lame ducks would walk again. It is deeply ironic that while Mrs Thatcher's governments were giving a kiss of life of sorts to some sectors of British industry, the very services traditionally associated with the nation's health and welfare – the NHS, the personal social services and social security – were, in the views of many, being crippled and asphyxiated.

The manifesto was clear that Britain was a shadow of its former self and that success in the future lay in restoring the past. We were reminded of 'the values we used to share' and 'the success and prosperity we once took for granted'. It went on to describe Britain as a society on the brink of disintegration and complained pointedly of a recent political past characterised by the politics of envy, the discouragement of wealth creation, and the legacy of a weak economy created 'by enlarging the role of the state and diminishing the role of the individual'. Together, these had 'crippled the enterprise and effort on which a prosperous country with improving social services depends'.

Britain in 1979 was portrayed as a failure – its values eroded, its economy disabled, its public services a greedy leech on a faltering and anaemic Exchequer. The inheritance was a poor one – or so it was alleged. After all, the economic miracle would not be wrought on a healthy body politic. This portrayal has since proved to be a successful and skilful one in crude electoral terms. It became the departure point for a far-reaching and imaginative process of desocialisation both structurally and attitudinally. Services and institutions were not simply diminished or dismantled *per se*, the very philosophical values and consumer expectations that underpinned them were themselves narrowed, lowered and disarmed to make practical change possible. Major social problems have not been resolved; they have, rather, been 're-defined' to fit the resources available and have therefore become 'manageable'. Nowhere, surely, can this have been more clearly or cynically illustrated than in the breathtaking flow of creative accountancy that massaged unemployment into submission below the three million mark.

Today, the 'bureau-speak' of value for money, effective prioritisation and better use of existing resources look less and less consistent with the government's professed intention 'to make services more responsive to the needs of the consumer' (DHSS, Cmnd 249, November 1987). This point has been most forcefully made by Conservative MPs apprehensive about new departures in welfare policy generally. We should not be too surprised by this. The 1979 manifesto did, after all, warn that anyone who searched in its text for 'lavish promise' or 'detailed commitments' would 'look in vain'.

A watershed in social policy

The General Election of 1979 is now believed by many practitioners and students of social policy to have marked a watershed in the development of the post-war welfare state and significantly to have called into question the principles, assumptions and value framework that had underpinned much of British social policy for the three previous decades. Two immediate challenges were posed to the welfare consensus. First, the new Conservative government brought with it, as all contributors to this book show, a determined economic regime and a reaffirmation of principles of self-help and value for money. Secondly, this was bolstered by and embroidered with an uncompromising social morality. The social and political consensus which had forged and sustained the post-war welfare state – the so-called mainstream Butskellite political tradition – came to be seen as the cause of and not the solution to Britain's social and economic malaise. Consensus was disparaged and then turned on its head.

These sentiments found increasing expression in the language of social policy in the 1980s. At the centre of a debate that ranges across social security, education and health to the personal social services, employment, law and order and housing, a familiar litany developed to the point where broad slogans such as 'value for money', 'deserving' and 'undeserving', 'nil cost remit', 'better use of existing resources', 'genuine need' 'self-help' and 'freedom and responsibility' were elevated to the status of key policy dictates. Occasionally, they were mistaken for policy ends in themselves. They are to be found in each of the major areas of social policy reviewed in this book.

The welfare state has become a moveable feast. The Conservatives have demonstrated more graphically than ever before that there is no single or uniform ideology of care. They have ensured also that practice should swiftly follow principle. And, even where they have sometimes momentarily appeared politically and electorally vulnerable, as for example on their care record in the last ten days of the 1987 General Election campaign when Labour seized the initiative on the NHS, a broad wave of economically-centred support has swept up behind them.

There are many among the ten million or so electors who voted Conservative at the last election who believe that the welfare state *is* just the sort of massive, profligate and impersonal bureaucracy that ought to offer more choice about where and how their children are schooled; where and how their elderly relatives are cared for, where and how best to utilise health care resources; and where and how best to make arrangements to support poor families and the unemployed while, of course, ensuring some measure of self-help and personal responsibility is fostered (if not imposed) and while retaining the incentive to work. Some have already reached the conclusion that the old-style universalist welfare state – providing services to all and funded overwhelmingly and directly from the public purse – will no longer do the job.

There are many and diverse reasons for this, some quite sophisticated, some rather less so. A number of standards have been energetically borne aloft: more choice, more competition, more efficient services, more freedom from debilitating taxation. There is, above all, the alleged dark side of the welfare state, apparently untrammelled in its capacity to induce indolence, passivity, dependency and atrophy. When John Moore spoke in September 1987 of an all-embracing and all-providing state with its theme of global care, he suggested that many of us were unaware of how sinister this can sound. In 1979 the Conservative manifesto had, after all, spoken of the enlargement of the role of the state as 'diminishing the role of the individual'. It portrayed the welfare state as discouraging growth and personal enterprise. The Health Service was painted as monolithic and immensely bureaucratic. The social security system was drawn as so complicated that even ministry officials did not understand it and as failing to bring effective help to those in greatest need, while discouraging the will to work. The broad canvas of the rule of law had been perilously stretched in the 1970s by, it said, a lack of respect, the undermining of authority, weak deterrents and perverse sentencing.

It was, then, entirely consistent for the Secretary of State for Social Services to seek to assure and remind the electorate after the 1987 election that 'the shape and pattern of the welfare measures enacted in those years too often had the effect of increasing people's dependence on the state and its attendant bureaucrats, and of reducing the power and control they might have hoped to gain over their own lives' (Moore, Conservative Central Office, 26 September 1987). Sitting in the audience, one might have been forgiven for concluding that the welfare state had already been consigned, intellectually at least, to the dustbin of history.

Of course, it has not. Rather, we are witnessing in the 1990s the emergence of a different welfare state – one that more closely mirrors the social, economic and ideological values of the modern Conservative Party – but one in which, nevertheless, the state does and will continue to have a part to play, if more reduced and constrained than hitherto. There are some creative and positive virtues in this, not least the opportunity to throw some new ideas into the ring. The most important truth to come to terms with is that the debates on the volume of service provision in the public sector may now be a relic, rather than a dynamic, in modern Tory social policy.

Defining the boundaries of welfare

There is, however, one element in the government's blueprint for the new welfare that it has chosen to significantly, perhaps deliberately, understate – its real effects upon the large body of consumers who have been dependent on the Beveridge welfare state for long periods and who find it difficult, and traumatic to adapt to the practical implementation of some of the ideas for diversity, pluralism and self-help in welfare that now proliferate. These are likely to include people with a severe physical disability; poor families where the head of the household is chronically sick or long-term unemployed and without skills; the recidivist petty offender; mentally ill people leaving large institutions to seek appropriate housing and care in the community; and young people with families crushed by a lack of employment and housing opportunities. It is instructive to recall Francis Pym's observation, borne of considerable experience as a leading Conservative front-bencher in Mrs Thatcher's early period of office, that 'Even in these materialistic times, governments are not merely Directorates of Economic Policy. Most economic theories have damaging social consequences if pushed to their extremes, which is why economic purism is dangerous to governments' (Pym, 1985).

It is, however, partly for this reason that ministers have sought to 'redefine' the social problems confronting them in such a way that reformulation diminishes their size and complexity. Existing resources consequently appear more generous, or at least more adequate, than before problem redefinition took place. Thus a major political crisis is transformed into an essentially administrative and manageable exercise. The explosive growth of single payments, passionately attributed to a significant growth in poverty, was dissipated by the introduction of a controversial Social Fund designed as much as anything to 'manage' the problem of poverty by using control over income maintenance to limit expectations and costs. Place enough obstacles in the claimant's path and there is a reasonable chance he/she will disappear from view, unable and unequipped to clear the new and complex hurdles. However, as we will show, a problem 'managed' may simply be a problem displaced, and those same claimants are now redirecting their needs and problems to housing and social services agencies and to charities. Poverty also provides a fine example of the other key element of problem redefinition – avoiding, where possible, mention of the problem altogether. It is interesting that many senior ministers do not refer to poverty at all, as if they do not recognise its existence or, if they do, they do so by some other expression. Elevating poverty to the status of a major political issue would tarnish the economic miracle the Government is bent on marketing to the rest of the OECD. The Prime Minister's own defence that more and more money is being diverted to meet the needs of the least well off is only superficially true.

As Ruth Lister shows in Chapter 4, when examined closely the evidence of public expenditure on social security during Mrs Thatcher's terms of office does not serve the Conservatives well. More people are now in poverty than at any other time in the post-war period and while in aggregate they command more resources than before, as families and individuals they have become steadily worse off under Mrs Thatcher's governments.

It is necessary to dwell on poverty in this way because it is a striking characteristic of the modern welfare state – some would say its chief dynamic – and it features closely in each of the contributions to this book. If ability to pay continues to gather strength as a chief buttress of the new welfare then the social, economic and moral divisions that Mrs Thatcher perceived in 1979 will persist and entrench and her promise to unite a divided and disillusioned people will ring hollow. Her Government has yet to address, still less overcome the central paradox of its policy that in allowing poverty to take the unremitting hold it has over a very large section of the population, perhaps as many as eleven million people, it continues to sustain the chief dynamic of the old welfare state that in turn leads to the dependency culture it is so critical of. Redefining the problem, massaging the statistics or diversifying the sources of welfare without extra resources will not succeed in thwarting this paradox in the long term.

A policy debate for the 1990s

It is for this reason that we attempt to review and assess the principal developments in key areas of British social policy in the last decade which continue to shape the face of the welfare state in the 1990s. Each of the contributors identifies the pathway leading to policy development from 1979. Each goes some way towards demonstrating that present initiatives have at least some roots in the recent past. In short, what is so often disdainfully referred to as 'Thatcherism' has not emerged entirely unexpectedly or without some historical framework. Some, moreover, point to significant creative and lasting initiatives instigated in the field of social policy in the period since 1979. Some of the cobwebs *have* been cleared away, bureaucracy *has* been trimmed and made more accountable and the prospects for diversity and choice in certain quarters of the welfare state *are* more imaginative and realistic than for some time.

The intention here is to establish what can be learned from the debates and policy shifts of the last decade and how this learning process might enrich and guide future patterns of social policy into the next. We begin in Chapter 1 with the personal social services (PSS). This chapter serves the additional purpose of setting the context for the book as a whole, commencing with a brief review of how taxation and the requirements of economic policy have shaped and had an impact upon social policy. Michael McCarthy sets out the principal challenges confronting the personal social services, not least those of demography, access to services and resources, and the continuing tensions experienced in upholding the civilising influences of the welfare state against a determined

Conservative drive to define the limits to welfare. He draws out the traditional goals and values of the PSS and sets these against the increasingly blurred boundaries between cash, care and capitalism. McCarthy argues that the personal social services, both in structural and in policy terms, are at a watershed and face in the 1990s a further period of change and challenge. Confronted by policy change that favours pluralism and competition in service provision; challenged to reassess and reformulate partnerships with the private, voluntary and informal care sectors; stretched and overburdened, and sometimes lost in a labrynthine riddle of statutes and codes of practice which sharpen the conflict between the roles of enabler and guardian on the one hand and of social control on the other: the personal social services are already caught up in a new era of welfare that owes as much to the mores and values of the market as it does to social service and care.

The NHS also faces uncertainty about its future. Caught between rising expectations and declining real levels of resources, the Government has baulked at the prospect of any major new investment of public funds and the NHS has caught a severe cold that threatens to deteriorate into something far worse. The Conservatives have for some time acknowledged the NHS as their particular Achilles heel. In 1986, with a general election still two years away, both the Prime Minister herself and her party chairman recognised the party's vulnerability on health and embarked on a determined public relations drive to demonstrate the success of the hospital building programme, the growing 'rationality' and economies imposed upon drug and equipment purchase and the apparent rise in the numbers of consumers using the NHS. Ministers have since boasted of a 20 per cent real increase in expenditure on the NHS since 1978, of which some £800 million represented capital spending on the hospital building programme and have continued to detail a range of health care, expenditure and patient statistics to support the Government's case that the NHS has improved and strengthened under its aegis.

Yet for all this, the Conservatives found themselves most vulnerable at the hustings in 1987 precisely on their treatment of the NHS. The fact that Britain spent only 5.9 per cent of its GDP on the National Health Service – placing it some way behind all but two of her EEC partners – seemed less of an issue to the electorate than the less tangible but far more passionately felt concern that the NHS was simply not safe in Tory hands. Tensions within the Conservative Party itself increased with the publication of Leon Brittan's proposal for *A New Deal For Health Care* which called for greater efficiency, more contracting out, an extension of 'hotel charges', a £1 fee for a visit to a GP. Also advocated were abolition of existing national insurance contributions and their replacement by a new two-tier scheme sustaining the NHS at a lower level of service provision alongside a greatly expanded private sector. The announcement that the Prime Minister herself was to chair a high-level review of the NHS starting in February 1988 was significant both for its timing and political weight and for the gross overdependence of the review on *economic* rather than healthcare terms of reference.

It had much to consider – the introduction of a health stamp; reform of the NHS structure into Health Management Units; consumer sovereignty and the enhancement of choice; tax relief on insurance premiums; the creation of internal markets in the NHS; the costs and future direction of nurse training; and vouchers for healthcare. Six months later, the Government opted for caution. The outcome of the review was more to do with adjusting and adding on to the existing structure and practices of the NHS than replacing them wholesale. For many Conservatives the outcome of the review has been disappointing and cautious. For others such caution may help them to retain their marginal seats at the next election. Public and professinal reaction to Kenneth Clark's White Paper *Working for Patient's* may yet prove bloody *and* decisive.

In Chapter 2 – Health – Judy Allsop picks her way through the healthcare minefield, identifying en route the most significant areas of pressure now directed at the NHS. She examines Conservative attempts to curtail the power of the health professions and to trim back a major bureaucracy with a perceived vested interest in NHS growth. In particular, she draws our attention to the shift in management style in the NHS, to the imposition of a new culture post-Griffiths, and to the adoption of business and commercial practices and values in healthcare. She argues that health policy in the 1990s will be firmly dominated by issues concerned with the management of the NHS and that the structural causes of ill-health and the need for preventive strategies remain firmly off the political agenda. She concludes that the NHS is being deliberately underfunded to create the need for and to stimulate the development of a private health care market.

The development of the private market is also, as Nick Raynsford illustrates in Chapter 3 – Housing – both a major feature and an overriding goal of Conservative housing policy in the period since 1979. The manifesto of that year had astutely perceived the electoral gains to be wrought from an extension of home ownership. 'Homes of Our Own' became a rallying cry at the polls and rapidly assumed a wider significance in the general policy clamour to assist and strengthen family life. For party managers, an extension of home ownership was seen as an unrivalled opportunity to increase the electorate's stake in Conservatism. In the short term, at least, the sale of council houses proved to be an electoral coup. Nick Raynsford views 1979 as a major watershed in British housing policy, marking an abrupt end to a relatively durable, if rather fragile, consensus. He argues that 'instead of a twin-tracked approach, involving the co-expansion of public rented housing and owner-occupation, 'the government has increasingly made clear its preference for private sector provision and its hostility to public sector housing'.

Warnings about the shortcomings in Conservative housing policy were posted as early as 1983 by the House of Commons Environment Committee which protested that this amounted to 'a policy of cuts and no more'. That view was painfully confirmed in 1985 when housing investment once more took the brunt of public expenditure restraint in the local authority sector; when the numbers of homeless soared; when the pro-portion of the housing stock requiring major renovation and repair reached a six-year high; when over two million dwellings were either unfit for habitation, lacking in basic amenities or required significant and expensive modernisation; and when it cost more to place homeless families in squalid bed and breakfast accommodation than it did to build them new homes.

Nick Raynsford examines the sources of this crisis and draws attention to swingeing real cuts in investment allocations to local authorities and to additional restrictions which have pre-vented them from using their own resources – including capital receipts from sales – to the full to provide new housing stock, though the latter is now under partial review. He notes, bluntly, that 'successive government ministers have made it clear that they see no role for local authorities as providers of new homes'.

Yet, while deliberately cutting a swathe through public sector programmes, the Conservatives have given unremitting encouragement to the expansion of owner-occupation and to the private rented sector. The casualty figures have inevitably risen steeply as a result – over one hundred thousand households were accepted as homeless by local authorities at the time of the last election and the costs of bed and breakfast provision for homeless families have been sent soaring.

Nick Raynsford addresses the dangers of council housing becoming a residual sector and the reduced prospects for the tenants who remain. He relates those prospects to the increasing socioeconomic divisions fostered by Government fiscal policy and questions the morality and absurdity of subsidy and tax relief for the well-off while so many people are caught in a warp of poverty, unemployment, poor-housing and ill-health. He already sees in the 1990s the patterns of the 1980s repeated and with them a further entrenchment of the 'increasingly stark divide between owner-occupation and public rented housing'.

The theme of poverty amidst wealth is developed further by Ruth Lister in Chapter 4 – Social Security. She reminds us that the first three Conservative manifestos – 1979, 1983, 1987 – have avoided mention of the term poverty altogether. Instead, there has been an emphasis on simplifying welfare, restoring incentives to work, targeting existing resources more effectively and tackling fraud and abuse. By incorporating each in the same general thesis on poverty, the Conservatives have sharpened to a fine edge the practise of 'blaming the victim'. Thus, poverty is frequently seen as the result of an unwillingness to work or to fend for oneself; it is a matter of indolence and preferred dependence. Hence the continuing emphasis on freedom and responsibility, self-help, and the propagation of distinctions between the 'deserving' and 'undeserving' poor that threads a path through modern Conservative social policy.

The poor have not shared in the rising prosperity of Britain in the period since Margaret Thatcher came to power. By 1987, some 7 million people were dependent on supplementary benefit compared with less than 4 million when the Conservatives came to power in 1979. While the rest of the population have enjoyed a rising standard of living, the numbers dependent on supplementary benefit/income support have almost doubled and the real value of that support has been eroded. It is this disturbing increase, in both the numbers of poor and the sheer scale of poverty in Britain after three successive Thatcher governments – and at a time when other advanced industrial nations have actively canvassed a replication of the British 'economic miracle' within their own electorates – which has caused the chorus of disapproval against the 1986 Act and against the social fund in particular.

Ruth Lister draws close attention to the Government's overriding aim to control social security spending and to achieve a social security system that is consistent with its overall objectives for the economy, observing that a sustained attempt was made to create an atmosphere of crisis around social security spending. The 1985 Social Security Green Paper made clear that social security was a millstone impeding economic growth and a determined effort was made to create a sense of crisis and generate public pressure for cuts. Even child benefit, that most universal of benefits, has, she notes, been and continues to be the subject of great uncertainty.

The Government's overall strategy has been a punitive and divisive one. Promotion of the 'less eligibility' principle, says Lister, has become a central tenet of policy. There has been a continuing, often damaging and spurious emphasis on fraud and abuse that has produced a hue and cry out of all proportion to the size of the problem. There has been the startling growth of what she terms 'DIY social security' and in the DHSS exporting its responsibilities to employers. We have also seen a pronounced shift in the direction of the concept, and soon the practice also, of 'Workfare' as the extraordinary means by which the Government can seemingly fulfil its wish to promote financial independence.

Throughout the last decade, the terms of welfare and those on which social security entitlement were founded, have been placed in question and redefined. The social fund became the ultimate test for proving the virtues of problem redefinition as a means of controlling welfare expenditure. Meanwhile, for the unemployed, who represent the major group in poverty, 'the continued emphasis on work incentives and "voluntary" unemployment has constituted a classic example of blaming the victim'. Sadly, observes Lister, 'it does not seem to have had much impact on public attitudes'.

The controversy of work incentives and the tendency to blame the victim feature closely in Chapter 5 also – Employment. Molly Meacher usefully juxtaposes the social and economic reasoning that has characterised the debate on employment and charges, as happened with social security, that the Conservatives had reached the conclusion before coming to power that the country could not afford full employment. She, like most contributors to this book, views 1979 and the election of the first Thatcher government as ending a post-war all-party consensus – in this case, in favour of full-employment. The macroeconomic, monetary and fiscal policies that had hitherto been used to control unemployment by sustaining sufficient demand in the economy were turned on their heads: 'Mass unemployment became the central weapon with which to tackle inflation.'

The casualties of this policy have suffered on two counts – loss of jobs on the one hand and government (and public) rejection on the other of their own efforts to find alternative employment. The value of shifting responsibility onto the 'victim' was clear from the outset. The 1979 manifesto spoke of 'restoring the will to work' and attributed much of Britain's economic malaise and its own overblown social security system to the unwillingness of many people to find a job. It made no bones about the reception such people could expect from a Conservative government: 'The rules about the unemployed accepting available jobs will be reinforced and we shall act more vigorously against fraud and abuse.' Shortly after, the Secretary of State for Employment chided people to 'get on their bike'. Sometime later a Secretary of State for Social Services spoke of the wellbeing of individuals as being 'best protected and promoted when they are helped to be independent, to use their talents to take care of themselves and their families'. All three statements amount to the same thing, if differently put.

This 'blaming the victim' syndrome has, as Molly Meacher shows, produced punitive policies towards unemployed people that include reductions in benefit, the introduction of tough 'availability for work tests', the undermining of their rights and their labelling as 'work-shy'. There is now the prospect of benefit being withheld entirely from those refusing jobs as 'Workfare' looms larger and nearer. Generally, they have been marginalised and excluded from the new and aggressive portrayal of Britain as a country only fit for 'producers'.

Molly Meacher questions the effectiveness of current employment schemes and examines the underlying flaws in the Government's ongoing efforts at problem redefinition in the field of unemployment which have resulted in successive changes in the way the unemployment figures are 'massaged' downwards. She draws attention to the knock-on effects and cost of unemployment to the other areas of the welfare state, notably the health service, social security and the personal social services, and concludes with a case for 'significant policy reversals' which would place full employment firmly at the centre of the political agenda and offer the prospect for beneficial social and economic change.

A recurring theme throughout the contributions here is that of 'freedom and choice'. Alongside a determined drive to improve alleged poor standards in our state schools, they have become a central feature of Conservative education policy. However, as Miriam David shows in Chapter 6 – Education – the apparent pursuit of excellence obscures a rather more determined quest for financial and political control of education. She describes how the first two Thatcher administrations focused on finance and on the economics of education rather than on the reform of institutions or the promotion of improved standards – a rather puzzling departure for a party that had so vigorously flown the flag of 'excellence' in 1979. In practice, finance became the determinant of policy – as it did in so many other areas of social policy. The consequence, says David, was that the 'conditions of change were, therefore, largely negative'.

Resources were diverted to private and independent schools through the development of the Assisted Places Scheme. Teacher training and certification were modified to ensure greater compatibility with new changes in courses and curricula – reflecting similar changes taking place in the NHS and the PSS also. The consequence, she argues, is that institutions at all levels are now more generally concerned with financial and educational accountability to the full range of their consumers than was routinely the case under previous governments.

If there is common ground with other parts of the welfare state such as the health service and the PSS with regard to managerial accountability and the infusion of business practices and a commercial culture, then there is also some overlap with employment strategies. Education has, says Miriam David, become an integral part of the revived economy, a vehicle for driving forward appropriately skilled personnel to take their places at the frontline of production. This has, in turn, fuelled tensions within the Conservative Party between those who view education reform as the promotion of standards of excellence and those bent on ideological fulfilment alone. The latter may be seen to have held sway in initiatives to reduce access to social and educational services by means of limitations in financial support and, says David, in the increased reliance on voluntary and family-based educational schemes and through parental involvement in the classroom.

Miriam David points to the emergence of, and to the attempts to consolidate, a culture of populism in education. She cites, in particular, the popularisation of the idea of 'a market place' in the education of our children. This popularisation has been assisted, in turn, by the debunking of existing state education programmes as monolithic, poorly conceived and managed, and by contrasting them sharply with new and allegedly dynamic Tory policies founded on the pursuit of excellence and a shift in control from local authority to consumer. This has been accompanied by the introduction of new financial and educational contractual arrangements and by competition between the sectors. 'Performance' has been redefined as having more to do with the measurement of cost-effectiveness than with 'the more elusive measure of academic achievement'. The real cost, concludes David, is more centralisation of resources and control, more hierarchy, a deeply contrived and imbalanced pluralism and the reinforcement of social, racial and sexual differentiation.

In Chapter 7 – Criminal Justice – we return to the thesis that 1979 marks a watershed in social policy and a radical departure from the post-war consensus. Rod Morgan reminds us that restoring 'the rule of law' was one of five objectives the Party had set for itself in the 1979 manifesto and that its criminal justice programme has excited considerable acrimony ever since. The question he puts and seeks to answer is 'whether this is because new policy directions have been taken or because criminal justice has been affected by broader strains and changes taking place in British life'. He goes on to demonstrate that, for the Conservatives, law and order is about enforcing the rules which 'naturally' govern the consumer market place.

From the outset, the Government gave a high priority to

re-establishing law and order and to providing the resources to do the job, not least for additional police recruitment. And while in 1979 the emphasis might have been placed on increasing manpower in the inner city to curb urban crime, more than a decade later the need to assuage the growing anxieties of its 'natural constituency' in the shire counties has persuaded the Government that tackling thuggish and often drink-related behaviour in the villages and the larger market towns is of political, as much as social, importance. There is, moreover, much common ground in the present debate on the alleged surge in crime in the shires and the proposals put forward by the Party more than ten years ago. The 1979 manifesto warned that violent criminals would face the full wrath of the law and assured the electorate that the excesses of wayward young thugs and hooligans would meet with a short sharp shock. Since then, sentencing has been reshaped by the 1982 Criminal Justice Act and the 1984 Police and Criminal Evidence Act has transformed, controversially, the major police powers of arrest, stop and search, detention and interrogation and has introduced a new Police Complaints Authority. The Act has drawn unremitting criticism from its critics and opponents that it has greatly increased police powers and seriously undermined civil rights and that it has opened the door to further oppression of and discrimination against minorities.

There has, in common with other areas of social policy cited in this book, also been the imposition from the centre of new and stricter means to control financial and managerial accountability and to measure cost-effectiveness and performance. Morgan addresses each of these issues in turn. He examines the Conservatives' record in the fight against crime and assesses the contribution other Government policies – in the economy, industrial relations, employment, social security, civil rights – may have made to the growth of crime and public disorder. He analyses the pattern of law and order expenditure over the last decade and sets this alongside a growth in manpower and the statistics on crimes solved. In a section devoted to 'Prisons: matching supply and demand', he examines some of the most volatile issues now confronting policymakers – the explosive growth in the prison population, the deep flaws in sentencing arrangements and the prospects for further abuse and unrest.

Morgan also offers some alternative ways forward. He proposes alternative ideas on prison building, sentencing, resourcing, and police accountability and control. And he warns that a tough law and order stance may actually prove to be both the Conservatives' Achilles heel as well as its spear. The very social, economic, industrial and civil changes the Conservatives have introduced or provoked since 1979 are, paradoxically, a key dynamic in their law and order policy and may have exacerbated tensions to a point where the boundaries between the bobby on the beat and the paramilitary tactical support units may be increasingly blurred.

In the final two chapters of the book we deal directly with the inescapable conclusions of modern conservative social policy. These are the enforced retreat from public service provision and its replacement by a fragmented pattern of private arrangements, substantially dependent upon the continuing and expanding goodwill and resources of the family, the informal carer and the voluntary association. Ultimately, there are the roles assigned to the private sector itself: entrepreneur, liberator, champion of the consumer, protector of the public purse. Roles assigned but not yet proven.

In the first of these – Community Care – Alan Walker argues that the main thrust of community care policies in the period since 1979 has been towards reducing the role of local authorities as service providers. At the same time, he says, the Government has sought to encourage, in an ad hoc and disparate way, the growth of informal, voluntary and private care 'under the guise of promoting a mixed economy of welfare'. He suggests that the very concept of 'community care' may be part of the problem, explaining that its political and public appeal obscures a jigsaw of ill-defined policies and mismatched resources, further hamstrung by unreal expectations. Walker argues that the survival of community care over the years as a generalised policy may owe much to the lack of clarity about its aims and content and a consequent uncertainty about what might replace it.

Beneath the attractive political veneer there lies a long history of policy discontents and a continuing attrition between health service and social service interests. Walker describes the history of community care in Britain as characterised by confusion and the struggle for power between those favouring institutional forms of care and those promoting community-based arrangements. Thus far, he adds, the former have been in the acsendancy.

This shows little promise of immediate change. The 1980s saw the active encouragement of the private sector, aided by cuts in the resources available to local authorities and by rate-capping. There was also the splendid bounty presented to the private sector by local DHSS offices in the payment of board and lodging allowances to residential and nursing home residents.

Alan Walker sees the promotion of the idea of 'increased choice' as an important but mistaken source of popular legitimation for the contrived and skewed expansion of the private sector. He sees the radical Conservative approach to social policy succeeding in some instances in overcoming institutional inertia and entrenched professional interests in the promotion of community care but asserts that the motivation for doing so is overwhelmingly economic. It is a quest for cost-efficiency rather than quality of service. Like other contributors to this book, Walker views 1979 as the break-point in the post-war consensus and he cites Norman Fowler's Buxton speech and the diminished role for statutory services outlined in it as firm evidence of the policy intent to force the retreat of community care into the backwaters of the family and the informal sector.

Walker concludes that the community care policy is deliberately fragmented and now woefully exposed to 'marketisation'. He sees the lack of resources locally as impeding and undermining the prospects for greater consumer involvement. The cumulative impact of these policy developments amounts to a residualisation of the local authority role in providing and developing community care services. He rounds off with a critique of the 1988 Griffiths Report, assessing its implications for consumers, staff, accountability and social care planning. He sees Griffiths as having given further impetus to the residualisation of public service provision and as a missed opportunity for building upon and developing further the many imaginative but unsung community care initiatives in the public sector.

In the concluding chapter – Private and Voluntary Welfare – Martin Knapp examines further the care and cost assumptions associated with voluntarism and private sector initiative. He begins by reminding us that 'volunteering' has its own costs, not least to the volunteer, and that far from being a cheap and easy option for providing care it does involve a 'transfer of time'. And despite the popular view that no one is coerced or compelled to 'volunteer', many people may feel 'morally bound' to assist or contribute to the welfare of others.

Martin Knapp also confirms the evidence presented by all other contributors to this book, that the welfare state in Britain, far from being a monopolistic and monolithic state concern, actually 'contains an almost bewildering array of transaction types between the funding, demand or patronage side of the economy and the provision or supply side'. He goes on to dispel some of the policy myths surrounding private initiative, pointing out that the alleged advantages of privatisation with regard to innovation, competition and choice may be rather more apparent than real. He raises important questions about, and counter-arguments to, the claims that privatisation provides competition which, in turn, guarantees more efficient production and responsiveness to consumer wishes. He observes, for example, that contracting-out to the private sector may well confuse and restrict choice because of the necessity for government regulation of quality or lines of accountability.

Many of the claims exerted by those favouring privatisation at all costs are clearly exaggerated and often flawed. The best way forward for the welfare state in the 1990s, suggests Knapp, should be through a multiplicity of service providers – in whatever sectors – since this offers the best chance for innovation and accompanying efficiency gains. The political drive to tear down the edifice of state provision may be judged, on the evidence presented throughout this book, to be precipitate at best and ill-judged at worst. The real answer to efficiency, says Knapp, may lie internally. In other words, public agencies and services could provide the answer themselves by being allowed and encouraged to put their own house in order, rather than being forced to seek an independent contractor to build another and different house altogether.

Perhaps the most significant evidence that Britain *already* has an arguably flourishing (though not necessarily entirely healthy) mixed economy of welfare is Knapp's observation that public support to the voluntary sector alone is now equivalent to at least 7 per cent of total central government expenditure on goods and services. There is every prospect that this figure will continue to grow. The consequences, positive or otherwise, will not be economic alone. There will be policy, planning, legislative, training, service and, above all, needs outcomes to address and resolve also. Successive ministers, as this book shows, have wrestled with the challenge of, first, creating and, subsequently, of developing and fine-tuning, a welfare state to meet the needs *and* the resources of their time. The splitting of the huge and unwieldy DHSS in 1988 was one of the more politically visible illustrations of the high-wire act governments believe the public expect them to perform. The wire is kept taut by ensuring that needs and resources are skilfully and fairly matched and that individual *and* collective responsibility are understood, accepted and honoured. These are key considerations and were lucidly set out by one of the most influential Conservative leaders of this century, Harold Macmillan, as we now go on to see. As we move into the 1990s, however, there are strains and tensions in the wire, and the safety-net for *both* consumers *and* ministers themselves looks less secure than ever.

1

Personal Social Services

MICHAEL McCARTHY

'There are, then, many possible ways of providing support. Equally, there are many possible ways of financing
it – whether from people's own resources, by social
security payments, by charitable funds, by central and
local government grants, or by explicit contracts of service
between public service agencies and private or voluntary
sector suppliers. It is only with an understanding of the
immense variety of potential care and through asking
the question, 'who does what best and how can they
be helped to do it?', that we can satisfactorily define
the role of the local authority social services department. That question has to be answered if we are to
make the best use of all available resources in meeting
need.' (Norman Fowler, 'The Enabling Role of Social
Services Departments', speech to the Joint Social Services Conference, Buxton, September 1984.)

1 Past and present

The economy, social services and taxation

Writing in 1938 in *The Middle Way*, Harold Macmillan set
out the principles and perhaps the boundaries also for what
might be termed in present political vernacular 'caring Conservatism'. At the heart of his argument lay a recognition that
the expansion of social services provision would have much to
do with economic strength. It was a pragmatic and realistic relationship that predicated the volume of welfare upon

increased productivity and sustained growth and it has echoed across the decades since, finding resonance in the policies of Conversative and Labour administrations alike.

For Macmillan, and many Conservatives since, a dividing line had to be drawn between the efficient organisation of society 'for the supply of the essentials of life which are the common need of all citizens' and a social and political structure which would take collectivism so far that it would punish any prospects of individuality.

There are a number of observations to be made here and each is fundamental to the analysis of the Conservative Party's approach to the personal social services put forward in this chapter. First, there is the emphasis on growth before expenditure. Next, there is some notion of 'boundary' in collective provision. This boundary is then explained to us as the provision of the essentials, the basics for a civilised life. Last, but certainly not least, there is also the value placed upon individual choice and liberty and, by implication, the balance that must be struck between freedom and responsibility.

If it sounds familiar, it should. The same views have been recited at length by a chain of Conservative ministers from Boyd Carpenter and MacLeod, to Joseph and Jenkin and, latterly, Fowler and Moore. The concern with setting moral, financial and libertarian boundaries to the provision of social services provides much historical common ground within the Party. Nowhere is this better illustrated than in a traditional Conservative preoccupation with the economy, with the role of taxation in encouraging or arresting growth and with the pull on taxation levied by what so many Conservatives over the last half-century have seen as the unbridled growth of welfare. Little more than a decade after Macmillan had set out his own boundaries for caring Conservatism and with the modern welfare state barely out of its cradle, a Conservative manifesto warned that 'Britain can only enjoy the social services for which she is prepared to work' (*This is the Road*, 1950). This phase demonstrated what has since become both a persistent feature and a continuing tension in the Conservative Party's approach to the personal social services.

The principal features were clear. Primarily, that the level of benefits and volume of services in the modern welfare state ought to be related to the nation's economic performance. Secondly, that selectivity and not universality should, where appropriate, be the key factor in determining their allocation. To many Conservatives, both in Parliament and in the wider electorate, the logic of financial control and of concentrating resources where they were deemed to be most needed was compelling. Conservative policy took it as axiomatic that improvements in welfare could only be made on the basis of improved economic performance.

The 1949 policy document *The Right Road for Britain* had endorsed the principle of basic minimum provision throughout the social services but not at unlimited cost to economic growth and social development. 'Tory spokesmen, therefore, stressed that production must precede distribution – the Social Services could not be expanded faster than the economy expanded' (Gamble, 1974). If the economy should falter then the implications were clear.

Old ideas recycled

By the General Election of 1964, Edward Heath, much influenced by the Bow and One Nation Groups, had come to conclude that five major policy changes were necessary for 'putting Britain right ahead'. One of these was the re-emphasis on selectivity and targeting in the social services. The welfare state was to be thoroughly overhauled and modernised to meet the requirements of the new 'competition policy'. Heath rejected any ideological role for the welfare state and rebuffed those who saw it as an instrument for achieving social equality. The social services were to have a more narrowly defined role as a casualty clearing station for welfare capitalism.

This view was emphasised by a number of Conservative spokesmen on social services when the Party returned to power again in 1970. Writing in 1973, John Selwyn Gummer explained 'Conservative social policy seeks the social services to set up people rather than drag them down to a dependence. Its preoccupation with help to the permanently needy is matched by the belief that it is best to ensure that as many people make provision for themselves rather than expect the state to undertake the task' (Gummer, 1973).

In the Conservative view for a transformation of the welfare state there lay the belief that expenditure on welfare was already beyond the means of a low growth economy struggling to modernise in the uncertain political and economic climate of the early 1960s. Rather than increase expenditure, it chose instead to redefine the terms on which welfare could be distributed. *Distribution* not volume of services became the key.

This view struck a particular chord in the late 1980s. Selectivity and targeting increasingly became euphemisms for cost effectiveness and for cuts in service provision as demographic trends and the changing scale and complexity of social need outpaced the resources available to the personal social services. A concern for good housekeeping was invested with an openly aggressive brand of moral philosophy that emphasised self-help, personal responsibility and a spirit of individualism as the primary considerations in imposing a new welfare consensus. At its most hostile this philosophy took the view that the personal social services could be threatening to the fabric of society by inducing, alongside social security, a 'dependency culture'.

The seeds of this view were long in the germination, however. Thus, when Norman Fowler spoke in September 1984 of the need for social service departments to 'enable the greatest possible number of individuals to act reciprocally, giving and receiving services for the well-being of the whole community' he was reaffirming views set out by Tory backbenchers and senior ministers in the Heath government a decade earlier. Similarly, when his successor, John Moore, spoke in September 1987 of the need to move forward on 'the long evolutionary march of the welfare state . . . away from dependence toward independence', he was essentially reworking Macmillan's warning that too great a reliance on the state for social services can 'compress the life of men into too narrow a pattern' (Macmillan, 1938).

Conviction politics

The governments of Margaret Thatcher have by no means invented a 'new' Conservative approach to the personal social services that is significantly and qualitatively different from the past. That it *appears* to be significantly different may have as much to do with the style of pursuit as it does with policy content. In the age of the conviction politician, a number of well-worn ideas have been recycled with a vigour and determination not previously experienced in post-war Britain and which allows little, if any, room for an alternative view.

A commitment to revolutionise industrial practices, to shake out the manufacturing and employment base and effect a sea change in economic thinking was always bound to have major consequences for *all* forms of public enterprise. It is not such a quantum leap after all to see that the repercussions would extend to the personal social services, to education, to social security and to housing. It is no latter-day conspiracy either, that the welfare state would be obliged to bear its share of a general rein-back of public expenditure. The sanctity and inviolability of the welfare state had been breached long before Margaret Thatcher came to power in 1979 and Labour Prime Ministers and their Chancellors have their own place in the hall of villainy. What the governments of Mrs Thatcher have dared to do is to go further and faster and to brook no opposition. The impact of this, both supposed and real, is all the greater because at a time of such unprecedented economic change, the welfare state was held by many to be a stabilising force in an otherwise deeply uncertain and disruptive equation.

Britain may now in the 1990s be at the point of arrival, but the point of departure is rooted in the distant past. In vilifying Thatcherism and in insisting that the welfare state has been under full frontal assault since 1979, it is too easy to forget that only five years earlier the evidence against the 1970-74 Conservative Government was so great and so emotionally charged that Peter Townsend concluded that it had 'represented a return to the more authoritarian and doctrinaire principles of Tory Social philosophy, which no Tory administration of the post-war years had dared to espouse'. Townsend saw then, as many do now, a revival of conditional welfare for the few and a tendency to blame the victim. Tory philosophy was seen as reaffirming 'the paramountcy of the values of the market' (Townsend, 1974).

Working with the grain of human nature

Conservative social policy after 1979 has substantially reaffirmed this position. The 1979 manifesto talked of a Party wishing to work with the grain of human nature, helping people to help themselves – and others. This was seen as the road to establishing personal responsibility and national success. Like Heath's competition policy, the new Thatcher Government set itself five tasks, of which the fourth stated the need for 'concentrating welfare services on the effective support of the old, the sick, the disabled and those who are in real need' (*The Conservative Manifesto,* 1979).

Most familiarly, perhaps, the Party stated 'the lack of money to improve our social services and assist those in need can only be overcome by restoring the nation's prosperity. But some improvements can be made now by spending what we do have more sensibly'. In an unmistakeable gesture of hiving-off and drawing-in the boundaries of collective provision, it stressed 'we must also encourage the voluntary movement and self help groups working in partnership with the statutory services'. It was a firm restatement that the Conservative tradition of 'growth before expenditure' would not only be maintained but would become the centrepiece of the new government's strategy for realigning popular welfare capitalism and integrating cash and care. It is to this that we now turn.

2 A mixed economy of welfare

Cash, care and welfare capitalism

The 1980s proved to be a significant period of change and challenge for the personal social services in Britain. The emphasis given in two major reports by the Audit Commission (1985, 1986), by the Firth Report on Public Assistance for Residential Care (1987), the Griffiths Report on Community Care (1988), the Short Report on Community Care (HC13 1984–5), together with the provisions of the 1986 Social Security Act, each took the personal social services further down the road to the integration of cash and care and to an extension of welfare pluralism in favour of private, voluntary and informal care arrangements.

The 1988 Griffiths Report reflected many of these beliefs and, in the clear context of cash-care policy boundaries, addressed itself to a review, on the one hand, of 'the way in which public funds are used' and, on the other, 'the options for action that would improve the use of these funds'. It was not concerned as some supposed with finding new resources or in offering targets for cost reduction, rather it addressed the use of existing resources. This has been a key feature of Conservative social policy in recent years and much of what the Audit Commission and Sir Roy Griffiths had to say is consonant with it. The language of care in recent years has come increasingly to resemble the language of capital and of the market place.

Writing during the first Thatcher administration, Neil Gilbert described 'welfare capitalism' as expressing

> a symbiotic relationship between a social and economic market that represent two dissimilar modes for the production and distribution of benefits in society. It bonds individual ambitions and collective responsibility. Capitalism encourages competition and risk-taking behaviour . . . the welfare state operates through a social market that provides a sort of communal safety net for the casualties of a market economy (Gilbert, 1983).

The very social, moral and philosophical structures that served to attenuate market forces are now increasingly exposed to them and may, with the passage of time, become *subordinated* to them. The popular image of the welfare state as a wholly publicly provided and collectively subscribed social institution has, for administrative, political and fiscal reasons, masked the *reality* of a system of institutions and services that are much more pluralistic in the way they are financed, constructed and distributed. The Thatcher Governments have shown beyond question that politics and capital *do* matter and cannot be isolated from considerations of social need.

The rejection by Norman Fowler of 'a single ideology of care' and his rebuttal of the view that the state should take overall responsibility for the financing and provision of care, amounted to a polite invitation to study the writing on the wall. We were encouraged to look a little closer in 1986 when he remarked that 'for all those in the personal social services a fundamental question must be whether we are making the best use of *all* of our financial and human resources' (Fowler, 1986).

It might be supposed that the evolutionary march towards independence described by John Moore in 1987 had a great deal to do with enhancing choice, uplifting the consumer and ensuring the effective delivery and fine-tuning of care. But it was rather more to do with revamping the personal social services; getting value for money; encouraging private and informal care initiatives; and about slowing the burgeoning growth of the welfare state. It was also about reviewing a major area of social and economic activity that had not been closely put under the microscope since Beveridge presented his report to the House of Commons in 1943.

Table 1.1 *Public expenditure on the welfare state 1987–8*

	£ billion
Social security	48.5
Health and personal social services	20.7
Education	18.0
Housing and environment	6.8
Total	94.0
(64 per cent of public expenditure)	

Source: adapted from Chancellor's Autumn 1987 Statement.

It was to be achieved by charges; by problem redefinition; by targeting; by residualising public services; by privatisation; by exporting the burden of care to families and to individuals; and through public regulation of private provision. The debate was and still is not about the future of the welfare state but about its future *shape*. As one writer eloquently puts it 'with the social market undergoing pressure to adopt the values and methods of the economic market, a third phase of welfare capitalism is on the horizon' (Gilbert, 1983).

The control of expenditure

When Margaret Thatcher took office in 1979, total public expenditure had risen to £70 billion or 44 per cent of GNP (Le Grand, 1982). Public expenditure has been rising both in real terms *and* as a proportion of total national output. In cash terms public expenditure rose from about £10 billion in 1963–4 to some £139 billion in 1984–5.

Le Grand and Robinson speak of 'social expenditure' rising by almost 250 per cent in real terms between the Conservative Governments of 1951 and 1979. Generally, social expenditure in this period may be seen to have risen *despite* changes in political hue. Gross expenditure on the personal social services rose from £1,900 million in 1980–1 to a planned expenditure of £2,950 million in 1988–9. Since 1984 financial *and* needs pressures have significantly pushed estimates up, so that for example the 1984 projected estimate of £19,130 million for expenditure on health and personal social

services in 1988–9 had been substantially overtaken and stood
at £20,680 after the 1987 estimates were submitted. See Table
1.1. The public expenditure and taxation White Paper, *The
Next Ten Years*, spoke of expenditure on health and personal social services as growing at about 16 per cent in real
terms between 1978 and 1984 'continuing a pattern of sustained
growth sufficient to meet demographic pressures'.

We shall return to the subject of demographic pressures shortly
but it is significant that the White Paper went on to add that 'the
pressures for additional expenditure continue to be strong and
there appears to have been little if any effect on the gap between
the services and expectations'. The perceived need to close this gap
may substantially explain why ministers have been so concerned
since to divorce general demand from specific need in both the
health and personal social services and to 'redefine' problems and,
in so doing, to rein back on demand and expenditure.

Taxation has become an increasingly important factor in the
economics of the personal social services. The reasons for its
prominence are both ideological and fiscal and the 'burden of
taxation' charge levied at the welfare state has proved to be a
useful Trojan Horse for carrying forward moral and philosophical
arguments also. Taxation is seen as affecting the performance of
the economy and national morale and efficiency. It is viewed by
some leading Conservatives as reducing the will to work and
inducing in others a 'dependency culture'. Since it underpins
public sector provision it is also blamed for the alleged lack
of consumer choice in the state sector and for monolithic social
institutions and services. The chief sin, however, is the serious
impact of taxation on Britain's economic performance over
many years, with the result that 'as public expenditure takes
a larger and larger share of GDP, so the public sector steadily
encroaches on the rest of the economy. This is a process which
could not be allowed to go on indefinitely (Cmnd 9189).'

Even where services, such as the personal social services,
were required to improve or expand, the Government warned
that 'there should be no general presumption that higher public
spending is inevitable if provision in these areas is to be improved,
given the scope for switching from the public to private sector and
for improved efficiency within the public sector'. The golden rule
since 1984 has been 'that finance must determine expenditure, not

Table 1.2 *Health and personal social services expenditure per head 1984*

Age group	Per capita expenditure (£)
75+	1,340
65–74	530
16–64	170
5–15	205
0–4	209
births	1,115
all ages	£305

expenditure determine finance'. There were, thus, two obvious ways of drawing back on public expenditure in the personal social services – by shifting increasingly towards private provision and by securing greater value for money in the public sector.

Consumer pressures

The pressure points are relatively easy to spot if we examine health and personal social services expenditure per head. Table 1.2 shows expenditure in the mid-1980s on an age group basis.

Expenditure continues to be polarised at the extremes of birth and old age. In 1985–6 elderly people and the younger physically handicapped accounted for 42 per cent of all personal social services expenditure with a further 20 per cent on children and 10 per cent on the mentally ill and mentally handicapped. Social work accounted for 12 per cent. There were similarities in NHS expenditure with the elderly again the chief consumers at 13 per cent. Elderly people occupied 40 per cent of all acute beds. Acute services in general accounted for the lion's share of NHS expenditure at 46 per cent. A further 11 per cent was spent on the mentally ill, 6 per cent on maternity, 5 per cent on mental handicap and 3 per cent on children.

Yet it is the source, rather than the disbursement, of expenditure in both sectors that is of more interest. With 85 per cent of NHS finance coming from direct taxation and 82 per cent of personal social services finance from block grants and rates, it is easy to see the large and vulnerable targets they present to a government seeking, on the one hand, to reduce taxation and finance tax cuts and, on the other, to promote the philosophy and virtues of the market. The growth of demographic pressures and of new and complex social needs have added to the financial imperative to 'reconstruct' the Beveridge welfare state and to deconstruct the post-war welfare consensus. In both sectors it is services to elderly people which are most at risk. The 1986 public expenditure white paper warned that demands for public services were becoming limitless because they were 'not restrained by the price mechanism which forces those making demands to balance them against costs'. The conclusion that the Conservatives were to draw from this was that 'wherever it is possible and sensible to do so, the Government is seeking to transfer the provision of services into the market sector'.

The vital part played by the personal social services and by social work in maintaining, repairing and renewing the social fabric is at best understated and at worst simply not understood. Expenditure on the personal social services is by no means luxurious. The reality is that a little money is having to acquire extraordinary powers of elasticity.

New wave pressures

The social fabric has been cruelly stretched by a predictable growth in the needs and demands expressed by traditional consumers such as the elderly, young children, people with a mental handicap and those with a mental illness. These have been further accentuated by the emergence of newer consumer pressures from unemployed people and their families, from drug-users, people with HIV-AIDS and their carers, from the growing ranks of the homeless, from young care-leavers and from ethnic minorities for whom the obstacles of access to services in the first place have been greatest of all.

Each has taken a toll on resources. Between 1979 and 1984 unemployment tripled in real terms. A report by the Association of Metropolitan Authorities in 1985 found that nine out of ten people seeking help from social services departments in Britain's major cities were unemployed and that most came from households where no other adult had a job (Balloch *et al.*, 1985). In May 1986, as the Conservatives were beginning to claim some success in slowing down the underlying trend in unemployment, a research monograph by Saul Becker and Stewart MacPherson of the Benefits Research Unit showed that poverty, through unemployment, was driving increasing numbers of people to seek the help, often inappropriately, of the local social services department. In 1986, over two million men, women and children were dependent on supplementary benefit and in contact with a social worker. Becker and MacPherson drew together considerable evidence from local authorities throughout Britain to show that 'financial problems are bringing people into contact with the social services department. The implication is simple but stark: claimants are poor *before* they become clients, but more and more are becoming clients *because they are poor*' (Becker and MacPherson, 1986).

The evidence presented in a number of studies (Balloch, 1985; Becker and MacPherson, 1986; Ridley and McCarthy, 1986; and Fimister, 1986) suggests that, with a few exceptions, social services departments generally do not cope adequately with the problems generated by long-term unemployment. Many have failed through lack of foresight, priority, training or resources, to record and assess the increasing impact of unemployment upon their work. It is not surprising, therefore, that practical and imaginative responses are few and far between. Certainly, departments are right to protest about their lack of resources to do the job and in some areas the task of providing any sort of practical help or guidance is Herculean. There is no excuse, however, for the view that the department 'did not see the problem coming and could not plan for it'.

The result is that many field social workers are ill-trained, ill-equipped and ill-prepared for the problems that now confront them through unemployment. Their uncertainty and lack of confidence in dealing with the financial complexities that arise only serves to reinforce the ambivalence of the department generally to this area of work.

Beyond the experience of poverty itself, unemployment has quite particular consequences for some groups and requires *anything but* the generalised or qualified responses that have characterised the efforts of some departments. For black people, in particular, the difficulties that may characterise their relationship with the local SSD are substantially wider than demography or unemployment alone. In many inner city areas there is an acute sense of alienation, a lack of any sense of community and, in some, the very family and neighbourhood networks on which the Conservative Government is so dependent in its vision of the future pattern of welfare have irretrievably broken down. In many instances the personal social services fail entirely to reach ethnic minority groups where differences in language, culture, aspirations, attitude and need continue to be major obstacles to service delivery and which fail regularly to impress upon the mainstream of service priorities.

Becker and MacPherson are right, nevertheless, to draw attention to the general failure of social services agencies to identify the part played by unemployment in other social work problems, not least since this might bolster the case for additional resources. Unemployment *has* added to social work caseloads and *has* lead to an overwhelming increase in the demand for financial and debt counselling and welfare rights advice. The social fund has already greatly extended these pressures. Unemployment has the largest single impact on child care and family problems and evidence links unemployment with mental illness, delinquency, family violence, drug taking, alcohol problems and the removal of children into care. Yet it has not emerged as a major personal social services issue requiring major social services investment. Unemployment remains firmly entrenched in the forgotten limbo of industrial change.

Three other 'new wave' problems have major implications for the personal social services in the 1990s and beyond. Alcohol, for example, is a presenting factor in a whole range of other, more conventional, social work issues. Effectively addressing, let alone resolving, the social consequences of alcohol abuse or alcohol-related problems has not been assisted by the benign way in which society continues to view the use of alcohol or by the reluctance of policymakers, professionals and public alike to admit alcohol as a factor in more conventional casework. The efforts of some social services agencies to confront and tackle the increasing incidence of alcohol-related problems continues to be hindered by the social acceptability of the drug and by a lack of resources for training, planning and staffing in social services departments themselves or in seriously under-resourced detoxification centres. Alcohol and hard drug abuse have both been subject to government attempts to detach them from mainstream social services provision and to export them instead to hard-pressed voluntary agencies.

Even allowing for a major sea change in policy in the 1990s, alcohol abuse is unlikely to excite the moral panic that characterised the public and government reaction to HIV-AIDS or hard drug abuse, both of which will continue to have far reaching consequences for the personal social services.

The moral panic now looks, with hindsight, to have been engineered – an exercise in agenda-setting by a government determined to define and tackle the problem on its own terms. Characteristically, the *social* problem of hard drug misuse acquired a law and order veneer. The fight against hard drugs has been politically visible and has been bound up with a general Conservative drive on law and order, while its social dimension has been substantially shaded. Continuing regional disparities in funding; a lack of training and suitable staff skills; shortfalls in information technology and an official persistence in viewing drug abuse as a criminal act seriously call into question the confident view of the House of Commons Social Services Committee that 'we can provide the right sort of administrative and financial structure which will deliver the preventive treatment and rehabilitive services which are required' (4th Report, June 1985).

There are parallels here with the government's response to HIV-AIDS also. At a major symposium on AIDS in March 1987, the Secretary of State for Social Services emphasised that the two developments which had most impressed him on a recent fact-finding tour to San Francisco were the extent to which the response to HIV-AIDS came from the whole community and that the range of care extended from hospice care to care in the community. The latter was seen as making the most significant contribution to care arrangements. Under Norman Fowler's guidance, the DHSS and the Conservative Government itself took perhaps a more constructive approach to HIV-AIDS than many of their critics were prepared to concede. There are now in prospect centres for the training of staff from health and social services disciplines; funding of fellowships; opportunities for clinical training for GPs; a pilot scheme for AIDS regional support centres; new training requirements for health care professionals; a rethink of nurse-training and some limited initiatives directed towards social services staff. But it is not nearly enough.

The limitations of the latter, explained by the need to finance other priorities, were brought more sharply into focus by the considerable costs of an expensive campaign of public education and television advertising which the government conceded had had only limited success. Two important issues loom for the personal social services. Foremost is the clear indication that statutory social work agencies and voluntary organisations are now having to shoulder a significant burden of care and support to those with HIV-AIDS. Secondly, there is the more general problem of ensuring that the Government maintains a continuing and meaningful commitment to tackling HIV-AIDS, not least in economic terms, and that it properly recognises and resources the role it has cast for both statutory and voluntary agencies in this process. Social services agencies have already faced up to and are now counting the cost of staff training and education; new counselling and care packages; the development of domiciliary, day care, residential and respite arrangements for those with HIV-AIDS; the emotional costs of staff burn-out following intense terminal care and bereavement counselling; finding and sustaining suitable foster care arrangements for children with HIV-AIDS; the costs of liaison with other agencies, the voluntary sector and NHS.

People with HIV-AIDS who wish to remain in the community with their families, partners and carers will require support to do so and this will, in large part, have to come from the personal social services. The costs are certain to be considerable and will add further to the financial dilemma of local authorities already straight-jacketed by the financial restraint of the 1980s.

The Conservative Government's response to HIV-AIDS remains, at best, cosmetic and is unlikely to offer relief to already-hardpressed social services agencies confronted by yet another string to the ever-lengthening bow of community care. The ninety-four recommendations of the 1987 report of the House of Commons Social Services Committee, *Problems Associated with AIDS*, have rarely looked to be in danger of implementation; Government support for the inspirational work of voluntary bodies like the Terence Higgins Trust, Body Positive or Scottish Aids Monitor is either minimal, or in some doubt or simply unforthcoming; efforts to address and tackle the drug dimension of HIV-AIDS have been feeble; and the prospect of long-term financial support of voluntary drug agencies is dim. Meanwhile, training needs and staffing levels in the personal social services have, with the exception of a handful of progressive departments in Scotland and London, been addressed only at the margin, while the challenge posed by HIV-AIDS is anything but marginal.

Mainstream pressures

The growth in numbers of elderly people assumed to be dependent upon the state for care or income maintenance has been seen as *the major* challenge confronting both the personal social services and social security throughout Mrs Thatcher's period of office. In his evidence to the Select Committee on Public Expenditure in 1986, Sir Kenneth Stowe, Permanent Secretary at the DHSS, described elderly people as 'the major source of pressure on social security expenditure' and as 'the single major challenge facing the DHSS'. For Norman Fowler they represented in 1985 'a certainty for which we must plan'.

The Conservatives are right to be concerned by the challenge posed by growing numbers of elderly people. Mistakenly, however, the Government has too often chosen to describe this challenge as a *burden*, not least in the sphere of social security and pension provision. The costs of maintaining SERPS into the next century have already proved too much to bear. The demographic trends *are*, indeed, significant. The population aged 85 or over is projected to double to 1.4 million between 1986 and the year 2025. Already, the elderly population over 65 has grown by 3.2 million since 1951 and is likely to increase by another 2.6 million by 2025. The balance of age groups is also set to change, so that those aged 65–74 years should comprise only 53 per cent of the total elderly population by 2025 compared with 57 per cent in 1986.

The implications for the personal social services, and for social security and health service provision also, are far-reaching. One likely outcome is a pronounced shift in demand for local authority services away from children towards elderly people at a time when enormous public and professional pressure is being exerted to develop *more* services to children and families. With local authority services already seriously reduced or residualised in some boroughs, the prospects for an extension of private provision of services, be they day care, residential care, sheltered housing, domiciliary care, or transport are significant.

The evidence is already substantial if we examine the growth of privatisation in the nursing and residential care sectors. Between

1981 and 1986, the open-ended provision of social security board and lodging payments had given such an impetus to the growth of private residential homes for elderly people that the number of residents had nearly doubled to 112,700 by 1986 (*Social Trends 18*, 1988). By contrast, the number of residents in local authority homes had *peaked* in 1981 and has been falling since, levelling off at 120,900 in 1986. Similar trends may also be seen in the expansion of private nursing homes and hospitals where numbers of elderly residents had doubled between 1971 and 1985 to reach 51,000. Meanwhile, the local authority sector is variously described as having been residualised and stigmatised as a service for the second-class citizen.

In the private nursing sector, a large question mark continues to hang over the *need* for the admission of many elderly people who, properly assessed, might be deemed perfectly fit to remain in their own homes supported by relatively minimal public or private home care services or who might move instead to imaginative and cost-effective private schemes of very sheltered housing. There has also been the attendant and unfortunate development of a North-South polarisation of private provision with the growth of private facilities in the South freely outstripping those in Northern England and Wales. While some local authorities have welcomed and encouraged this development, seeing in it an opportunity to alleviate consumer pressures on their own services and to redirect scant public resources elsewhere, others protest that their own services have been diminished and subjected to unfairly subsidised competition; that their staff have been bound up with uneconomic inspectoral and regulatory duties; and that they face the prospect of having to cope with new uncertainty as the government rethinks the relaxed social security arrangements it has allowed to develop.

Even so, the Social Security Minister, Nicholas Scott, in 1988 openly and enthusiastically endorsed a further expansion of private residential care and a greater independence for the private sector from local authority control. Too often, however, profit has loomed larger than quality and standards in the outlook and practice of many private companies providing care and services to the elderly, to people with a mental handicap and to those returning to the community from psychiatric hospitals. There are some progressive and responsible exceptions, not least in the provision of very sheltered private housing for elderly people, and rehabilitative services for those with a mental handicap, but it will take time for those quality services to expand to meet the clear demand available. Few private companies have shown interest in providing residential services or care for the severely disabled or the chronically sick elderly. Consequently local authorities and the NHS confront the possibility of operating not only a residualised and stigmatised service for elderly people in the years to come but also a *characteristically different* service where need is much more concentrated than before. Elderly people will be at the sharp end even in their own homes.

One recent estimate put forward by local authorities suggests that there will be an additional 175,000 elderly people requiring help with bathing and washing all over by the end of the century and 50,000 more elderly people requiring assistance to get in and out of bed. (Walker, *The Care Gap,* 1986). The implications for PSS and health service resources are all the more significant given that over half of the elderly population over 65 are said to experience a 'limiting longstanding illness'.

In 1987–8 approximately 30 per cent of personal social services expenditure was allocated to home care services. There have been, however, striking variations in provision of home help hours between authorities – from one hour to twenty hours weekly according to the Audit Commission (1985) and from around 6.8 full time equivalent home helps per 1,000 elderly over 75 to 44 per thousand. Expenditure on these services within authorities has also varied markedly from 13 per cent of local budgets to 44 per cent (Audit Commission 1986). The Commission has also pointed to gross local authority expenditure on people over 75 varying by as much as a factor of 5.

The Government has done little, however, to isolate myth from reality in its persistent presentation of growing numbers of elderly people as a burden on a society which can ill-afford them. The advice given to elderly people by both the Prime Minister and her former Junior Health Minister to cash in on their principal capital asset, their home, *may* be a realistic and flexible option for *some,* but is not for the overwhelming majority, many of whom are to be found located in the poorer of the 'two nations of old age'. Such advice is also a symptom of the confusion that equates rising numbers of elderly directly with a matching rise in the demand for services. While there are clear areas of demand-growth for some sections of the elderly population, it is unhelpful to manufacture and sustain the myth that old age and dependency are automatically synonymous.

Balancing care

It is the *balance* of care which perhaps provides the most significant challenge for the Government and local authorities in this decade. Undermined by cuts in central funding and uncertain about demographic trends, many local authorities have not planned for the increase in numbers and the changes in need expected between now and the end of the century. Many have been unable or unwilling to tackle mismatches in the balance between private and local authority residential care; others have remained politically unreceptive to voluntary and private care arrangements for their elderly ratepayers; and many others have lost out in joint finance and community care funding arrangements with better organised Health Authorities.

Community care arrangements have proved particularly vexatious for some authorities who have rightly questioned the Conservatives' commitment to the principle and their neglect of the practice. The Government might well insist that existing arrangements represent poor value for the taxpayer but it has been hoist by its own petard by the Audit Commission which states bluntly that 'much of the replacement for hospitals is in the form of residential and nursing home care; and more effective community services are not being adequately developed' (Audit Commission, 1986). The Government is only now awakening to the crisis of confidence it has provoked in the local authority sector as a result of its encouragement of private residential care through social security subsidy. The exponential growth of the latter has left a bitter taste for local authorities repeatedly sent packing with the Treasury's rebuff that there is no public money for an expansion of community-based services for the elderly. The fact is that central government, by using the control of resources to shape and determine need, has added further to the mismatch between services and people that the Audit Commission so lucidly exposed.

The Audit Commission might also be thanked for galvanising a faltering debate on community care in general. Arguments for structural change; a throughgoing critique of present planning and funding arrangements; calls for the coordination of social security policy with community care expenditure; the delegation and decentralisation of managerial authority; and the alignment of agencies – public, private and voluntary, thoughtfully bridged the gap between the Short Report on Community Care (House of Commons, 1985) and the Griffiths Report in March 1988. These reports on what is a substantial part of the future of the personal social services in Britain surfaced during a period when the confidence and sense of direction of local authorities had taken a battering. Pointers to a stronger presence for the health service in the community and a blurring of traditional roles and professional boundaries in respect of 'cash and care' have not improved the view in some quarters that the personal social services are drifting.

Many of the concerns that feature in the provision of social services to elderly people are to be found also in the field of mental handicap. Central government has remained pre-occupied with the politically visible issue of hospital closure and deinstitutionalisation without either properly preparing the community for the consequences of this programme or in any way realistically acknowledging in policy terms that the great majority of people with a mental handicap *already* live in the community.

It is in the care of elderly and mentally handicapped people that Mrs Thatcher's governments have most clearly sought to demonstrate that the frontiers of state provision may be vigorously rolled back and the tasks and burden of care can be cheaply 're-exported' to the community itself. The old cliché that care in the community has become care *by* the community is amply proven. Savings might be made in the short-term and the Treasury may well utilise these to finance tax cuts and, in turn, to stimulate macroeconomic growth. In the long term, however, the social and economic costs could prove untenable for carers, consumers and society alike. Already, the increased pressure on carers and the continuing and often unresourced needs of people with a mental handicap can be seen in the growth of admissions to mental handicap hospitals for short-term respite care. Many of these admissions result from a lack of care or housing resources in the community with the consequence that a new class of long-stay mental handicap patient has developed.

Inevitably, local authorities have responded variably to a range of influences including the availability of joint finance;

uncertainties about long-term planning and resourcing; the punitive nature of rate support grant settlements and their own
schedule of political and social priorities. The Audit Commission itself noted that, perversely 'in the current climate
of restraints on local government expenditure, those authorities that wish to develop community care policies must either
make equivalent cuts elsewhere in their budgets, or they must
transfer a disproportionately high burden of cost onto local
ratepayers' (Audit Commission, 1986).

Local authorities are also having to provide services to 10,000
or more people with a mental handicap than they had to ten
years ago and are also having to meet the needs of 17,000
more mentally ill people. If the Conservatives persist in insisting
that the personal social services must bear their share of public
expenditure restraint while, at the same time, they continue
to encourage a global policy of care in the community, the
crisis envisaged by the House of Commons Social Services
Committee will be earlier and deeper than imagined.

The smaller numbers of children with a mental handicap
currently in our schools and the larger and growing number of
young adults with a mental handicap, together with a significant
increase in numbers over 40 years of age with a mental handicap,
mean that parents are accordingly older and less able to cope and
that pressures on local authority services are increasing. To com-
pound the situation further, needs are increasingly concentrated
in the inner city where the population is less mobile and where
authorities are most likely to be rate-capped and overwhelmed by
consumer pressures generally. For local authorities there is now
the dual prospect of having to meet the needs, on the one hand, of
their traditional client group, i.e. those who would *not* be admitted
to long-stay hospitals and, on the other, of those in the past who
would have been admitted but cannot now enter hospital because
of closures and the programme of deinstitutionalisation.

The Audit Commission advocated 'a change in organisational
and financial arrangements . . . to match changes in the patterns of
care and the increasing burden on local authorities'. It called also
for 'serious consideration' to be given 'to assigning responsibility
for this client group to local authorities, with resources transferred
to them from the NHS where appropriate'. The alternative it
argued might be that the 'totality of services may contract

unacceptably'. This, as we shall see in the next section, is a spectre that stalks the personal social services generally.

3   Welfare into the 1990s

'A wider conception of social services'

In September 1984, Norman Fowler, in a major speech on the future of the social services, expressed his hope that the ideas he had been putting forward for a 'new role for social services departments' would become the subject of 'more extended debate and consultation', and that such a debate must 'develop further the idea of a strategic and enabling role for social services departments'. The Secretary of State had reassessed Seebohm and found in it strong arguments for 'a wider conception of social services'. He saw this concept of 'enabling' as 'fundamental to the role of social services departments that I want to promote'.

In announcing his intentions for a review of the personal social services, Mr Fowler's view was that society must increasingly look away from the state for the provision of care and must tap instead what he and his colleagues believed to be 'a great reservoir of voluntary and private effort'.

The government clearly saw a number of advantages in dismantling and narrowing existing arrangements. 'A wider conception of social services' offered the opportunity to reduce expenditure and shed responsibilities; it would reshape and control expectations; it would provoke new ideas and new initiatives; it would offer an opportunity to compare practice and policy between sectors; and it would strike a curiously populist chord, finely tuned to the Thatcherite emphasis on freedom, self-help and responsibility, which would enable tens of thousands to 'give something back to their own local community by participating in social support'. Ultimately, society would come to recognise the family as the frontline of care, that the closest circle of support should be friends and neighbours and that voluntary organisations and charities could step in thereafter. The social services department would be firmly recast in the mould of 'enabler' rather than direct provider, facilitating and perhaps co-ordinating the efforts of these other sources of support.

This view of the future was not confined to an outline of the mechanics for shifting responsibilities for care, it was also about setting in train new processes of socialisation that would alter expectations and perceptions about the levels and the nature of care. Statutory social services in this vision of the future would have a secondary role 'to back up and develop the assistance which is given by private and voluntary support'. There would in future be no single ideology of care. There would be no further wrangle about *who* provides because *somebody* would eventually – if only by default. There is very little in this vision, however, about consumer needs or aspirations, or about the future patterns of resources; little attention is paid to the need for accountability or for open access to services or to issues of ethnic, gender or cultural sensitivity. No mention is made of equality of treatment or of standards in education and training. As a vision of the future, it is at best partial and at worst deeply flawed.

Social services departments would have three paramount responsibilities;First, they would have a comprehensive, strategic view of *all* the sources of care available in their area; second, they would recognise that direct provision is only *part* of the local pattern and that other forms of provision and other roles for statutory agencies are both available and to be worked at; Thirdly, social services departments would have as their primary task, not direct service provision but, rather, monitoring and supporting the other sources of care which exist or which can be somehow developed within or by the community itself.

Departments thus face the prospect of becoming *integrators* of other services. This would involve a number of developments. We can expect to see a greater sharing of responsibilities and closer collaboration with the other *statutory* services. This would result in a 'strategic overview' that seems to overlook the fact that the other statutory services have their *own* complex and apparently 'intractable' problems. The blueprint for the 1990s also requires greater committments by departments to both redistribute *and* make more effective the use of existing resources – a requirement wholly consonant with the emphasis placed on value for money and targeting throughout the 1980s. The real twist in the storyline will come through wholly new initiatives to exploit resources on offer from outside the traditional net, i.e. from the business community, from charitable foundations and from philanthropic trusts and independent social welfare organisations. This is particularly important to grasp since 'extraneous resourcing' of this type (if indeed it is possible), is so clearly central to the blueprint.

It is for this reason that the resources needed for the new role social services departments are developing in the 1990s 'are not the bulk supplies of money, plant and personnel needed to provide new services. Rather, they are the less tangible requirements of change; leadership with vision to strike away from the safe franchise of traditional practices . . . conditions in which staff use resources creatively and to best effect' (Fowler, 1984).

Marketing and regulating the PSS

The very suggestion of a regulatory role for social services departments in the 1990s and beyond begs the question, Regulation of what? The Conservative Party has long cherished ambitions of privatising social services where possible and, where it is not, of offsetting public expenditure through selective charges. While the influences, variously, of Seldon and Harris in the late 1960s and more recently of Hayek, Minsford, the Centre for Policy Studies and the 'public choice school' have each developed further the arguments for a more market-oriented approach to welfare, the fact is that charges were an early feature of the post-war welfare state. They have been 'an integral part of the historical development of the welfare state' (Judge and Mathews, 1980; King, 1987).

Writing in 1976, Roy Parker ascribed five separate purposes to the use of charges: to reduce the cost to taxpayers of providing a constant supply of service; to reduce those costs by reducing demand from consumers and lowering the level of supply; to shift priorities from one group to another; to prevent waste or abuse arising from a free and open-ended service; to act as 'symbols' or 'ideological marker flags' (*Journal of Social Policy*, vol. 5, 1986). Charges may also be seen by the local authority itself as a means to some financial autonomy or the means by which increasingly scarce public funds are supplemented.

No doubt this partly reflects a general pressure to attract revenue against costs at a time of public expenditure constraint and rising consumer expectations. There is every reason to suppose that charges will become a firmly entrenched and much more developed feature of the 1990s landscape. *The Next Ten Years* in 1984 did, after all, look to offsetting public sector costs either by shifting service provision into the private sector and/or by introducing or increasing charges for local authority-provided services. We can safely add a third option also. This would provide for local authorities to charge *each other* for the services they are most cost-effective at providing and would resemble the recent development of an 'internal market' between hospitals and health authorities within the NHS. Thus we might expect to see a situation in which one local authority buys in the whole or part of its home help services from another, while in turn 'exporting' its own cost effective community transport arrangements to a third.

The Next Ten Years, however, clearly favoured privatisation where possible, noting that the lack of a price mechanism in the public sector made demand virtually limitless. The way out of the vortex would be simple 'wherever it is possible and sensible to do so, the Government is seeking to transfer the provision of services into the market sector' (Cmnd 9189).

The Conservative blueprint for social policy in the 1990s does not so much resemble a wholesale abdication of state responsibility for either funding or provision of services, as, rather, a reformulation of what those responsibilities really mean. Service boundaries, resource allocation and assessment and the means to 'police' and review each are key determinants of the new welfare. The orthodox role of the state as primary provider and funder is increasingly giving way to the state as an *enabler* (i.e. Community Care), as a *subsidiser* (i.e. private residential care) and as a *regulator* (private residential and nursing care). The state will continue to have a strong and continuing role in planning and monitoring welfare but its role in direct production has diminished and will diminish further. This inevitably raises questions about what actually constitutes, and how we may best promote and defend the 'public interest'. Can this be best determined by private means or by public means or by public supervision of private production?

One key myth that will be severely tested is that privatisation will necessarily lead to a reduction in public expenditure. Evidence, not least from the experience of private residential care, suggests that public funding is and will remain a key dynamic in encouraging and sustaining private welfare initiatives. The spectacular growth of private residential care has been massively assisted by the injection of over £1 billion of social security benefits in the latter half of the 1980s alone, much to the rancour of many local authorities struggling to provide services at the margins. Yet the local authorities may still hold the ultimate ace in any private welfare blueprint. Their experience, staffing and training, their direct local knowledge and political accountability and their expertise and professional strengths suggest that 'the more the state depends on the private production of welfare, the more it is drawn into extending its responsibilities for the public regulation of such provision'. The development of the personal social services in this decade is likely to be characterised by a significant culture-shift away from the orthodoxy of 'public versus private' and in favour of the *principle* of 'horses for courses' (in which there will be many more private entrants) and the *practise* of 'stewardship' in regard of regulations, assessment and the quality of care provided. In time we may see this developed further with local authority 'stewards' playing a key part in the accreditation and pricing policy of private producers, and requiring satisfaction in each before the latter are able to enter the market. In short, the price of a major extension of market principles in the personal social services may yet be some concession from Conservative privateers that such a market must be properly regulated and governed by some form of public accountability.

This may prove too much to bear for some private producers and their supporters since it holds the prospect, in their view, of being 'held to ransom' by the regulating agency. The report of the Joint Central and Local Government Working Party on Public Support for Residential Care (The Firth Committee) put the cat amongst the pigeons by concluding that the financing of residents should rest solely with the local authorites and that this should be accompanied by local authority assessment of the care needs of people requiring financial support in private and voluntary homes.

The difficulties ahead may be seen in the divisions which took place within the Working Party itself. Local government members argued that professional assessment should be extended to people receiving social security benefits in the private and voluntary sectors in order to 'inform and protect' them. The central government members of the Firth Committee were neither persuaded that social security expenditure would be much reduced by assessment nor were they convinced of the merits of assessment itself. In the final analysis the likelihood of an extension of assessment was seen to depend on who ultimately assumed responsibility for financing residential care in the private sector. This one issue offered a startling microcosm of all the key arguments raging around 'public versus private'. The private sector wants to expand further but requires public money to enable it to do so.The Conservative Government would like to encourage further expansion but is now counting the cost. A compromise would see the local authorities acquire a regulatory role that would also meet calls for greater and more professional control over standards of care and service provision: The private sector, meanwhile, regards this as a gun at their head and argues that some local authorities would simply use assessment to disadvantage them in the competition for clients. And the Government itself is not at all convinced that the best way to further the cause of privatisation, even allowing for the need to improve standards and extend professional assessment, is to deposit another half a billion pounds of public money into the hands of the very bodies they have so long regarded as the principle targets for financial restraint.

Postscript – whatever happened to the Green Paper?

When Norman Fowler spoke of reshaping the personal social services, there was an immediate expectation of a Green Paper. The Green Paper has not emerged, however, or certainly not in its traditional form. But Mrs Thatcher's governments have prided themselves in upsetting political and administrative convention and the personal Social Services have not escaped the treatment. In fact, the 'Green Paper' is all around us and has been since early 1984, some months before the Secretary of State even began to speak of it.

It is there in *The Next Ten Years* which so determinedly set out the case for expenditure determining demand and which so rigorously sought to apply fiscal policy to social need. It can be found in the 1986 Social Security Act which introduced the social fund, controversial new arrangements for liaison between social fund officers and social workers and which has since resulted in the 'clientisation' of social security claimants. Its spirit is invested in the boundary changes for social services and Health Service professionals set out in the primary health care White Paper *Promoting Better Health Cmnd 249* (November 1987), the Cumberledge

Report *Neighbourhood Nursing – A Focus For Care* (HMSO, 1986) and parts of the nurse training document *Project 2000.*

It is to be found also in the outcomes of a number of major public inquiries on child abuse, not least the reports on the Jasmine Beckford and Tyra Henry cases and the Cleveland Child Abuse Inquiry. It stares out from the pages of the Social Services Inspectorate reports on *The Registered Homes Act 1984* (1987) and *From Home Help to Home Care* (1987): And it may be most fully detected in the 1985 and 1986 reports of the Audit Commission on social services for elderly people and community care respectively. Latterly, the Wagner Report, *Residential Care: A Positive Choice*, and the report by Sir Roy Griffiths, *Community Care: Agenda For Action*, on the way in which public funds were and could be used to support community care, were seen by many as cornerstones of a loosely-writ 'Green Paper' on the future of the personal social services.

Griffiths and Wagner each raised fundamental issues, about the future shape and direction of the personal social services. Both offered the prospect of achieving more flexible and more pluralistic care arrangements than hitherto and full implementation of both would do much to progress the reality of consumer choice.

Both, however, to different degrees, were less clear about where the resources to achieve this could come from. On the other hand, the support of both reports for the local authority to retain 'lead status' in community care and residential care, despite efforts to couch that support in other terms, was much less attractive to ministers whose low regard for local authorities as service-providers had become less and less disguised. Ministers clearly interpreted some of the more imaginative initiatives put forward as little more than unhelpful additional pressures to win more local authority resources. Wagner's call for a social care service at home and the development of *real* alternative care packages which exhorted the government to move away from a resource-led in favour of a needs-led service may at the time have been immensely attractive to social services staff and to consumers but it ran contrary to everything the Conservatives set out in *The Next Ten Years* and in the 1986 Public Expenditure White Paper, and since, about controlling need and ensuring that resources determine expenditure.

The emphasis placed on choice, on quality and on individuality of care, and on the need to transform the image *and* reality of residential care from that of a 'last resort' to a 'positive' care choice may have been welcome but hardly radical, since Wagner was both coy and uncertain about how and with what resources this was to be achieved. Even as it was launched, there was an expectation that the report would simply founder because it had chosen to ignore the stricture that for any policy or initiative to have a chance of success it must be *costed*, and costed cheaply and effectively. This was a serious oversight which flawed and undermined some fine principles and sound ideas.

Sir Roy Griffiths was more exact in what he believed was required to make funding of community care more effective. Griffiths was perhaps general rather than uncertain about resources and his critics may have missed the point that drawing up or making the case for new resources was not in his terms of reference. Griffith's recommendation that a Minister for State for Community Care be appointed as someone who would be 'seen by the public as being clearly responsible for community care' was long overdue and was designed to give encouragement and purpose to the coordinative and strategic measures the Government itself has favoured for community care for some years. On the other hand, such an appointment has always had the disadvantage that it would steer expectations back into the path of central government at a time when it so clearly has wished the community itself would get on with the task.

It was in recommending the responsibilities of the social services department that Griffiths was most revealing. A continuing emphasis on the needs of both individual consumers and their carers was welcome, if predictable. More interesting was his call for departments to establish local plans, priorities and service objectives in consultation with other agencies, including those in the voluntary and private sector, and to examine *all* resources available in a local community *before* implementing policy. The script could almost have been written by Norman Fowler and it took forward logically the ideas the latter had set out in September 1984. Griffiths also found common cause with Fowler's earlier calls for an extension of welfare pluralism and emphasised that social services departments need not be direct providers of care of services. He, too, raised the prospect for the 1990s of the regulatory role for departments, to which we referred earlier, recommending that departments 'act for these purposes as the designers, organisers and purchasers of non-health care services and not primarily as direct providers, making the maximum possible use of voluntary and private sector bodies'.

Griffith's major thrust, lay, like Wagner and Firth, in the area of residential care and its link with community-based services. Local authorities would have responsibility for assessing the need for residential care and for meeting the costs of caring for people who could not pay for themselves. Whether local authorities actually want or could cope financially with expanded 'topping-up' arrangements is quite another matter and if implemented could plunge local and central government into yet another confrontation over the adequacy of resources. Some local authorities would no doubt also contest the establishment of joint planning bodies representing all welfare 'contributors' and encompassing the full spectrum of community service provision, despite the fact that pragmatically and historically Griffiths was quite consistent with ideas advanced by the House of Commons Social Services Committee and the Audit Commission. There was close consistency also in the recommendations for improved local authority community care programmes. Even the relatively fresh idea of central government specific grants targeted to match defined responsibilities and conditional on local authority performance, and fidelity to central government policy, remained consistent with central concerns to establish value for money, local responsibility and the overall priority of the centre.

It may still prove to be the case that Griffiths's 'mistake' was that he came too *close* to succeeding in his efforts to take the Government at face value and to find solutions to the continuing policy impasse on community care and to have done so, as some have overlooked, 'within the resources available'. He may have disappointed Treasury ministers in finding no case for cost reductions and in identifying the problems besetting community care in terms of roadblocks, notably the perversity of Rate Support Grant, and not in terms of vehicles, i.e. local authorities and health authorities. His reaffirmation of earlier concerns about the lack of bridging finance and his fierce criticism of the lack of care packages for mentally-ill people returning to the community cannot have endeared him to ministers either. Nor can his support for the Audit Commission's conclusion in 1986 that 'what is *not* tenable is to do nothing'.

Elsewhere, however, Griffiths did succeed in raising the profile of welfare pluralism and encouraged ministers in his call for full stimulation of the private sector and recommendations for the extension of competitive tendering and means of testing the market. His criticism of local authority information systems, their lack of management accounting and the promotion of vouchers and credits for local services should all figure powerfully over the next few years. Its greatest fault could be that it took *too* balanced a view. And balance, as the last decade of social policy has shown, is not a luxury that the conviction politician can easily comprehend or afford.

2

Health

JUDITH ALLSOP

'The NHS has done the health of the people a dis-service because it has prevented the development of more spontaneous, organic, local, voluntary and sensitive medical services that would have grown up as incomes rose and medical science and technology advanced. If it were not for the politically controlled NHS we should have seen new forms of medical organisation and financing that better reflected consumer preferences, requirements and circumstances.' (Arthur Seldon, *The Litmus Papers: A National Health Dis-service*, London, Centre for Policy Studies, 1980.)

1 The NHS: policies and principles

The policies of Mrs Thatcher's governments have been framed by a commitment to a number of general principles. First, economic issues have taken precedence over social concerns. In the interests of creating an enterprise economy, the aim has been to reduce public borrowing and expenditure. Social spending has been a particular target; thus annual plans, outlined by the Treasury, have set the targets and limits for the spending ministries including the Department of Health and Social Security (DHSS). Second, the aim has been to transfer the burden of welfare provision away from the state towards the family and community. Third, a priority has been placed on increasing the role of the private sector and the principles of the free market have been used to increase competition within the public sector. Lastly, and most fundamentally for

53

the New Right, the individual is seen to have a right to, and responsibility for, choice and action.

These principles have provided an ethos for Thatcherism, although outcomes in the measurable terms of public expenditure have been modest. Public expenditure grew in real terms by 7 per cent between 1978–9 and 1986–7 (Gretton and Harrison, 1987).

The NHS has posed something of a dilemma for Conservatives in the light of these over-riding aims. It is very largely financed from taxation; it is free to all citizens at the point of use and it covers a comprehensive range of services in the areas of cure, care and prevention. It is, furthermore, a service where the professional providers determine the quantity, and level of service, and have considerable monopoly power over both governments and service users. There are difficulties in achieving policy objectives, and shortfalls can be put down to a lack of resources from the centre.

The NHS is a large and complex institution. In 1986, it employed over 800000 staff and attracted £20 billion in public funding (OHE, 1987). The high public profile of the service and the suspicion that its principles are on the point of erosion, is, as Enoch Powell a former Minister of Health pointed out, a consequence of the structure and funding of the service (Powell, 1966). There is no intervening tier of local government. Public criticism is a way of service providers gaining salary increases for themselves, as well as gaining resources for patient services. Furthermore, health care has an emotional appeal and is popular. The 1986 Social Attitude Survey (Taylor-Gooby 1987) confirmed that health care was the sector which most people ranked first in their priorities for extra government spending. Opinion polls have, on a number of occasions, indicated that the public prefer extra funding for the NHS to tax cuts.

Partly as a consequence of these factors, it has been harder for Conservative governments to introduce radical reforms in the NHS than in other policy areas. There have been constant reassurances of good intent. This was well-illustrated in the pledge given by former Secretary of State for Social Services, John Moore. At the Conservative Party Conference in 1987, he declared that: 'It [the NHS] is a British vision, not one that belongs to any political party . . . There is no way this long proud tradition is going to be abandoned – certainly not by a Conservative government. We are committed to the health service in principle and we are committed to it in practice' (NAHA News, November 1987). Nevertheless in 1988, the NHS came under a Prime Ministerial review.

The low levels of growth in expenditure, or 'cumulative under-funding', during the 1980s brought a sense of crisis, so that the NHS may now be at a watershed in its development. Time was bought by a substantial and fully-funded pay rise for doctors and nurses in April 1988, but the circumstances were created for the consideration of radical change. The review may ultimately herald a significant shift in public responsibility for health services or it could simply mark a movement towards tighter management of the hospital sector and a more mixed economy in the caring services.

Whatever its longer-term outcome, Thatcherism has brought into relief some of the more deep-seated problems in providing health care in the second half of the twentieth century. Behind the immediate cash crisis lie a number of structural and other factors which have increased the demand for health care in all industrial societies. Section 1 of this chapter examines these issues, and the public policy response during the 1960s and 1970s. Section 2 outlines Conservative policies during the 1908s indicating continuity and change, while Section 3 considers policy options in the 1990s.

Pressures on the NHS: Demography, Technology, Equality

Bevan's vision of a universally available and comprehensive health service has set the paradigm for health policy in the UK since the 1940s. However, from the 1960s onwards there has been increasing central direction and control of the policy process as health care costs have risen due to social and demographic change. Crossman captured the issues succinctly when he referred to the pressures of demography; the pressures of technology and the pressure for equality of provision (Crossman, 1972). The three are inter-related. As medical knowledge has advanced, a greater variety of treatments have become available. Diagnosis has also been aided by technological innovations. Public awareness of the possibilities of medical intervention has increased, as well as expectations about efficacy. The numbers of health care professionals have risen, and so has the proportion of the population who are elderly. Both factors have led to a greater demand for health services. Furthermore, the principles of the NHS dictate that what is available in one part of the country, should be available in another.

Governments during the 1960s and 1970s, whether Conservative or Labour, aimed to plan and deliver health care through what Webb and Wistow (1982) refer to as governance, resource and service policies. The health service was reorganised in 1970, and the nursing and medical professions restructured. A variety of measures were introduced to control and allocate resources, while a number of committees, commisssions and consultative documents laid down guidelines for the development of services for mentally ill and handicapped people. The 'Cinderella' services, as they were then called, were given priority. During this period, the pressures for more resources were met within a set of conventions. Although NHS budgets were cash-limited from the early 1970s, allocations were increased on the basis of allowances for demographic and technological change, and service development. Pay awards were usually met in full by the Treasury.

However, despite its achievements, the NHS was criticised from a number of directions. The Right argued that it was inefficient, bureaucratic and unresponsive to users. The Left concurred, but attributed inadequacies to professional dominance and inadequate funding. The Left were also concerned that the NHS had failed to achieve sufficient equality of access to services. Several studies had indicated that the poor received worse services, while the middle classes had benefited disproportionately (Townsend and Davidson, 1986; LeGrand, 1982). More fundamental criticisms came from academe. McKeown demonstrated that the improvements in health status which had occurred over the last century were due to environmental factors rather than medical interventions, or health services (McKeown, 1979).

From the vantage point of the 1980s, it is possible to argue that Bevan's 1946 Act, although a major legislative achievement, introduced certain biases in health policy and a lack of institutional flexibility. The emphasis on universal provision (translated into equal treatment for equal need) has meant that less attention has been paid to achieving minimum standards and updating facilities. Governments have been more concerned with staff and resource inputs and less with outputs of service, and outcomes of treatment. There has been more emphasis on health services for populations organised within hierarchical regional groupings and less on specific groups, such as elderly people, poor people, women, ethnic minorities, for whom service linkages across institutional boundaries are important. Perhaps most critically, there has been more emphasis on the treatment of illness than on the prevention of ill health. Health policy in the UK has been dominated by issues concerned with the management of the NHS.

Although this chapter is concerned mainly with areas where governments have actively intervened to change the direction of policy, what Bachrach and Baratz (1971) refer to as 'non-decisions' are also relevant to understanding the significance of policy choice. There are issues critical to health which have been *kept off* the policy agenda. A wider view of health policy which deals with the health status of populations, and differences in health status between groups within populations, the causes of ill health and the maintenance of good health, have concerned doctors and academics, but not on the whole, governments, particularly Conservative ones. Such issues have been marginalised through specific health education programmes.

Concentration on the NHS reflects a policy choice about intervening at the level of the individual and providing an illness service, rather than via a wider strategy concerned with improvements in standards of living. The 1942 Beveridge Report was based on proposals for an inter-related set of welfare measures dealing with income support, housing, employment and education as well as health. In 1980, the Black Report outlined a programme for a wide range of measures for public policies drawing on knowledge of the inter-connections between standards of living, environmental factors and ill health (DHSS 1980). Governments have not chosen to pursue the interconnections to achieve a 'healthy public policy'.

2   Conservative policies for the NHS in the 1980s

Incremental change: patients first, the Griffiths Report and general management

Policies shaping the operation of the NHS during the 1980s were characterised by both continuity and change. One theme was the search for a means of increasing central control, while diffusing responsibility for service provision and consumer choice to the health authorities at the periphery. *Patients First* was a consultative document published in the early months of the 1979 Conservative Government (DHSS, 1979). It led to a simplified NHS structure in 1982. The changes arose logically from criticisms of the over-complex structure made by the Merrison Commission (Royal Commission on the NHS, 1979). The Area tier of administration was abolished, and there are now 190 Health Districts in England, accountable through 14 regions to the Secretary of State. Different arrangements exist in Wales and Scotland. The Welsh Office and the Scottish Home and Health Department pursue slightly different policies (Hunter and Wistow, 1987).

Patients First signalled a change of language and rhetoric. The emphasis was on patients (though not yet consumers) and the Districts were identified as the bodies responsible for determining policy to suit local needs. Yet, in practice, their ability to do so was to be tightly constrained through budgets set by the DHSS, and by Regions. For example, since the early 1980s the DHSS has issued instructions to Districts requiring them to make efficiency savings annually. Regions were identified in *Patients First* as strategic planning authorities, and a top-down review process was introduced in 1983. This proved to be a powerful mechanism for upward accountability in meeting targets within resource and service policies.

The Griffiths Inquiry (DHSS, 1983) and the subsequent implementation of its proposals for the introduction of 'general management' into the health service brought another crucial change of emphasis. The centre can now ensure that the lower tier authorities are more accountable, yet at the same time their responsibilities have increased. The Griffiths Report is of significance, too, because it represents a diagnosis of the problems of delivering health care via a publicly funded and regulated service. It spelt out the 1980s solution acceptable to Conservative politicians.

Roy Griffiths (then a director of Sainsburys) concluded that the NHS suffered from 'institutionalised stagnation'. It was an organisation where change was difficult to achieve and where there was a lack of clarity about objectives: 'the NHS [could not] display a ready assessment of the effectiveness with which it is meeting the needs and expectations of the people it serves. Business men have a keen sense of how well they are looking after their customers. Whether the NHS is meeting the needs of the patient and the community, and can prove it is doing so is open to question.' There was a recognition in the Report that the authority to make decisions was exercised by a number of groups, notably the medical profession. Spending decisions had a ripple effect upward through the organisation, but there was no mechanism for either predicting or controlling costs. This point had been clearly demonstrated by a number of studies during the 1970s (Klein, 1983; Hunter, 1982; Elcock and Hayward, 1980).

The aim, or spirit, of the Griffiths recommendations was to introduce the concepts and methods of business management into the NHS in order to change the organisational culture. Central to this enterprise was the appointment of a single person at Regional, District and Unit level to replace the former professionally-based team. The general manager had responsibility for running their part of the organisation within allocated budgets. The general management task was to provide 'a driving force for developing management plans and accepting personal responsibility for this'. This was to ensure 'appropriate levels of service, quality of product, meeting budgets, cost improvement, productivity, monitoring and rewarding the staff, research and development and initiating the measurement of health outputs'.

The changes proposed by Griffiths were quickly introduced, along with some features of the business world, such as short-term contracts for general managers and performance-related pay. At the centre a Health Service Supervisory Board was established with functional heads responsible to a Chairman. It was intended that the Board should operate independently of the Minister but following the resignation of the first incumbent, the Minister for Health chairs the Board. Within the health authorities there was an attempt, though not a particularly successful one, to recruit managers from outside the health service.

The Griffiths diagnosis of the ills of the NHS was widely accepted. The structure and culture of the service was ill-suited to adapting to change: setting priorities and objectives, monitoring and evaluating. In order to carry out these tasks successfully, however, managers had to face the problem of an inadequate database. Although there was a great deal of information about the activity of the NHS and about the input of resources – staff, capital and revenue – this was not in a form which made it possible to itemise the costs of care for each patient. Nor was it possible to trace patients' treatment over time so as to evaluate effectiveness. Without this sort of data managers could not meet some of the requirements of their new posts.

Since the mid-1980s, therefore, considerable effort has been expended in developing and implementing methods for increasing efficiency and effectiveness. Some DHSS policies have simply been top-down directives to save money. The National Audit Office commented that in some instances it was difficult to distinguish between savings, and cuts in services (National Audit Office, 1986). The Korner Reports (DHSS, 1984–6) made recommendations about the kinds of databases which Districts should develop. These are now being implemented and health authorities should be in a better position to understand and control their activity. There are also experiments in some authorities in developing clinical budgeting, and other systems to enable clinicians and managers to make choices within financial constraints.

The introduction of general management can be represented as a continuing search by the centre for control over the use of health resources. However, it also marks a change of ethos from the organic view of the NHS epitomised in the 1979 Royal Commission. Here, the producers of health care were viewed as having legitimate interests. Their well-being was necessary to patient care within a consensual, participative, if somewhat paternalistic, model. Now, health care is viewed as a series of goods provided for consumers by specialists who must be controlled and managed by a cadre of expert managers. Their line of accountability is upwards to the controllers of resources (ministers and civil servants) at the centre. These managers have been encouraged to use their entreprenurial skills to raise money from alternative sources and to develop partnerships with the private sector in ways outlined below.

Continuities: policies for regional resource allocation, and for community care

An area where there was a clear continuity of policy between the 1970s and 1980s was in relation to the redistribution of resources from better endowed to less well-off Regions. One of the major problems for all health-care systems is that areas with higher concentrations of population and income tend to have better health services. These area inequalities persist over time. The UK is no exception, and for the first thirty years of the NHS, inequalities were perpetuated by a funding system of incremental growth based on historic costs.

In 1976, the Resource Allocation Working Party (RAWP) proposed a formula for resource distribution according to need (DHSS, 1976). Carrier has called RAWP 'the most significant attempt at planned change in the NHS since its inception' (Carrier, 1978). Simply put, the RAWP formula provides a basis for assessing relative need within Regions, then dividing the national resource for the NHS and setting targets for the gradual equalisation of resources via a series of annual budgets. The formula is based on weighted population figures – the population of the Region with allowances for age and sex, because the proportions of elderly and young people will affect the need for services. The inclusion of standardised mortality ratios (SMRs) provides a proxy weighting for morbidity. These figures form the basis for an allocation of funds which is then further adjusted for cross-boundary flows (patients living in one Region but treated in another) and SIFT, an allowance for the extra costs generated by teaching hospitals in the clinical training of medical and dental students.

The RAWP formula was first applied to the NHS budget in 1977–8. At this time, there was a 27 per cent difference between the best endowed Region (needs in relation to resources) and the poorest (Mays and Bevan, 1987). After ten years, the gap between the best-off and worst-off Regions had narrowed substantially. Birch and Maynard (1986) calculated that with the exception of North-East Thames and North-West Thames, all Regions were within 4 per cent, above, or below, their RAWP targets. During the 1980s therefore, the resources for some Regions grew while for others there were substantial reductions. What is not known is how extra resources have been translated into services, and the consequences of this for patient care.

The intention of the RAWP policy was that funding on criteria of need should be applied by Regions to Districts. However, Regions followed different strategies which were not always spelt out. There are still large differences between Districts in resources according to need. For example, Mays and Bevan note that among the teaching Districts, the largest variation is between Nottingham at 92 per cent of the target (100), and Paddington and North Kensington at 197 per cent. Although there has been considerable criticism of RAWP, particularly from areas which lose most from the exercise, it is likely that it will remain the basis of distributing NHS funding for the foreseeable future. A DHSS Working Party (DHSS 1986b) concluded that the RAWP formula remained the best available measure of need.

The second resource policy – priority funding for elderly, mentally ill and mentally handicapped people – also has service implications. Health and local authorities have been expected to develop a range of services in the community, rather than in residential institutions. In 1976, the consultative document, *Priorities for the Health and Personal Social Services in England,* outlined target spending for the priority services, with relative reductions in the acute hospital services (DHSS, 1976). The document was seen as a new departure as, for the first time, an attempt had been made to establish priorities throughout the health and social services (Owen, 1976). However, unlike RAWP, the policies for community care have proved difficult to implement.

Overall target figures for resource allocations were quickly abandoned. A later government policy document, *Care in Action* (DHSS, 1981), simply requested Districts and local authorities to develop community care. Funding was limited to specific projects. Two examples are 'dowry funding' to facilitate the movement of patients from a long-term residential setting into the community, and financing for joint health, local authority or voluntary organisation schemes. Some Regions have set aside special development funds to replace long-stay hospitals with community-based facilities.

The impact of policies for community care is difficult to assess, as a wide group of agencies spanning the public, voluntary and private sectors are involved in providing services. Nevertheless, it is clear that the role of the health sector hospital has decreased. The average number of beds occupied daily in mental hospitals and units declined by 37 per cent between 1971 and 1986 and a similar trend is observable in the case of mental handicap. Other changes have occurred also, lengths of stay have declined and out-patient facilities increased. The numbers of out patient attendances grew two and a half times over the period (Central Statistical Office, 1988, p.126). The number of places provided by local authorities, voluntary and private agencies usually in small units, increased.

Table 2.1 shows that the rate of increase in the private and voluntary sector was more rapid than that of the local authority, although the latter provided well over half of the home and hostel accommodation for mentally ill, and handicapped people.

The rate of growth of community care facilities has varied considerably in different parts of the country. The Audit Commission Report, *Making a Reality of Community Care* (1986), was highly critical of the pace and direction of development. It suggested that good innovative practices were patchy. The subsidy payments through Supplementary Benefit had distorted the market by creating perverse incentives. Local authorities had been encouraged to reduce local publicly-provided facilities, while the unplanned growth of private homes drew people away from their locality in an insufficiently regulated way. In short, in this policy area, while there has been continuity in the overall aims, the means adopted by Conservative governments has shifted community care from the public sector to the private, and diffused responsibility. Systemic and market factors have led to a variety of outcomes.

The 1988 Griffiths Report, *Community Care: Agenda For Action*, was commissioned by the Secretary of State for Social Services to propose an action plan for community care. The Report was clear in its principles. The primary means by which people are enabled to live normal lives in community settings is through informal networks. 'Families, friends, neighbours and other local people provide the majority of care in response to needs which they are uniquely well placed to identify and respond to' (Griffiths, 1988).

Table 2.1 *Homes and hostels for mentally ill and mentally handicapped people: Great Britain 1976–80*

	1976	1981	1985	1986
Mentally ill people:				
number (000s) of places in local authority homes	2.9	4.8	5.4	5.5
in registered private and voluntary homes	1.7	2.3	3.4	4.0
Mentally handicapped people				
number (000s) of places in local authority homes	9.0	14.2	17.0	17.9
in registered private and voluntary homes	3.3	3.6	8.4	9.9

Source: Central Statistical Office, *Social Trends 18*, London, HMSO, 1988.

The first task of the state was therefore to strengthen the network of carers. Social service authorities, it was argued, must identify where networks have broken down. They must design, arrange and purchase care services rather than provide them in a monopolistic fashion. The Report supported a mixed economy approach to community care. It proposed that local authorities should have a clear and major responsibility for planning all aspects of community care. Central government, it suggested, should set clear objectives and arrange the necessary transfer of resources to local government to match defined responsibilities. The Griffiths Report posed a dilemma for the Conservative government. Change required investment. There was a conflict between macroeconomic and social policy objectives, and between planned change and laissez faire. During the 1980s, considerable effort had been expended in curbing the powers and levels of spending in local authorities, yet the Griffiths Report recommended a new, local authority-based funding mechanism to provide community care.

New directions: primary health care

Unlike their predecessors, the Thatcher governments have promoted the development of primary care. Primary care services, using the definition of the DHSS (1986a), include the community health services run by Districts and the family practitioner services (FPS); that is, services provided by GPs; dentists; pharmacists and opticians under contract to Family Practitioner Committees (FPCs). During the 1980s, the FPS element of health service expenditure grew faster than other parts of the NHS, from 21 per cent of the NHS budget in 1977, to nearly 23 per cent by 1987 (OHE, 1987 Table 4.1). The growth was largely attributable to the increase in the cost of prescriptions and items of service payments for doctors.

In 1985, FPCs were given free-standing status, that is they had full responsibility for managing the contracts of family practitioners. They were no longer administratively accountable to the Districts but directly to the Secretary of State. Their functions were expanded from a purely administrative, to a planning and monitoring role. They are now expected to collaborate with DHAs and local authorities to 'secure and advance the health and welfare of the people they serve'. They must establish baseline provision of primary care; identify local needs, opportunities and constraints;

and determine aims and policies and how these might be achieved. They must produce annual programmes, and longer-term strategy plans to review progress periodically (Barnard and Wood, 1986).

These new powers are of most importance in relation to the work of GPs. Since the inception of the NHS, GPs have worked largely independently – like a number of small businesses. They have provided general medical services for those who are registered with them. Collectively, GPs cover virtually the whole population. Their contractual requirements are open-ended. They must be available for consultation at their surgery premises for at least 20 hours per week. They, or their deputies, must be accessible to their patients in emergencies at other times. They must practise from surgeries of a certain standard. Otherwise GPs, within certain limits laid down by the FPC and a national body, the Medical Practices Committee, may work how and where they please.

As a result, there is considerable variation in the type and quality of general practice. For example, in one area a group of GPs may work within a primary care team, from up to date, purpose-built premises, and employing practice nurses, a practice manager or other specialist staff. They may have attached DHA community nurses and social workers. They may cover for each other's night calls and provide a service for their well patients, such as visiting their elderly patients regularly; carrying out routine child health surveillance; screening for hypertension, cervical cytology and other conditions. At the other end of the spectrum, a practice may provide basic emergency services with no additional staff in poor premises, using deputising services for cover.

The main aims of the new powers for FPCs and the proposals of the White Paper, *Promoting Better Health* (DHSS 1987), were to strengthen the powers of FPCs to improve services and encourage activities which promote good health at a primary level. General practice is seen as the cornerstone of health care. GPs are gate-keepers to the rest of the health system as they refer patients on to expensive, specialist services. Care and support may be provided in general practice for vulnerable people outside a hospital setting and illness may thus be detected at an early stage. The GP register is the best source available of population data and therefore of use in any form of screening for illness (see Allsop and May, 1986, ch. 8). The 1987 Health and Medicines Bill proposed that FPS budgets for contractors should be cash-limited. Providing that these are set at levels which give FPCs the capacity for manoeuvre, this may increase FPCs' capacity for managing their practitioners.

Conservative policies in the primary care arena reflect contradictions and tensions between practical policy concerns, and ideology. If hospitals are to be used effectively and prevention developed, primary care should be strengthened. However, professional interests are strongly represented and the potential for a private market is small. The present government has been locked into extensive negotiations with the medical profession and has not, as yet, been prepared to enter into open conflict. Nor have they been prepared to invest to achieve change. In consequence the rhetoric of the new FPC managerialism has been greater than the reality.

Prevention: individual versus societal change

It was argued in the introduction that Conservative governments have been determined to keep the social structural determinants of ill health off the policy agenda. This can be illustrated by three examples. First, in his foreword to the Black Report (DHSS 1980), the then Secretary of State for Social Services, Patrick Jenkin concluded that additional expenditure on the scale implied by the Reports' recommendations 'is quite unrealistic in present, or any forseeable economic circumstances, quite apart from any judgement that may be formed of the effectiveness of such expenditure in dealing with the problems identified'. Second, in a Report for the House of Commons' Agriculture Committee (1987) on the use of pesticides, the Chairman warned of the danger of traditional secrecy and recommended that the effect of pesticides on water supplies should be monitored. Agricultural interests on the Committee scuttled any suggestion of an agreed majority report emerging.

Third, and more recently, the Acheson Committee on Public Health in England found its terms of reference were narrowly drawn. Despite its preference for a broad definition of public health as 'the art and science of preventing disease, prolonging life and promoting health through the organised efforts of society', the Committee was instructed to exclude aspects of public health which were shared by the DHSS and other government departments. Its own view was that these policies 'can have implications for health and that consequently there is a need for effective co-ordination of such policies if health is to be improved' (DHSS, 1988, p.2,1.6).

Where Conservative health policy has taken a preventive outlook, it has focused on changing individual behaviour rather than on the removal or modification of health hazards which might involve policies to reduce disadvantage or the regulation of private interests. Edwina Currie, for example, as a junior Minister at the DHSS, made a number of highly publicised speeches on the effects of smoking and poor diets on health. She attributed the high mortality and morbidity rates in the North of England to individual choice and lifestyle. The shift of emphasis towards prevention in general practice, welcome though it may be, also centres on education and on the offer of screening programmes to individuals. The abolition of the Health Education Council, an independent quango, and its replacement by a Health Education Authority under the direct purview of the DHSS, has ensured that the focus on individual behaviour change is sustained.

The AIDS epidemic has presented the Government with a dilemma. Are AIDS sufferers to be responsible for their own fate? The Government's response has been contradictory. It funded a media campaign on an unprecedented scale to change sexual behaviour, yet such campaigns have had a limited effect in other areas of health education. Although some extra resources have been made available, the government has been reluctant to underwrite the expansion of hospital and community facilities for AIDs patients. Conflicts have arisen within the Conservative Party in relation to AIDs and other competing claims for resources. Moral questions have arisen as to whose needs should be met.

Resourcing the NHS

It was stated at the beginning of this chapter that one of the themes of the Thatcher administrations has been the aim to reduce and rationalise social expenditure. The NHS has fared less badly than housing, education and the personal social services for reasons outlined earlier. There has been a small element of annual growth but this is low compared to growth rates in the 1970s (see Table 2.2 below). Set against most other comparable countries, expenditure on health in the UK is a lower proportion of GDP. Table 2.2 shows the proportion of GDP devoted to health, and per capita expenditure, in different countries.

Furthermore, a recent King's Fund Institute Paper demonstrates that per capita expenditure in the UK is nearly 30 per cent below the level which could be expected if compared to the GDP/health expenditure ratio in other countries. This is the case for both public and private expenditure (King's Fund Institute, 1988, p.10).

By the 1980s, approximately 85 per cent of NHS funding derived from taxation, 3.2 per cent from charges, and 11.8 per cent from national insurance contributions. In recent years the share from taxation has declined while the share from other sources has risen (OHE, 1987, Table 2.7a).

Demographic changes, alterations in the pattern and incidence of disease and technological innovations have each added to the demands for health services. The overt aim of Conservative health ministers has been to contain overall expenditure while seeking to manage the interaction between supply and demand more efficiently. They have sought to increase value for money; that is, they have aimed to increase outputs for

Table 2.2   *Health care expenditure in selected Western countries 1982*

	Expenditure per person (US$)	% of GDP spent on health
Australia	828	7.6
Belgium	534	6.2
Canada	981	8.2
Denmark	746	6.8
France	931	9.3
Germany	874	8.2
Ireland	436	8.2
Italy	441	7.2
Japan	602	6.6
The Netherlands	836	8.7
UK	508	5.9
USA	1388	10.6
Sweden	1168	9.7

Source: OECD *Measuring Health Care: Expenditure, Costs and Performance.* Social Policy Studies no. 2, Paris, OECD, 1985.

Table 2.3 *Public expenditure on health in England 1980/1–1986/7 (volume expenditure*: annual increases, per cent per year)*

	Hospital and community services (current)	FPS (current)	NHS (total)
1980/1	3.0	−1.2	2.8
1981/2	2.0	2.0	3.0
1982/3	0.8	3.5	1.6
1983/4	0.0	2.0	0.9
1984/5	−0.1	2.8	1.4
1985/6	0.2	−1.1	0.1
1986/7	2.7	2.9	2.4

*volume expenditure refers to cash spending adjusted for changes in the prices of health sector inputs.
Source: adapted from R. Robinson and K. Judge (1987) *Public Expenditure and the NHS*, London, King's Fund Institute.

virtually the same resource inputs and to use these more effectively.

In some respects, Conservative governments have been able to demonstrate considerable success in achieving greater economy and productivity. The DHSS Annual Reports for 1985 and 1986 indicated that greater numbers of patients had been treated in fewer beds. Between 1971 and 1986, the number of inpatient discharges and deaths (that is the numbers of patients treated) increased by 24 per cent even though the daily number of beds available fell by 22 per cent. Day care attendances increased by nearly half between 1981 and 1986 (Central Statistical Office, 1988, p.124). There has been increased throughput. However, the question remains as to whether resources have kept pace with demand. Some have disputed the meaning of the figures (Bosanquet, 1985; the Radical Statistics Group, 1987), while others accept improvement in productivity, but argue that this has been insufficient, and masks local shortages.

By the late 1980s, there was a chorus of criticism that the NHS was underfunded. In 1985–6 waiting lists increased by 3 per cent, while in September 1986, in England alone, 61 per cent of urgent cases had been on the waiting list more than one month. Twenty-six per cent of non-urgent cases had been waiting for more than a year (Central Statistical Office, 1988). There is difficulty in establishing how far waiting lists are themselves a construct. They reflect GP behaviour and expectations as well as objective needs. However, there are signs which indicate that NHS resourcing is not keeping pace with the conventional measures of demand. In 1986, the Social Service Select Committee commented:

> Taking into account efficiency savings, on the most favourable interpretation of the Government's own data for the last five years, the Government has done no more than half what, by its own admission, should have been done: resources for the hospital and community health service ought to have grown by 2 per cent in volume terms, but they have actually grown by only 1 per cent since 1980–1. The most telling way of representing the shortfall is to say that between 1980–1 and 1985–6 the cumulative total underfunding on the HCHS [Hospital and Community Health Services] current account was £1,325 billion at 1986–6 prices, after taking full account of the cash-releasing cost improvements (Social Services Committee, 1986, p.xiii).

In 1988, the Social Services Committee concluded that the underfunding had risen to almost £2 billion (Social Services Committee, 1988, p.xiii).

The DHSS reply to these criticisms is that activity is more important than volume of expenditure (what can be done with the resources, rather than what services can be bought). In their review of health service expenditure, Robinson and Judge (1987) comment that volume increases in 1986–87 have shown higher rates of growth, but that this has been too little too late. Table 2.3 below shows the figures.

There are a number of factors which may explain the concern about health service funding at the beginning of the 1990s. Cumulative underfunding has affected in particular the most visible part of the NHS, the hospital services. Health Districts have been affected differentially depending on whether they are RAWP–losing or gaining. The experience of shortages is compounded by a lack of nursing staff. Wards in some areas have been closed because of difficulties in recruiting nurses with the appropriate specialist qualifications. However, Government supporters would argue that for those who work in the service, creating a sense of crisis may be used as a way of winning extra resources. Conversely, Government

detractors might respond that underfunding the NHS creates
an opportunity for expanding the private market.

Market mechanisms in the NHS

A second commitment of the Thatcher governments has been to
increase the role of the market. Market mechanisms have been
used in a variety of different ways: first, to increase the supply
of resources to health care from alternative sources; second, to
extend the use of the price mechanism within the NHS, and third,
to limit demand, thereby diverting it to the private sector. The
pursuit of these strategies also has the effect of meeting another
commitment of the Conservative Party, shifting the responsibility,
or burden, of care to the family and the wider community.

The overall supply of resources going to health care has
been increased by encouraging private insurance, particularly
for groups and companies where subsidies were introduced in
1980. The numbers of persons privately insured increased sharply
from 1979 to 1982 but then levelled off. Paradoxically, contributions
to private sector insurance appear to have grown fastest when
the NHS was also growing. The proportion of the population
contributing to private insurance is still relatively small: 9 per cent
of the population (Central Statistical Office, 1988).

Prescription charges and charges for dental treatment have
risen steeply. In relation to the optical service, a voucher system
for those with low incomes has replaced the former system of
subsidised lenses and NHS frames. There are now plans to
abolish the free sight test. As a consequence of these measures, there has been a slight rise in the proportion of NHS
income derived from charges. There is no good source of data
for people who pay directly in cash for their medical care,
although it is known that almost a quarter of elective surgery
is carried out privately (Gretton and Harrison, 1987).

NHS managers have been encouraged to generate income
from external sources by selling their services to the private
sector or by raising funds from charitable bodies. Although
some Districts have developed in this direction, particularly
in hard-pressed inner London, this activity remains very much
at the margin. It has been the result of crisis management
rather than a consequence of a planned strategy.

As to the second area, the interface between supply and demand, a number of measures have been used to lower costs. For example, the hotel services of the hospital and community services must now be put out to competitive tender. In 1985–6, a saving of £42 million was recorded by the Regions. Over half of this was due to savings from lower in-house tenders for services. This moved the Social Services Committee to comment: 'We wonder how long health authorities will be able to sustain such reductions in costs, in the face of understandable pressures for real wage increases for low paid ancillary staff' (Social Services Committee, 1986, p.xx). The quality of services may have been reduced as a consequence of competitive tendering and it is likely that there are hidden costs as work previously carried out by ancillary workers is shifted to others such as nurses.

In the third area, limiting demand, there are some clear examples. The prescribing for, and making up of, spectacles has been privatised and de-regulated. There have also been a large number of covert rationing mechanisms. The increase in the size of waiting lists is one example. In some areas there is a shortfall of beds related to demand – for example, intensive care beds for very premature babies and open heart surgery. Overall, demand in health care tends to be limited by supply. Ultimately, the governments of Mrs Thatcher have controlled the purse strings and have aimed for a lean and economical NHS.

3   Challenges and options for health policies in the 1990s

Changes in the pattern and incidence of disease

Before speculating about the future direction of health policy, it is appropriate to examine some of the factors which will determine the demand for health care. The major determinants relate to the demographic structure of the population and the pattern and incidence of disease. These rarely change quickly, and have sustained pressure on the NHS for some decades.

Demographically, Britain has moved from a pattern of high birth and death rates in the early nineteenth century, to low birth and death rates in the mid to late twentieth century. Elderly people in general (over 65) will increase their representation within the total population from 14.8 per cent in 1984, to a projected 16.3 per cent in 2013. The proportionate increase in the numbers of the very elderly (over 75) will be slightly higher. For those at the furthest end of the age spectrum, the over-85s, the proportionate increase will be most marked of all.

On average, elderly people consume nine times more health care expenditure than those between 16 and 65. Expenditure on the hospital and community services for the latter is £90 per capita per annum, while for those over 75 the costs are £925 (Robinson and Judge, 1987). Extra resources will be needed simply to keep pace with the increase in the population in dependent groups. In service terms, there will be a high demand for acute hospital care where repairs of different kinds can improve the quality of life – for example, hip replacements, coronary artery, bypass graphs, cardiac pacemakers and corneal transplants. Currently, at any one time, approximately two-thirds of hospital beds are occupied by people over the age of 65 (DHSS, 1988). Some elderly people stay in hospital longer than is necessary because no alternative is available.

Wells suggests that in the future pharmaceutical advances will contribute further to the management out of hospital of chronic illnesses such as asthma, angina, Parkinson's disease and peptic ulceration (Wells, 1987). However, the need for support from professional and other carers for home-management will be crucial in maintaining the quality of life of elderly people, and those who are mentally ill or handicapped.

Apart from diseases of the ageing process, it is difficult to predict with accuracy changes in the pattern and incidence of disease. Disease categories are not fixed, perceptions of conditions alter and new classifications occur. Moreover, consultations with a medical person may take place more readily for conditions previously accepted as normal.

Overall, there has been a small but steady increase in average longevity for men and women. The most substantial reductions in death rates have been in the younger age groups, particularly in infant mortality rates. Although there has been a recent rise, infant death rates are very low. The death rate from infectious diseases has continued to fall. Doll (1988) declares that the two major epidemics are now coronary artery disease and lung cancer. In 1986, the former caused 31 per cent of deaths. This is among the highest rates in the developed world. Lung cancer is also a major cause of death in middle age for men, and other forms of cancer, for women. There has been a significant increase in alcohol-related diseases and in the occurence of drug abuse. Among the chronic conditions, the prevalence of senile dementia has increased.

It is unlikely that these disease patterns will change significantly into the 1990s. Susceptibility to disease depends on a variety of factors – genetic, environmental and behavioural factors. However, childhood circumstances, and poor environmental and working conditions, can have cumulative effects over time. Particular lifestyles may bring additional risks. Doll suggests that coronary artery disease is now being contained as a result of changes in individual behaviour – largely through the reduction in smoking and alterations in diet. But there are new and lethal infections where the incidence is increasing, such as acquired immune deficiency syndrome (AIDS), and hepatitis B. The challenge of HIV-AIDs has prompted the Chief Medical Officer, Sir Donald Acheson, to state that controlling the spread of infection must be regarded as an issue of prime importance to the future of the nation (Acheson, 1986).

Inequalities in health status between social classes

The incidence of most diseases, measured by mortality ratios, has a social class gradient. For example, the overall SMR for social class 5 is five times higher than for social class I (DHSS, 1980). There are also marked regional differences in health status which are not wholly explained by income and occupation structures. These inequalities in health have been much researched and discussed in recent years, although not, on the whole, by Conservative politicians. When the latter have made comment, the causes are attributed to individual lifestyles. Just as there are different explanations for the persistence of inequalities, so there has been a debate about trends and their meaning. Reviewing the issue, Carr-Hill comments: 'the poor do die earlier than the rich but early deaths (before 65) are slowly declining so that inequality is both increasing and becoming less important quantitatively. Beyond 65, inequalities persist although there is no clear trend . . . the incidence of morbidity is becoming an increasingly important aspect of inequalities . . . [they] are likely to follow closely inequalities in income' (Carr-Hill, 1987).

The patterns of disease strongly suggest that policies for preventing ill health should figure prominently on any government agenda, and that the costs of health care will continue to rise due to demographic factors. To date, although the NHS has failed to alleviate the inequalities in health, it *has* provided treatment and care for those who are ill, particularly the acutely ill, and has greatly reduced the financial anxiety associated with illness. However, spending, both public and private, on health care in the UK is low compared to other comparable countries; facilities are both insufficient and out of date. Pressures for more health spending will increase in the future.

At a general ideological level, there are two opposed responses to this dilemma – the egalitarian and the libertarian. The former argues for increased state expenditure in the interests of equity; the latter defines health and health care as a personal responsibility and considers that individuals should have greater freedom to contribute more to their health care, and have more choices in treatment. Should this occur, then the divisions and polarisation within society will increase, and standards of care will tend to diverge further. The main question at the beginning of the 1990s is – will the NHS continue to be a largely publicly-funded service, or will there be widespread destructuring through private funding and private provision?

Therborn and Roebrock (1986) in their analysis of the welfare state suggest that political changes must precede any rollback of the welfare state. (Although their view is that the population structure of post-industrial societies makes the welfare state virtually irreversible.) The political changes to which they refer are: 'a division, demoralisation, a decomposition and at least a political marginalisation of the broad coalition of socio-political forces that supported the welfare state expansion'. They consider that this may occur if there is an increasing dualism in economy and society, within an elistist political system. It is not difficult to identify ways in which the UK in the 1990s has some of these charcteristics.

The Conservatives, are now nearing the end of their third term of office under Mrs Thatcher. The Party was supported in 1987 by less than half the electorate (42 per cent). In large parts of the country it has few representatives. The opposition parties have fragmented. There are signs of a dual economy. High rates of unemployment and low incomes in some areas and sectors have been accompanied by high incomes and buoyant employment prospects in others. Overall, incomes have risen faster than prices, but the divergencies in income and wealth have increased. Some argue that these changes have created an underclass: those on welfare benefit, unemployed young people and the inhabitants of inner city housing estates (Macnichol, 1987). Against this background, policy options can be assessed.

Policy options for the 1990s: financing the NHS

Paying for health care became a critical issue at the end of the 1980s and a full account of alternatives can be found in the King's Fund Institute Paper, *Funding the NHS* (1988). The focus has been on alternative methods of financing the hospital and community health services. This sector accounts for 70 per cent of the health budget and has been under the greatest pressure. New Right policy bodies, such as the Institute of Economic Affairs and the Centre for Policy Studies (1988), have already proposed moving to a voucher, or health credit system. This could be used towards the purchase of private health insurance or exchanged for treatment within either the public, or the private health system. Compulsory insurance on the French or German model has also been considered, and there are suggestions that this can be topped-up by private insurance.

Health Maintenance Organisations (HMOs) have developed in the US as a method of voluntary insurance which gives total care from a partnership of doctors for an annual subscription. The aim is to set the price at a level which keeps clients fit, yet generates a profit for the providers. Health Management Units (HMUs) are a variation of this which retains a tax-funded system but replaces health authorities with management units which buy services for patients from GPs, consultants and hospitals. The funding is brought to the HMUs with patients (Adam Smith Institute, 1988).

All these schemes aim to achieve a number of objectives: first, to contain or reduce costs to the state; second, to shift costs to the consumer; third, to make health costs more visible to consumers and providers; fourth, to increase competition between suppliers; fifth, to increase choice for consumers, and sixth, to develop a larger private health sector and, in doing so, reduce the tax burden. The disadvantages of many of the radical funding proposals are that administrative costs would increase and there would be more difficulty in ensuring overall efficiency and effectiveness in resource use. Problems of distribution and equity also arise. Those in greatest need of health care are likely to be those least able to pay, and possibly those least able to make the choices posed in a consumer-led system. There is also a risk of dual standards developing between public and private care. This is, of course, an unknown factor. It is often assumed that the private sector is efficient, effective and responsive in a way which the public sector is not. However, perfect competition is an ideal, and so is the concept of the rational consumer. Patients are inevitably in a weak position in relation to exerting market pressure and are unable to judge the quality of health care.

In the author's view radical changes in NHS funding are unlikely on practical grounds. Not only do they have considerable disadvantages administratively, but they increase costs overall. Some proposals, such as HMOs or HMUs, would take a considerable time to implement as they would disrupt convential ways of working. Even the less far-reaching proposals such as the introduction of an internal market to reward the most efficient hospital for certain types of operation – hip replacements, for example – might take years to implement. Abel Smith (1988) argues that such a system could have considerable distorting effects. He maintains that such changes are unlikely as they could not be established securely prior to the next election.

At the present time, a wide spectrum of opinion supports the maintenance of a publicly-funded NHS. It is a system which has contained costs, and where the administrative cost element is particularly low. It has treated more patients each year at lower unit costs. Moreover, it has received strong support from the medical profession through unprecedented joint statements from the Royal College Presidents, and also from the British Medical Association, the National Association of Health Authorities and the Royal College of Nursing. In the early months of 1988, there were a series of partial strikes by health workers in support of the Service.

The most popular, and simplest method of funding the NHS would be through an increased Exchequer contribution from taxation. However, this is against current Conservative policy. The 1988 Budget introduced tax cuts while controversy over the

NHS raged. There are alternatives although they, too, increase public expenditure. Extra resources could be raised by earmarking a specific health tax, or introducing a tagged National Insurance contribution. More likely,under a Conservative government, is the use of a variety of methods to draw in extra resources. Market mechanisms to encourage internal competition may be introduced on a small-scale, experimental basis. Private sector provision may be encouraged by incentives for individual insurance schemes or direct payments for elective surgery to create 'a market in queue jumping'. Certainly the pressure to increase value for money will continue well into the new decade.

Even if radical changes do not occur, a new paradigm emerged in the 1980s which moved consideration of the NHS beyond the assumptions of the 1940s. This cut across the political spectrum. In future, the principles of business management will inform decision-making and alter the balance of power, particularly in hospitals. There will be emphasis on developing tools for greater control including the pricing of health care inputs and the measurement of outcomes. This may lead to a relative decline in the autonomy of doctors.

Some examples will illustrate the point. A number of mechanisms are being developed such as costing for types of treatment within diagnostic categories. These can be used to set budgets and establish levels of activity. Pricing items which contribute to particular treatments will enable choices to be made between competing claims. Methods of using data to assess the advantages of new technologies are also being developed. Jennet, for example, has argued for more 'rational rationing' in the assessment of new technologies (Jennet, 1984; Thwaites, 1987).

A greater concern for the efficacy of medical interventions is also likely in future, although there are considerable difficulties involved. Maynard, Williams and others have devised ways of assessing the benefits of treatments in terms of added life years (QUALYs) (Maynard, 1987). The use of QUALYs or other rationing methods may involve moral judgements as well as statistical assessments. Implicit in such rationing methods is a shift in decision-making from clinicians to managers. The assumption is that better use can be made of health care resources by reducing the clinical autonomy of doctors as it has been traditionally defined. Such a shift raises questions about how health care users, and their families could, or should, be involved in decisions about their own care.

Whatever the future form of health service funding it is certain that there will be continuing pressure to reduce lengths of stay in hospital. There will thus be increasing demand for nursing homes for the frail, vulnerable or convalescent as well as for support services out of the hospital. Nursing homes are far less developed in the UK than in North America and it is probable that the private sector will extend in this area. Such private sector development may occur as a result of rising expectations and personal incomes as much as state action, particularly if there is continued NHS underfunding. For those using health services, the development of a more mixed provision and the use of economic criteria on the provider side are likely to change the relationship between health workers and patients and thus increase individual and family responsibility for choosing between alternatives.

The challenge for those who take a more socialist view of health care is to incorporate into a state-financed service lessons learnt from the 1980s about managing health services, and more flexible ways of delivering care which allow choice. A socialist agenda would give a high priority to redressing the inequalities in health status. This would involve economic and fiscal policies to redistribute income, reduce unemployment and improve environments. Socialists are against unmodified private markets as they increase inequality but there is a growing acceptance of markets, if their discriminatory effects can be curbed (see *New Statesman*, 10 March 1987).

Further issues for the 1990s

Irrespective of matters related to funding the health services and particular sets of values, there are two issues which should concern governments into the 1990s, regardless of political party. The first relates to the supply of the largest group of health workers – nurses – the second to the regulation of private interests. A major difficulty in the 1990s will be a shortage of nurses, particularly in some specialisms. The number of potential recruits to nursing will fall as a consequence of demographic factors. Furthermore, nurse training, as a result of the Report of the UK Central Council for Nursing, Midwifery and Health

Visiting in 1986 – *Project 2000* – will undergo considerable change. Both factors will contribute to a reduction in the numbers of nurses available. It is possible that a different division of labour will develop as larger numbers of people with caring skills will be needed. Whether these are paid, or unpaid, and at what level of renumeration, are questions of power and politics.

A second issue is the regulation of public and private interests which create health hazards. Pressure groups have often prevented intervention and investigation. Opposition can come from public bodies, as in the case of some local authorities on fluoridisation of water, or private ones. In the past, Conservative governments have been reluctant to curb the activities of private interests. They have set up new regulatory bodies, but the privatisation of utilities, such as water, is likely to require greater Government regulation. The destructuring of the care industry has led to new ways of monitoring. Although, during the 1980s, measures to protect the interests of the frail and vulnerable have lagged behind the drive towards a mixed economy of provision.

Conclusion

This chapter has aimed to describe Conservative policies for health, and health services during the 1980s in the context of past policies and the principles of Thatcherism. It is clear that the inherent dilemmas of providing health services have been thrown into sharper relief by the insistence on economy in public spending. New ways of ensuring value for money and a more mixed market of provision have developed. This inevitably places more responsibilities on individuals, families and communities for choice.

Viewed as a whole, Conservative policies for the NHS reveal contradictory tendencies. The overriding concern with economy in health service spending has deprived the NHS of funding for investment in change. While managers at the coal-face have been urged to ensure value for money, they have frequently not been given the means to do so. In relation to both hospital, and primary care, the implementation of changes has been on a 'no-cost' basis. Parsimony may in the end defeat its own purpose.

However, perhaps the central paradox of Thatcherism is that a reduction in the role of the state in service provision and direct funding, may have the effect of increasing state activity in other respects. For example, a more mixed market in care brings further responsibilities for regulation. Moreover, governments cannot withdraw from the major commitment to the supply and training of health service personnel, or from threats to public health. Finally, radical changes in an institution as large and powerful as the NHS may carry the risk of electoral defeat.

3

Housing

NICK RAYNSFORD

'There may be important connections between housing conditions and demands on the personal social services but research has not so far established and quantified the various relationships.' (John Patten, Parliamentary Under-Secretary of State for Health and Social Security in a reply to the House of Commons, May 1985.)

1 The postwar consensus

Although housing has been the focus for much fierce political controversy in the post-war period, there was nevertheless a broad measure of consensus, at least on fundamental principles, in the first three and a half decades after 1945. It was recognised that large-scale investment was required to replace old and unsatisfactory housing and to build the new homes necessary to overcome the housing shortage. It was accepted that a framework involving both public and private investment was vital to the housing programme. It was agreed that this framework should be subject to planning control by public sector agencies, both to ensure the maintenance of good standards of accommodation and to avoid the social and environmental consequences of unplanned speculative development. That was seen not only as the cause of many problems in the overcrowded industrial cities, but also as a serious potential threat to the survival of the countryside in the post-war era, with 'ribbon development' and 'urban sprawl' encroaching on undeveloped rural areas. The impact of the

Figure 3.1 *Housing tenure in Great Britain 1914–84*

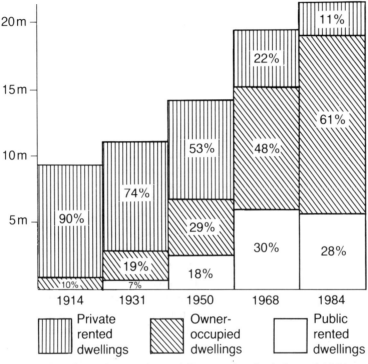

Sources: Social Trends, Housing and Construction Statistics and AMA estimates.

post-war consensus was considerable. Housing conditions and tenure patterns changed dramatically. Large-scale provision of rented housing by local authorities and other public agencies such as New Town Development Corporations offered the prospect of good quality homes to millions of families who had previously lived in overcrowded and often squalid accommodation. Simultaneously the rise in real incomes, the expansion of credit opportunities and the impact of government subsidies contributed to a rapid expansion in owner-occupation. By 1968, as is seen in Figure 3.1, the private rented sector which in 1914 accounted for 90 per cent of all housing was down to 22 per cent. Owner occupation had grown from 10 per cent to almost 50 per cent and public rented housing now made up 30 per cent of the total.

In general these trends were seen as positive. Privately rented housing had been the focus of most of the perceived problems of the pre-war era. Most lacked basic amenities such as baths and indoor WCs and tenants were often subject to financial pressures or harrassment. Indeed the Conservative Government's attempt to revive private renting in 1957 by a Rent Act which reduced tenant security was both unpopular and unsuccessful. It opened the door to the spectre of Rachmansim, which in turn justified the restoration of tighter controls on the return of a Labour Government in 1964.

However, although the twin-pronged attack on bad housing from the public sector and owner-occupation was successful, in many respects it also contained the seeds of many future problems, few of which were recognised at the time. Increasing concentration on two main sources of housing (owner-occupation and public sector renting) meant a reduction in opportunities for those groups who did not qualify for either, such as single people or childless couples on low incomes. The costs of moving in the one sector, and the bureaucratic allocation rules in the other, created increasing obstacles to mobility for many households. The adoption of new building methods allowing the rapid production of apparently cheap and high density housing estates led both to the creation of huge, inhumane and unpopular environments, and unforeseen structural and maintenance problems. New forms of indebtedness emerged as people overstretched themselves to obtain owner-occupied housing or found themselves unable to afford to repair and maintain their homes. Others encountered financial difficulties after a marital breakdown, or reduction of earnings, or could not cope with the costs of new heating systems. Hence the paradox that at a time in the late 1970s when official publications (the 1977 Housing Green Paper) breathed complacency about improving conditions and prospects, the number of people homeless was reaching new peak levels and new legislation to define local authority responsibilities to the homeless (the 1977 Housing (Homeless Persons) Act) was necessary.

So while the achievements of the first three and a half decades of the post war era were substantial, many problems remained, and policy adjustments were needed to remedy some of the new challenges created by both the successes and failure of the expansion of owner-occupation and public rented housing.

Table 3.1 *Housebuilding starts and completions, Great Britain 1976–86 (thousands)*

	Starts		
	Public	*Private*	*Total*
1976	170.8	154.7	325.4
1977	132.1	134.8	266.9
1978	107.4	157.3	264.7
1979	81.2	144.0	225.1
1980	56.4	98.9	155.2
1981	37.2	116.7	153.9
1982	53.0	140.5	193.4
1983	48.0	169.8	217.7
1984	40.2	153.7	193.9
1985	33.6	161.8	195.3
1986	30.8	173.7	204.4

Source: Department of the Environment Quarterly Housebuilding Statistics.

2 The end of consensus

Policy adjustments within the overall consensus were not however the hallmark of the Government elected in 1979. Indeed the subsequent decade saw a dramatic shift in housing policy. Instead of a twin-tracked approach involving the further expansion of both owner-occupation and public rented housing the Government increasingly made clear its preference for private sector provision and its hostility to public sector housing.

Public sector house building has been reduced progressively largely as a consequence of government expenditure cuts. Inheriting a declining programme from the outgoing Labour government, the new Conservative policy was not to reverse but rather to accelerate the reduction as can be seen from Table 3.1.

Initially this approach was justified on the grounds that the private sector would 'step in' to replace the reduced public sector provision. However this has not been the case. After a collapse during the recession of the early 1980s, private house construction has recovered to levels between 150,000 and 170,000 a year, only just above those achieved in the mid-1970s. (see Table 3.1). The combined public and private sector output

Figure 3.2   *Housing investment programme allocations, England,*
1978/9–1985/6

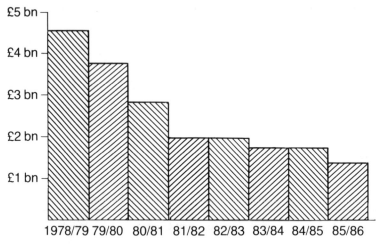

Source: Hansard, 8 January 1985, Table prepared by SHAC.

has dramatically reduced and indeed is insufficient to keep
pace with new household formation and the need to replace
worn-out homes (NFHA, 1985).

The Government's justification for the cut in public sector
housebuilding has since changed to one of outright hostility to
public sector provision. As is shown in Figure 3.2, investment
allocations to local authorities were cut by around two-thirds in
real terms, the most severe of all public sector expenditure cuts
since 1979. Furthermore, restrictions have prevented authorities
from being able to use their own resources, including capital receipts from sales, to the full to provide new homes.
Successive government ministers have made it clear that they
see no role for local authorities as providers of new homes
(Waldegrave, 1987).

While deliberately reducing public sector housing programmes
the Government has given maximum encouragement to the
expansion of owner occupation. The two are, of course, directly
connected. For the rapid increase in owner-occupation, which
averaged over 320,000 dwellings a year between 1980 and 1988
– more than double the rate of new housebuilding for sale –
depended on a large-scale transfer from other tenures (HMSO

1976–86). This partly reflected the continuing decline of privately-rented housing, but primarily was the product of the sale of a million former council homes under the Right to Buy.

The loss of rented housing

The inevitable effect has been a dramatic reduction in the supply of rented housing. There were in 1988 1,200,000 fewer rented homes, from all sources, than in 1979. This represents the worst loss of rented housing ever recorded in Britain. Until the beginning of the 1980s, new public housing more than compensated for the decline in private renting. This is no longer the case (HMSO, 1976–86, Housing Policy Review, 1977).

Private renting has continued to decline. Since 1979 half a million homes have vanished from the private sector. The Government attempted to stem the decline by introducing changes in the 1980 Act that weakened the protection of tenants with resident landlords and provided for higher and more frequent rent increases. The same Act introduced 'assured' and 'shorthold' tenancies in an attempt to bring more properties back on to the market – with no great success. Only around 3,000 of these assured tenancies were created in total and over 2,000 of these were leasehold schemes for elderly home owners rather than homes on the rented market (Kemp, 1988). The government has neither kept nor published detailed statistics on 'shorthold' lettings, but the figures compiled for the first year's lettings in Greater London showed only 300 shorthold tenancies created in the course of the year while 16,000 private lettings were withdrawn from the market over the same period.

While far more households own their own homes, there are still a considerable proportion who cannot afford to buy, or who choose to rent. The reduction in the number of homes available for renting has not been matched by a falling demand for rented housing. Shelter, the housing charity, has identified at least one and a quarter million households registered on council waiting lists (AMA, 1986; Bramley and Paice, 1987). This should not been seen as an accurate measure of need, for waiting lists are notoriously inaccurate. However it cannot be dismissed as an overstatement of the scale of the problem. While

Table 3.2   *Households accepted under the Housing (Homeless Persons)
Act, England 1978–86*

Year	Acceptances
1978	53,110
1979	56,750
1980	62,920
1981	70,010
1982	74,800
1983	78,240
1984	83,190
1985	93,980
1986	102,980

Source: DOE Homelessness Statistics

Table 3.3   *Net revenue expenditure on bed and breakfast hotels by local
authorities in London, 1981/2–1987/8*

	£
1981–1982	4,332,679
1982–1983	6,032,893
1983–1984	8,498,657
1984–1985	12,460,637
1985–1986	25,544,000
1986–1987	62,802,000
1987–1988(e)	99,540,000

Source: 1981–5, GLC Housing Research and Policy Report no. 4
'Temporary Accommodation, Counting the Cost'. 1985/6–1987/8,
London Housing Research Unit Survey of London Boroughs, 1987.

some of those registered may not be in immediate need, many
others in urgent need have let their registration lapse because
of the lack of realistic prospects of rehousing. The shortage
of council housing means that even families with the highest
priority can wait many years for a home of their own.

   The clearest evidence of housing shortage is provided by
the growing problem of homelessness (McCarthy, 1986). Over
100,000 households were accepted as homeless by local authorities
in England in 1986, almost precisely double the 1978 level (see Table
3.2 and 3.3). These figures substantially underestimate the true

scale of the problem. More than twice as many households applied as were accepted, and a significant but unquantifiable number of homeless people would not even have made an application. This reflects the fact that most single and childless people are excluded from the rehousing provisions of the Housing (Homeless Persons) Act. It is a chilling reminder of the inadequacy of these statistics that most of the people who actually sleep rough do not feature in the official homelessness figures.

The shortage in rented housing means that many of the hardest-pressed local authorities do not have sufficient homes to meet their responsibilities for rehousing homeless applicants. They have no option but to place homeless people in bed and breakfast hotels. The overwhelming human and social case against housing homeless families in B & B has been made forcibly and repeatedly. However, it was John Patten MP, the former Minister of Housing, who provided perhaps the most devastating critique of current policies when he revealed that it cost almost twice as much to accommodate a family in B & B – at an average cost of £12,000 a year – as it did to meet the cost of building a new council house (House of Commons Debates, 16 January 1987). As the housing crisis worsens, the numbers accommodated in bed and breakfast hotels have continued to rise. Sadly, bed and breakfast has also become one of the few options available to single homeless people. The costs are such that few people in low-paid work can afford such lodging. So for those who still – despite more restrictive Board and Lodgings regulations – do qualify for assistance from the DHSS, bed and breakfast is often both the last resort and a trap which keeps them unemployed (Conway and Kemp, 1985).

Sub-standard housing conditions

Conditions in bed and breakfast hotels and multi-occupied houses have been repeatedly exposed in both official and unofficial reports. They represent the most extreme examples of slum conditions – continuing squalor, overcrowding and exposure to the risk of fire and disease. It is perhaps no accident that the homeless families forced to live in these conditions are most likely to be those facing the greatest deprivation and discrimination, including ethnic minority households, young families with small children, and single parents (Conway and Kemp,

90   *Housing*

Table 3.4   *Unfitness and disrepair, England 1976 and 1981*

| | Number of dwellings (thousands) | | % change |
	1976	1981	
Unfit	1,162	1,116	−4
Fit but lacking basic amenities	921	390	−58
All dwellings needing repairs in excess of £9,500*	859	1,049	+22
Fit but needing repairs in excess of £9,500*	395	574	+45

* at May 86 figures
Source: AMA, from DOE English House Conditions Surveys 1976 and 1981.

1985). As yet, however, there is little indication that either appropriate legislative measures or sufficient resources will be provided to ensure that the problem is tackled.

There is a similar policy vacuum in relation to the repair and improvement of other categories of sub-standard housing. It is true that few homes now lack basic amenities as a result of the clearance and improvement policies of the past three decades. However, an increasing number of homes are falling into disrepair and by far the greatest number are owner-occupied. The most recent house condition survey in London showed that 49 per cent of substandard properties were in the owner-occupied sector (AMA, 1987). Many elderly home-owners have neither the means nor the inclination to carry out expensive and disruptive repairs to their properties. Home improvement policies have failed to respond to these changes. Emphasis has continued to be given to the installation of amenities and to improvement rather than repairs. Resources available for improvement and repair grants have, in any case, been slashed as a result of cuts in local authority spending. The implications of declining housing standards in the private sector, and the failure to pursue realistic renewal policies, are grave (see Table 3.4). The greatest public and media attention, however, has been focused on the problem of sub-standard council housing. Many of the worst problems are found on the high-density, high-rise and system-built estates which are a legacy from the 1960s. But while there are undoubtedly very serious structural and social problems affecting a number of such estates, the problem is much wider. Many older, traditionally built estates are also in need of renovation and repair. The total number of properties requiring some work is estimated at almost 4 million, at a cost of around £19 billion (DOE, 1985).

Most local authorities have been struggling to provide a service to tenants despite declining resources and accelerating problems of disrepair. At the same time there has been growing recognition that old-style council bureaucracies were often remote and unresponsive and failed to provide a service that met modern aspirations. Management sometimes broke down under pressures of rent arrears, empty properties and vandalism. Estates were often poorly designed, ill-lit and unsafe, especially for women. Many authorities have responded imaginatively, by decentralising housing services to a neighbourhood or estate level, and involving tenants in decision-making and design. It is ironic that while local authorities have tried to find innovative responses to government criticisms of poor management, they have been increasingly denied the resources to implement them.

There are dangers that council housing will become a residual sector. Declining standards, due to shrinking resources, put pressure on families who can afford it, to move out. Many have bought their council homes at discounted prices, taking the best housing out of the public sector. Others have bought homes in the private sector. Increasingly, those who remain council tenants are those with few choices. At the same time, local authorities have attempted to end the discrimination which used to exist towards sections of the population in greatest need, black households, women-headed households, and the homeless. It is therefore these households who will be trapped in poor and deteriorating council estates. Furthermore, policies designed to promote 'care in the community' and the resettlement of those who in the past were accommodated in institutions, has made greater demands on public housing to cope with many vulnerable people with special needs and problems. But these new demands have come at a time when local council's services are being squeezed by political and financial pressures, and are least able to meet them. Indeed, local authority attempts to widen allocations to provide homes

Table 3.5 *Mortgage tax relief*

	Exchequer cost of MIR (£m)	Mortgagors (thousands)	Average cost per mortgagor (£pa)
1979/80	1,640	5,900	280
1980/81	2,190	5,900	370
1981/82	2,290	5,900	390
1982/83	2,460	6,180	400
1983/84	2,750	7,500	370
1984/85	3,500	7,750	450
1985/86	4,750	8,000	590
1986/87	4,750	8,200	580

Source: House of Commons Debates, 12 May 1986, col.346W,
25 November 1983, col.322W.

Table 3.6 *Housing subsidy and rate fund contributions to local authorities, England 1978/9–1986/7*

	Exchequer subsidy (£ million)	Subsidy per dwelling (£)	Rate fund contribution (£ million)	Rate fund contribution per dwelling (£)
1979/80	1,274	257	321	89
1980/81	1,393	281	433	119
1981/82	884	180	420	114
1982/83	441	92	434	149
1983/84	350	75	497	143
1984/85	379	84	458	167
1985/86(e)	457	105	523	167
1986/87(e)	477	na	na	na

Source: Parliamentary written answer, 12 May 1986, col. 362.

for single and childless people may be jeopardised by pressure
to use all available lettings for homeless families.

Increasing divisions

The 1980s witnessed increasing division in the housing market,
division between the North and South, division between tenures,
and division between those with a decent home and those
without. Nowhere are these divisions more marked than in
respect of subsidies.

Mortgage interest tax relief was equivalent in the late 1980s to a subsidy of £4.75 billion, while rather less than £1 billion was allocated in government and local authority subsidies to council housing (see Table 3.5 and 3.6). Means-tested subsidies to those in greatest need have been cut, yet mortgage subsidies to households on higher incomes have gone unchecked. Over £1 billion a year has gone to households with incomes in excess of £20,000 a year (House of Commons Debates, 9 April 1986). Both the Duke of Edinburgh's Inquiry into British Housing and the Archbishop of Canterbury's Commission on the Inner Cities concluded that this subsidy system was inequitable, expensive and inefficient. What is more, by contributing to accelerating house price rises, it works against first-time buyers, especially in the South-East, who find the cost of entry into owner-occupation too high.

Despite the Government's commitment to home ownership, there was little in housing policy during the 1980s to commend itself to low income home owners. House prices rose sharply, and interest rates remained uncomfortably high. As a result of both high repayment costs, and growing unemployment and financial difficulties, the rate of mortgage default increased dramatically. The number of properties repossessed by Building Societies rose from 2,500 in 1979 to 20,000 in 1986 (see Table 3.7). Ten per cent of all homeless households accepted by local authorities in England lost their homes as a result of mortgage default (Kelly, 1986). As with policies for repair and improvement of older homes, subsidies to home-owners are manifestly failing to assist those in greatest need.

The 1988 Housing Bill

The 1987 Housing White Paper (HMSO 1987), published shortly after the Conservatives won their third successive term in office, signalled a further departure from the post-war consensus. The White Paper openly stated the Government's wish to diminish the role of local authorities as providers of housing, and the subsequent Housing Bill gave emphasis to measures designed to secure the transfer of much council housing into other ownership. However, while the Right to Buy continued as a main theme of policy, the Government had clearly recognised that with an increasingly poor and disadvantaged group of people living in council housing, the scope for large-scale transfer

Table 3.7   *Mortgage arrears and repossessions by building societies,
United Kingdom 1979–86*

Year to	Mortgages over six months in arrears	Repossessions
December 1979	8,420	2,530
December 1980	13,490	3,020
June 1981	15,880	4,240
June 1982	23,840	5,090
June 1983	33,910	6,680
June 1984	36,780	9,140
June 1985	52,890	13,040
June 1986	66,930	20,020

Source: Building Societies Association.

into home ownership was diminishing. So the Housing Bill
introduced the concept of a transfer of council housing into the
hands of other landlords, either through the 'tenant's choice' or
'opt-out' scheme, or through straightforward takeover of council
housing in designated areas by government-appointed Housing
Action Trusts. In parallel, the second key element in the 1988
Housing Bill was the decontrol of privately rented housing,
and the encouragement of a higher-rent 'independent' rented
sector comprising private landlords and housing associations.
The two policies inter-relate, in that the Government anticipates
private landlords and housing associations taking over substantial
numbers of former council properties. Indeed among all except
the most fanatical advocates of the private rented sector, it is
now recognised that the prospects of reviving private renting,
other than by a transfer of properties from the public sector,
are remote. In London, where the private rented market has
traditionally been larger than average, and where Rent Act
evasion has become widespread, the market continues to decline
by an estimated 17,000 dwellings a year despite the fact that more
than half the private lettings are outside Rent Act control (HMSO,
1976–86). This gives little comfort to those who glibly argue that
the removal of controls will stimulate the market.

While the underlying ideological motives behind the new
policies are clear – making further reductions in public sector
provision and encouraging a transfer into the private sector – the

practical implications are confused. Enabling private landlords and requiring housing associations to charge higher rents may satisfy 'market' ideology but is hardly calculated to encourage council tenants to opt for a change of landlord. Few tenants have shown any enthusiasm for voting for a rent increase. Equally it is difficult to see 'market rent' accommodation attracting many potential takers when they could buy a house for rather less than the outgoings in rent. Their mortgage payments would qualify for 25 per cent relief up to a level of £30,000, whereas their rent payments do not. Those who could afford a market rent, and do not have an overwhelming reason against buying (for example they are going to move in the near future) are far more likely to opt for owner-occupation and the prospect of some additional capital gain.

A further inherent contradiction is, paradoxically, the potential *increase* in cost to the government, as a consequence of the high proportion of tenants dependent on housing benefit to meet all or part of their rent. Here the problem is compounded by a departmental split between the Housing Ministry, based in the Department of the Environment, and the DSS, which carries responsibility for housing benefit. Indeed the sharp and frequent cuts in housing benefit between 1983 and 1988 indicate all too clearly the DSS's reluctance to pick up the financial tab for the Department of the Environment. The outcome is a housing benefit scheme which no longer provides effective assistance to those in low-paid work and others such as pensioners with savings or occupational pensions which take them above the Income Support level. Yet these are the very people likely to be priced out by higher rents. Only for those on the lowest income levels, including those on income support, will housing benefit cover the bulk of or all of their rent. And the fear of escalating benefit costs as their rent levels are forced up, has prompted the DSS to set 'ceilings' for housing benefit.

These unconvincing attempts to square the circle of higher rents and higher benefit costs, highlight the inherent contradictions of the attempt to reconcile social responsibility with private profit.

3   Prospects for the 1990s

The 1990s are therefore unlikely to see a radical transformation in the pattern of housing provision in Britain, despite the Government's wishes and rhetoric. Instead, the patterns of the 1980s seem likely to be extended. Some further extension of owner-occupation can be expected, in part reflecting demographic trends and in part the lack of realistic alternative options for obtaining housing. However, Britain already has an unusually high percentage of the population owning their homes, and the scope for substantial further increases in the tenure is probably limited. Indeed, some commentators already foresee a saturation point being reached at around 70 per cent. One of the constraints on further expansion of owner-occupation is likely to be the increase of problems with the tenure. Indeed it will be less easy to see owner-occupied housing as one homogeneous entity. Not only will there be dramatic (and often unbridgeable) price differentials between areas, but there is likely to be an even sharper division between those making sizeable capital gains out of their homes in the South-East,and those no longer able to maintain their homes in adequate condition, or no longer able to afford the mortgage repayment. Indeed the number of people at risk of homelessness from the owner-occupied sector may well continue to rise.

Increasing polarisation within the owner-occupied market is therefore probable. So, too, is an increasingly stark divide between owner-occupation and public rented housing. The prospects for public sector rented housing are of continuing decline. This does not necessarily imply a large-scale transfer of properties to other landlords, though some can be expected, particularly where the local authority is keen to dispose of all or part of its stock to another landlord. However, with new building likely to be brought almost to a complete stop, and with continuing sales under the Right to Buy even at a reduced level, some further reduction in the number of council homes seems inevitable. However, perhaps more significant and more worrying is the likely decline in the sector's standing and public image. The Government is explicit in its wish to see the sector diminished, and is all too ready to criticise the sector's failings. It will not provide investment finance for new building. At the same time it requires the public sector to accommodate the poorest, most vulnerable and most disadvantaged sections of the population. This points inexorably towards a 'residual' role, in which an ageing and increasingly unpopular housing stock will be occupied only by those who can find no way out, an 'underclass' condemned to a ghetto existence.

The 'independent' rented sector is likely by contrast to appear increasingly disparate. At one end there will be high-cost market rent accommodation for the small group of people – including overseas visitors and businessmen – who can afford it and who do not want to buy a home. We can also anticipate a continuing lucrative trade in bed and breakfast hotels and multi-occupied houses, where the return available from crowding large numbers of people into often squalid property makes renting an attractive speculative venture. This is particularly true where public sector subsidies in the form of housing benefit or board and lodging allowances underpin the whole financial calculation. The desperation of local authorities, required by statute to secure accommodation for the homeless, and with a dwindling supply of homes with which to meet the demand, will also probably guarantee the continuation of this lucrative trade in human misfortune. At the other end, the rump of the 'old' private rented market comprising older, generally poor condition property occupied by ageing tenants who still retain Rent Act protection, will continue its long decline. In between, some new developments may be initiated by financial institutions and building societies, particularly if the Government feels inclined to offer direct subsidies. However, these are unlikely to be on a scale even sufficient to offset the decline of the 'old' private rented market, let alone make good the parallel loss of public rented accommodation. Some growth can be expected from the housing association movement, though this too is likely to become more diverse. The larger associations with strong asset bases and the scope to raise private finance may well enjoy significant growth, while many of the smaller locally-based associations may cease any further development. The higher rent levels implicit in the new finance and subsidy arrangements could also prompt changes in allocation policies, with some associations moving up market to find tenants able to pay the rent, and others conversely moving down market to take, disproportionately, tenants on maximum housing benefit whose rent will be met in full.

Although the scale of their growth numerically may be less than the Government hopes, the further development of housing associations in the 1990s will be significant in that it is likely to be the only source of additional housing options for many disadvantaged and low income groups. However, there may well be a problem of affordability for those not in receipt of full housing benefit.

Dependence on benefits is likely to become an even more marked feature of both the public and housing association sectors. Whereas in the 1970s on average around 40 per cent of council tenants received help with the rent from the DHSS or in rent rebates, by the 1980s around two-thirds of council tenants were on Housing Benefit, despite cuts in the benefit scheme which had reduced potential entitlement. This reflected the transfer of wealthier tenants out of the sector through the Right to Buy, an increase in unemployment and poverty among tenants, and 'real' increases in rent levels, making it harder for many on the margins to cope without claiming benefit (Kemp and Raynsford, 1984). Among housing associations, almost three-quarters of tenants are currently thought to be receiving housing benefit (NFHA, 1988). The very rapid withdrawal of benefit as a tenant's income rises above the income support level, creating a poverty trap in which 90p out of every extra £1 can be lost in tax, national insurance and reduced housing benefit, reinforces this dependency on benefit and provides an active disincentive for those out of work to seek employment. These factors all suggest an increasingly polarised housing market in the early 1990s with a high proportion of public sector and housing association tenants trapped into their 'dependant' status, in marked contrast to the good fortune of those enjoying falling real costs of housing and potential capital gains in the buoyant areas of the owner-occupied market.

We can expect a continuing rise in the incidence of homelessness for three reasons. In the first place the shortage of low-cost rented housing will inevitably leave many low-income vulnerable households with no prospect of obtaining an affordable home. Secondly, higher rents and reduced security in the private rented sector are likely to increase the numbers at risk of losing their home. Thirdly, the rising trend in the proportion of people homeless from the owner-occupied sector (now at 10 per cent of all homelessness households in England) is likely to continue for economic and demographic reasons. Those with little purchasing power after a relationship breakdown and those struggling to cope with high repayment or repairs costs are obviously among those groups most at risk. How far the Government will expect local authorities to continue to exercise responsibilities towards the homeless is as yet unclear. Increasing demand at a time when public sector stocks are being run down obviously creates a potential for crisis, with the policy options divided between those which would increase the supply of housing to meet the demand, and those which would reduce the effective demand by diminishing statutory obligations towards the homeless.

The state of the housing stock is likely to be a continuing cause for concern. The reduced investment in public sector provision means an increasingly ageing stock which will continue to need attention. Some of the worst estates may be turned around by specific intervention, for example by government-appointed Housing Action Trusts. However, the underlying problems are unlikely to go away. In the private sector, much will depend on new policies towards improvements and repairs which were awaited from the mid to late 1980s with increasing impatience. Indications that the Government may favour a means-test for home renovation grants could ensure that the finances devoted to renovation are targeted more successfully to those who could not otherwise afford to carry out the work. Alternatively it may have an opposite deterrent effect. Much will depend on the nature and style of the means-test.

Of all housing policy issues the one on which there is the most need, and least likelihood of reform, is the subsidy system. The case for change is overwhelming, but the political pressures against change are formidable. Mortgage interest tax relief, albeit expensive, inequitable, inefficient and indiscriminate, goes to around eight million households, who are thought to be an almost insuperable political obstacle to reform. By threatening this against any party which suggests even modest changes, one political party can effectively block the others, and indeed the period since the 1977 Housing Policy Green Paper has been characterised on all sides by fear of action rather than any coherent approach. In this negative climate the best hope for reform has been a 'withering' away of the value of subsidy by holding the qualifying ceiling at £30,000. This has not, however, prevented the total cost rising to £4.75 billion, though it has had one perverse effect of penalising first-time buyers on slightly higher than average earnings in London and the South-East. As they now have to pay approaching £60,000 even for a modest starter home, the £30,000 ceiling is in some cases proving an obstacle. The other recent attempt to contain the cost of Mortgage Interest Tax Relief by ending entitlement on home improvements will also have the curious effect of discouraging owners on modest incomes from undertaking improvements. Yet at the same time those paying tax at higher rates will continue to get more benefit than everyone else. It would be nice to think that a government with a majority of 100 in the House of Commons would feel confident enough to 'bite the bullet' on this issue, particularly as it could justify reform on the basis of the need for better targeting and the need to redistribute subsidy within the owner occupied sector. However, with the Prime Minister known to be resolutely opposed to any change, this is probably unlikely.

There is an alternative

The continuation of current trends and the impact of the 1988 Housing Bill all point to a position in the early 1990s in which there will be increased and increasingly visible divisions between the 'haves' and 'have-nots', as well as sizeable unmet housing needs. This is not, however, inevitable. The adoption of different policies could, within a relatively short timescale and certainly by the end of the century, achieve a dramatic transformation. That is because there is no longer a massive shortage of housing as there was, for example, at the end of the war. The way in which Britain's housing is currently distributed, allocated and subsidised is wasteful and often inefficient, and there are still significant local shortages. However, a sustained programme of investment to remedy these shortages, coupled with action to ensure that the stock is better maintained and more equitably distributed to meet needs, could achieve major advances over a period of no more than a decade.

The starting point is the reaffirmation of the principle of public responsibility, which underpinned the post-war consensus. Instead of abdication to market forces and the interests of the private sector, the Government would once again need to take a lead in defining investment priorities and clarifying responsibilities and rights through new legislation. There would certainly be a need for an expansion of the rented housing programme but this does not mean a return to the crude 'numbers game' approach of the 1950s and 1960s. We have learned the lesson that an emphasis on quantity at the expense of quality is almost always a mistake in housing. Almost every decision to restrict the standard of provision from the 'don't give them baths' attitude of the 1930s to the inadequate TIC standards of the late 1980s, which made adequate central heating impossible to achieve in many schemes, can be seen to be short-sighted and mistaken.

Restoring a rented housing programme does not mean restoring a municipal monopoly. Local authorities have an important role to play in improving housing conditions in the 1990s, but within a pluralist framework which actively encourages more provision by housing associations, co-operatives and other social agencies. Not only does this offer greater potential choice to the public but it will also promote good practice and new approaches as different suppliers learn from the experiences of each other. The involvement of tenants in all stages of the housing process is another fundamental principle which should distinguish the policies of the 1990s from those of past decades. In some instances this will involve directly fostering co-operative housing projects, but even when more traditional landlord/tenant relationships continue, tenants must be more extensively and effectively involved in key decisions affecting their homes, such as the design of new buildings or improvement schemes and day-to-day management practices on their estates. The aim must be to promote a radical transformation in the attitudes of public sector housing managers from seeing tenants as supplicants and often as a nuisance, into treating them as customers. This transformation will hopefully be achieved by persuasion rather than coercion, but where necessary tenant's rights will need to be enchanced by legislation.

This will apply also in other tenures. New rights to security will need to be given to private tenants, while home owners should receive more rights of redress against builders or architects responsible for shoddy work or design. The introduction of a housing 'log book' system and controls on the scale of charges made by estate agents would help to simplify the process of moving home and reduce the costs.

One of the fundamental policy objectives must be to reduce the rigid divisions between tenure which so inhibit opportunities for mobility at present. Providing more choice between renting and buying and enabling people to move into more suitable accommodation at different stages of their life must make sense. Currently, this is often impossible because of the chronic shortage of appropriate rented housing and the subsidy system which gives such disproportionate advantages to owners.

So elderly owners remain in homes which they are no longer able to maintain properly because no suitable rented housing is available, while young people overstretch themselves to buy for fear that if they miss the boat they may never again be able to afford it. Developing a full range of different housing types, including shared accommodation and group homes for those seeking more supportive accommodation, as well as more provision for single people who wish to live independently, will also be a very necessary part of the programme.

Creating a more rational housing market in which people are able to exercise greater choice will require a reform of the housing subsidy system. This will not be easily accomplished because of the formidable political obstacles already mentioned. However, it cannot be overlooked if we are to end the inequities which so distort the market and consumer choice at present. Nor will it be a simple matter of cutting back on current subsidies to home owners. Some must be reduced, for example the continuing subsidy to those on high incomes, but others, notably first-time buyers and poorer owners facing unexpected expenditure, for example for repairs, may actually need more public subsidy. So redistribution *within* the owner-occupied sector, as well as in favour of renters will be essential. In the case of public and social rented housing, rents will need to be set at levels which avoid excessive dependence on means-testing. This would allow Housing Benefit to revert to its proper role as a 'safety net' for the economically non-active and those on very low wages rather than being the main form of subsidy to the rented sector with the consequent 'poverty trap' problems.

One of the other key objectives of the subsidy system should be to encourage the good maintenance of the housing stock. A simplified and reformed home improvement grant system, together with new arrangements to enable home-owners easier access to finance for major repairs, will be required. In the public sector, investment in the modernisation of older and substandard estates will be vital to avoid any further deterioration in the stock and the creation of more 'sink' estates.

More emphasis on getting older and under-used or empty properties converted and into full occupation will be needed in all sectors, backed up by measures to enable properties left needlessly empty to be taken over and brought into use by a socially responsible landlord. This would apply equally to public and private empty housing. Expanding the supply of rented housing will help to contain and indeed reduce the rising tide of homelessness, while the encouragement of a pluralist framework should help local authorities avoid being relegated into a 'residual' role. However, this will depend on clear obligations being placed on the other social housing agencies to accept responsibility for a full range of needs and not simply to select those most likely to prove ideal tenants.

Many of our cities are currently segregated rigidly between owner-occupied areas and council housing estates. Breaking down these rigid divisions should be another policy objective. The further acquisition of council housing under the Right to Buy may over a period involve an increase in the proportion of owners in formerly council rented areas. Conversely more fluidity between tenures, and the transfer of some formerly owner-occupied housing into renting can work the other way. This could in part be achieved by enabling elderly home-owners to trade in their homes (which could subsequently be rented) in exchange for suitable sheltered accommodation where they would receive a higher level of care than would have been possible in their former home. At the same time, a requirement on local authorities to plough back all 'right to buy' receipts into the provision of more rented housing would encourage more acquisitions from the private sector (as it would be decidedly quicker than constructing a new home). Such policies sustained over a decade or two could help to break down the divisive 'mono-tenure' patterns which exist today.

A 'mixed' economy – involving both public and private sector contributions as well as an expanded social housing sector – would be the hallmark of British housing policy under these proposals, as it has been for most of the post war era. But the objective would be to ensure that it was more truly 'mixed' and less obviously divided – by area, by tenure, by quality of housing and by esteem – than it as at present.

4

Social Security

RUTH LISTER

'The most obvious division of society is into rich and
poor; and it is no less obvious that the number of the
former bear a great disproportion to those of the latter.
The whole business of the poor is to administer to the
idleness, folly and luxury of the rich; and that of the rich,
in return, is to find the best methods of confirming the
slavery and increasing the burdens of the poor.' (Edmund
Burke, from *A Vindication of Natural Society*, 1756.)

'The boundaries which divide what is politically thinkable
from the unthinkable have been significantly shifted. And the
wolves in the Treasury, always ranging abroad in hopes of
bringing down a social benefit, learnt their lesson and have
since come back for more'. (Donnison, 1982, p. 209.)

The thesis of the first section of this chapter is that there has
been a watershed in social security policy as the unthinkable
has become the 'doable'. However, there are two qualifications. First, many of the roots of the present Government's
policies can be traced back to earlier administrations – both
Conservative and Labour. Second, while we will outline here
the damage wreaked on the social security system during the
first two terms of office, we will also show that wider political
concerns and a bedrock of political pragmatism served to temper
the government's ideological fervour. The actual implementation

of policy has, thus, on occasion, lacked the courage of the ideological convictions which had informed it.

1   The Record: 1979–1987

Setting the scene

The 1979 manifesto and the first Public Expenditure White Paper set the parameters for subsequent social security policy. The manifesto (and those that followed in 1983 and 1987) made no mention of poverty. Instead, having implicitly abandoned the previous Conservative administration's proposals for a tax credit scheme, it promised 'we shall do all we can to find other ways to simplify the system, restore the incentive to work, reduce the poverty trap and bring more effective help to those in greatest need . . . And we shall act more vigorously against fraud and abuse' (Conservative Party, 1979).

The Public Expenditure White Paper of the same year stated bluntly, 'public expenditure is at the heart of Britain's economic difficulties' (HM Treasury, 1979), a thesis already embraced, if less enthusiastically, by the Callaghan Government. It was not long before it was made plain that social security spending was regarded as a prime culprit. At the same time, Ministers were at pains to stress, as Sir Geoffrey Howe made plain in his first Budget speech, that 'our general policy is to make substantial reductions in public expenditure but that must not be done in a way that bears unfairly on the most vulnerable members of society' (House of Commons Debates, 1979a).

His comments reflect a continuing ambivalence in Conservative policy towards the poor. (This ambivalence has been negotiated by a refusal to define poverty. Instead Ministers and government documents use the sanitised language of 'the most vulnerable', 'low income', 'those in greatest need' and implicit assumptions are made about the relative deservingness of different groups). On the one hand, the Government has been inflenced by New Right notions of individual responsibility; of the need to reward the successful and therefore not 'featherbed' the unsuccessful. On the other, despite Malcolm Dean's much quoted observation that it is 'a government which does not feel guilty about the poor' (Dean, 1980), it has felt the need constantly to reaffirm its commitment to protecting the 'most vulnerable' (a narrowly defined group) in line with traditional One Nation Toryism, though One Nation Tories themselves have not been impressed.

The central themes of improving work incentives; reducing social security spending; targeting help on those in greatest need; and tackling fraud and abuse, determined policy changes implemented during the first two terms. With the exception of the last of these they were to re-emerge alongside a reduction in the role of central government so as to promote self-reliance and independence as the key objectives of the Fowler Green Paper published in 1985.

These themes, and the underlying assumption that social policy is subordinate to economic policy, were not in themselves new either to Conservative or Labour governments. But, as Peter Golding has argued, 'in combination and in the exuberant insistence with which they have been proclaimed and implemented [they] represent a significant shift away from the post-war consensus' (Golding, 1983, p.10), for which the ground had been well prepared over the previous decade.

1980: continuities and discontinuities

1980 was an important year of transition for social security policy. It saw two key pieces of legislation and the first stage in the Conservatives' crusade against fraud and abuse. The first 1980 Social Security Act, in particular, illustrated both the continuities and discontinuities with the past. The main part put into legislative form the much criticised nil-cost 'rough justice' supplementary benefits review carried out under the previous Labour government. Official estimates indicated about 1.75 million losers as against half a million gainers. The review's emphasis on simplification so as 'to fit the scheme to its mass role of coping with millions of claimants' (DHSS, 1978, para. 1.14) accorded well with the new Government's priorities. However, the latter refused to implement the review team's principal recommendation: the extension of the long-term supplementary benefit rate to the unemployed. The failure of James Callaghan's Government to do this reflected its own anxieties about work incentives and the likely reaction of a public unsympathetic to the unemployed. The new Government's reforms were also harsher than those originally proposed in their treatment of clothing grants – a clear cutback in provision that was never officially admitted.

The impact of the other main provision in the 1980 Act which ended the uprating link between pensions and other long-term benefits and average earnings has endured longer. This represented a clear break with previous Labour policy. It has been estimated by the House of Commons Library that the effect of breaking the earnings link during a period in which average earnings consistently out-stripped prices was, by April, 1987, a loss of £7.15 for a single pensioner and of £11.30 for a couple. The House of Commons Library has also estimated that this one change constituted about half the total savings made as a result of social security cuts between 1979 and 1987. As such it has clearly been one of the most significant measures taken. Yet, its impact is not fully appreciated.

It was, however, the 1980 Budget which represented the watershed in post-war social security policy. In the words of David Donnison, 'From time to time in the course of its history a nation crosses a watershed in its political journey – a point at which the whole landscape of popular assumptions and aspirations seems to change. The crest of the watershed we have just crossed was so clearly marked that I almost heard the crunch as we passed over it. To be precise, it was at about 3.00 pm on 26 March 1980 – Budget Day' (Donnison, 1982, p.206). The crunch came in the form of a 9 per cent cut in the real value of child benefit (despite earlier promises that it would be treated as a priority) and the unheralded announcement of the Social Security (No.2) Bill. For the first time ever, a government was prepared openly to legislate for a cut in the real value of the main national insurance benefits for those below pension age (through the imposition of a 5 per cent 'abatement in lieu of taxation') and for the actual abolition of benefits (the national insurance earnings-related supplement payable for the first six months of sickness, unemployment, maternity or widowhood). The Act also restricted the benefits paid to occupational pensioners and those involved in trade disputes. In the latter case, the increase in the direct financial costs of industrial action for individual workers and in the indirect costs for trade unions clearly bolstered the Government's industrial relations policy (see Booth and Smith, 1985).

Shortly before the Budget, the Government had stamped another mark on social security policy with the announcement of a major drive against fraud and 'abuse' to which end 1000 extra staff were to be allocated. Although pursued with greater conviction and vigour, this was not, however, a new departure. The number of special investigators and fraud prosecutions had already increased during the 1970s. The 1970 Conservative Government had set up the Fisher Committee to report on the issue. The 1974–9 Labour government had felt impelled to respond to public hysteria, fuelled by the popular press and certain Conservative politicians, with a special Co-ordinating Committee and fraud action plan. The atmosphere created provided the perfect context for an incoming government keen both to crack down still further and to cut spending on social security (see also Golding and Middleton, 1982).

Policy themes and developments

Moving on from 1980, a number of changes in social security provision have represented a response to policies formulated elsewhere. An important force for progress has been the EEC Directive on equal treatment of women and men. This underlay the extension to married women of the right to claim the main means-tested benefits and, under pressure, the removal of direct sex discrimination from non-contributory disability benefits and the invalid care allowance; in the latter case only after the UK had been taken to the European Court.

Less positive has been the impact on the DHSS of the Government's economic policy – both its aims and its effects. The Fowler Green Paper restated the central aim of a 'social security system consistent with the Government's overall objectives' for the economy (DHSS, 1985, vol.1, para.1.12), in particular the reduction in public expenditure and improved work incentives.

(i) Public spending and the Treasury wolves. A sustained attempt was made to create an atmosphere of crisis around social security spending. For instance, the 1985 Green Paper warned that it must

not become a 'millstone' impeding economic growth; earlier the Prime Minister had dubbed it a 'time bomb' (Wicks, 1987, p.96). Ironically, it was the Government's own economic policy that had encouraged the growth of social security expenditure during the early 1980s. In particular, the massive increase in unemployment recruited large numbers to the supplementary benefit ranks. Sharp cutbacks in housing expenditure fed directly into the housing benefit budget through higher local authority rents and contributed to higher expenditure on board and lodging as housing became more scarce. These increases in expenditure led in turn to successful and sustained pressure for benefit cuts.

This was the background against which the annual saga of the benefits uprating was played out. While it is certainly true that, as Donnison predicted, the Treasury wolves came back for more after 1980 (and the wolves roam in the Treasury whichever party is in power), they did not always draw as much blood as might have been expected from their initial success. Each autumn the headlines warned of further substantial cuts. But, thanks to the rallying of the Tory 'wets' and, in the case of pensions, an earlier prime ministerial pledge, a further full frontal assault on benefit levels was averted for some years. Indeed, the 1980 cuts in unemployment and child benefit were made good in 1983 following backbench pressure.

Instead, housing benefit was offered up as the sacrificial lamb. Following a steady series of cuts, mainly aimed at the 'tapers' and non-dependant deductions, about £250 million had been cut by the time of the Social Security Act 1986. The Act has since meant the loss of a further £650 million, two-thirds of which results from the requirement that everyone will have to pay at least 20 per cent of their rates bill (although an element of compensation is being provided through the other main means-tested benefits). The Treasury's insistence on cuts has marred what would otherwise have been a sensible, if limited, reform of the housing benefit scheme.

In addition, civil servants wielded the scalpel to effect an endless stream of minor cuts in complicated bits of the system, outweighing on balance the minor improvements that were also made from time to time. As Paul Johnson observed 'the incrementalism that allowed the welfare state to grow so silently is now used to effect its quiet contraction . . . the multiplicity of these individually small administrative changes amounts to a concerted, yet concealed contraction of the welfare state' (Johnson, 1985, p.33). This contraction was also used as a means of paving the way for the implementation of the Social Security Act 1986 so that its full impact on expenditure could be gauged.

One benefit which the Treasury wolves had long been hoping 'to bring down' was child benefit, having attempted to stall its introduction under the Labour government. After 1980, with the exception of a 35p. cut in child benefit's real value in 1985, they were kept at bay. But annual attempts to freeze it or at least cut its real value finally paid off with the advent of the new Social Services Secretary, John Moore, who accepted that child benefit should be frozen in 1988. Despite wide-ranging protests including from within its own backbenches, the Conservative Government decided in the Autumn of 1988 not to increase child benefit again in 1989 in favour of targeting limited resources on those it described as most in need.

(ii) Work incentives. An improvement in work incentives – both for the unemployed caught in the 'unemployment trap' and for the low paid caught in the 'poverty' trap' – has been a consistent objective. It is, however, an objective which has been pursued more wholeheartedly with regard to the unemployed than the low paid. In the case of the former, improving work incentives was consistent with the desire to reduce social security spending. In the case of the latter it was the victim of this same public spending policy which has favoured the cheaper means-tested benefits, a prime *cause* of the poverty trap, at the expense of the costlier child benefit, which the Conservative Party had itself earlier promoted as a *solution* to it (see also pp.116–17).

Paul Johnson reminds us that "New Right" ideas about restoring work incentives seem old hat to anyone familiar with the Edwardian debates on the poor laws, (Johnson, 1985, p.1). The 'less eligibility' principle enshrined in those laws has always acted as a more or less visible brake on benefit levels. But, under the emotive banner of the 'why work? syndrome', the 1979 Conservative Government promoted it into a central tenet of policy. As noted already, it was a primary motive behind the cuts contained in the Social Security (No. 2) Act 1980 and behind the subsequent extension of the tax net to a number of benefits. It also prompted a steady erosion in the real value of child support for national insurance beneficiaries, achieved through an administrative sleight of hand. Dressed up in the more positive guise of equity between social security claimants and the low paid, it has been used to justify various other cuts such as those in supplementary benefit single payments. At the same time, persistent demands for a better deal for the long-term unemployed, in particular through the extension of the long-term supplementary benefit rate – a cause pressed by a number of Conservative backbenchers – fell on ears deafened by the refrain 'why work?'.

A parallel obsession has been the notion that in many cases unemployment is not voluntary. The rules defining 'availability for work' have been tightened significantly alongside greater surveillance of the unemployed under the Restart scheme. At the same time, the maximum penalty for 'voluntary unemployment' has twice been doubled, to 26 weeks from 6.

The continued emphasis on work incentives and 'voluntary' unemployment has constituted a classic example of 'blaming the victim'. Yet it does not seem to have had much impact on public attitudes which,as measured by a number of polls, appear to be more sympathetic towards unemployed claimants than before the Conservatives came to power.

(iii) Care or control? The other major element of the 'blaming the victim' syndrome has been the continued emphasis on 'fraud and abuse'. A firm clampdown was listed in the 1983 manifesto as one of the main achievements of the first term. Additional special investigators; the much criticised and since withdrawn Specialist Claims Controls; Department of Employment Regional Benefit Investigating Teams; and the demonstration project presented by the infamous Operation Major incident[2] were all enlisted in the war against fraud. Less public was the shift from prosecution as an indicator of success to the recovery of overpaid benefit following a 'non-prosecution' interview. In 1988, the *Training for Employment* White Paper was used to announce the allocation of further resources to fraud investigation as part of a nationwide 'drive against fraud and abuse' (Department of Employment, 1988, paras 7.18 and 7.19).

Perhaps the most damaging response to a perceived problem of 'abuse' was the cutback in provision for those in board and lodgings. 'Costa del dole' headlines and Conservative backbench pressure lead to a series of increasingly draconian measures, arrested temporarily by setbacks in the courts. Young people were the main victims, allowed to claim ordinary board and lodging payments in any one area for only between two and eight weeks. Although these time limits are being abolished, it is predicted that the benefit provision proposed for this group will be so inadequate that young people simply will not be able to afford to live in lodgings in the first place.

Another group subject to increasing control has been the black community. Complaints have grown about the increase in passport checking, partly a product of the introduction in 1980 of the legal power to hold a sponsor liable for the maintenance of an immigrant relative. Although the original proposal in the Fowler Review for a presence test was dropped, under the new income support scheme claimants who entered the country within the previous five years are subject to a special interview with the information forwarded to the Home Office. These developments have to be seen in the context of a more general use of welfare services as an arm of immigration control (see Gordon and Newnham, 1986).

Perversely, the successive increases in the number of staff devoted to fraud work occurred at a time when the Government effected an overall reduction in the number of civil servants. Thus, at a time of steady growth in the claimant population, the staff-claimant ratio worsened, undermining the DHSS's attempts to improve the quality of service provided.

(iv) Rolling back the boundaries of the central state. The commitment to a reduction in the number of civil servants has motivated a number of important policy developments that have shifted responsibility for the administration of benefits from central government.

The most important of these has been the introduction of the housing benefit scheme, already under consideration by the 1974–9 Labour government following its abandonment of the attempt to achieve fundamental reform of housing finance. Responsibility for meeting the housing costs of supplementary benefit was transferred to local authorities, who already administered rent and rate rebates, without a unification of the scheme itself. The result was, in the words of *The Times*, 'the biggest fiasco in the history of the welfare state' (*The Times*, 1984), as authorities were not given enough time and resources to deal with the transfer. In the end, although the object was a reduction in public service staffing overall, local authorities took on more officials to deal with housing benefit than the DHSS had shed.

The combination of administrative chaos and politically sensitive cuts forced a review of the scheme within a year of its full introduction; this was subsequently subsumed under the wider Fowler review.

As we argue below, local authorities are also likely to face pressure to act as a safety net of last resort with the introduction of the social fund, as will charities. There has also been a more overt shift of responsibility to charities for the disbursement of benefits. A grant was made to the Haemophiliac Society to pay out grants to haemophiliacs infected by the AIDS virus and to the Independent Living Fund for those with severe disabilities who stood to lose as a result of the Social Security Act 1986, in a belated and rather desperate attempt to counter widespread criticism.

Another way in which the DHSS has divested itself of responsibilities has been by passing them over to employers. The first step was the introduction of statutory sick pay (SSP) in place of sickness benefit for the first 8 weeks, extended to 28 weeks, of sickness. This was also used as a means of improving work incentives by the application of taxation to SSP and the payment of a reduced rate of benefit to the low paid. The next step was to shift the main responsibility for the payment of maternity benefit to employers under the Social Security Act 1986. An attempt under the Act to make employers responsible also for the payment of family credit failed in the face of widespread resistance.

Finally, we have what Carol Walker has dubbed 'do-it-yourself social security'. The introduction of a postal claims form represents 'a more pervasive and insidious method of privatising administration', she argues. The effect has been to transfer responsibility for the identification and correct presentation of needs 'from the benefits system to claimants themselves' (Walker, C., 1987, p.108).

(v) Promoting self-reliance and independence. The reduction in the role of the state has also had a clear ideological aim.

Of five 'beliefs' outlined in the Fowler Green Paper, 'most important of all' was that 'social security must be designed to reinforce personal independence rather than extend the power of the state' (DHSS, 1985, vol.1, para.6.6). The theme was later taken up by Social Services Secretary, John Moore, who declared that 'the next step in the long evolutionary march of the welfare state in Britain is away from dependence towards independence' (Moore, 1987).

The Fowler Review's most visible contribution towards shifting responsibility from the 'pillar' of the state to that of the individual has been in the promotion of private pensions subsidised by public tax reliefs. The original proposal to abolish the state earnings-related scheme was abandoned in face of overwhelming opposition, but the 'modifications' made instead are thought to have seriously weakened the scheme, and in particular those elements that favoured women and other groups unable to build up a continuous contribution record.

An earlier, leaked, document from the Family Policy Group had suggested that 'more could be done to encourage families – in the widest sense – to reassume responsibility for the disabled, elderly and unemployed 16 year olds' (*Guardian*, 1983). Considerable progress has been made with regard to the last group. A series of benefit cuts have undermined the benefit position of young people, culminating in the lower benefit rates for single childless under-25 year olds under the Social Security Act 1986 and the removal of the right to benefit from most 16 to 17 year olds under the Social Security Act 1988. This last change is 'designed to avoid the damaging effects for young people of moving straight from school into the benefit culture' (DHSS, 1987).

The social fund has been justified in similar terms. In a letter to the Chair of the Social Security Advisory Committee, the Social Security Minister explained that 'it has been a consistent objective of the reforms to give people a sum of money within which they manage for themselves, reducing their dependence on the "benefits culture" for extras' (Scott, 1987). In fact, the concept of the 'benefits culture' is a relatively recent addition to the government lexicon, reflecting the ideological framework provided by John Moore. Critics have countered that a reduction in dependence on the 'benefit culture' will be matched by an increase in dependence on local authority social services departments and private forms of assistance such as families, charities and loan sharks. Indeed, charities have already felt the impact of the cutbacks in clothing grants in 1980 and the 1986 single payments cuts and have expressed considerable concern about the implications of the social fund for them (see e.g. Morley, 1988; Pugh, 1987).

The discretionary social fund, from which the Government's own Social Security Advisory Committee in an unprecedented move asked to be disassociated, introduced a number of fundamental new principles into social security policy. For the first time, part of the basic safety net is subject to a cash limit. The guidance issued to social fund officers makes it crystal clear that keeping within the budget is a more important consideration than meeting people's needs. The iron grip of the budget gives rise to a convoluted system of prioritisation which reeks of distinctions between the 'deserving' and 'undeserving' poor. Provision is made primarily by way of loans (or more accurately advances of benefit) rather than lump sum grants. Less than a third of the initial budget was available for grants, representing an 83 per cent reduction from the pre-August 1986 levels of expenditure on single payments (Cohen and Davies, 1988, p.6).

While discretion is nothing new – it was one of the major problems of the supplementary benefits scheme which lead to the 1978 review – the removal of an independent right of appeal is (although there is no such right of appeal for housing benefit). The complete removal of rights is underlined by the legislation's use of the term social fund 'applicant' rather than claimant – another example of the Government's skilful use of language.

The roots of the social fund can, in fact, be traced back to various earlier attempts to stem the tide of lump sum payments in 1966 and 1980. The 1978 review team had even recommended restrictions on the right to appeal against decisions on lump sum grants using very similar arguments to those used to justify the denial of an independent right of appeal under the social fund. This should not, however, blind us to the significance of the social fund's introduction. It represents a clear attempt to reduce expectations of what the state will provide for some of the poorest in our society. Although single payments represented only a small fraction of the total social security budget, their replacement by the social fund was, in the words of the Social Services' Correspondent of *The Independent*, 'the one great symbolic change' in the Social Security Act 1986 (Timmins, 1988).

(vi) Targeting help to those in greatest need. The numbers dependent on supplementary benefit nearly doubled between 1979 and 1987 from 4.37 million to over 8 million (House of Commons Debates, 1987a). This was mainly as a result of the increase in the number of unemployed but also, to a lesser extent, reflected increased dependence due to cuts in non-meanstested benefits. It was officially estimated that the 1980 cuts in national insurance benefits alone pushed 110,000 claimants onto supplementary benefit. Since then entitlement to national insurance benefits has been chipped away, pushing more people onto supplementary benefit (or in the case of many married women leaving them without any benefit at all). According to DHSS estimates, the most recent erosion of entitlement, contained in the Social Security Act 1988, will mean a further 300,000 people forced to turn to means-tested income support.

Similar developments have occurred among the working population. Each cut in child benefit has been accompanied and justified by a less expensive improvement in the real value of means-tested support for poor working families; first family income supplement and now family credit. It was officially estimated that the 1988 freeze in child benefit would push 15,000 more families into the means-tested net. Similarly, the abolition of the universal maternity and death grants by means-tested help under the social fund has further extended means-testing's tentacles. Higher rents and health charges also mean more people forced to rely on means-tested assistance to meet them.

Increases in the numbers dependent on means-tested assistance are hardly a new phenomenon. Previous governments have, however, presided reluctantly over such increases while still paying lipservice to the Beveridge goal of reducing dependence on means-testing – though there have been sections of the Conservative Party advocating selectivity as a positive virtue since the 1950s. The Heath government started out showing some enthusiasm for means-testing with the introduction of FIS and a national rent and rate rebate scheme. But by the time of the 1974 election its enthusiasm had waned, in the face of low take-up and the discovery of the poverty trap; tax credits were on the table and it was being stressed by Conservative Central office that FIS was brought in only as a temporary first aid measure (Conservative Central Office, 1974, p.337).

In 1980 ministers relied on the protection of the supplementary benefit safety net and improvement in FIS to demonstrate their commitment to protecting 'the really weak and needy'. By the time of the Fowler Green Paper, in 1985, 'targeting', the user-friendly modern euphemism for means-testing, had been elevated into a primary objective of government policy. Nevertheless, the Green Paper did not follow through this objective to its conclusion and stopped short of advocating the means-testing of child benefit and the more drastic cuts in national insurance that had been feared.

Although the actual extension of means-testing was not as significant as the rhetoric suggested, the Social Security Act 1986 did represent a further shift in the centre of gravity of social security policy. Means-tested benefits are now explicitly presented as the fulcrum of the system. Many of the reforms introduced in 1988 represent an attempt to rationalise the main means-tested benefits in search of the holy grail of simplification *without* tackling the underlying problems associated with means-testing. These include the long-recognised problems of low take-up and the poverty trap, which is now ensnaring more poor families than ever. It is officially estimated that the number of low-paid workers facing effective marginal tax rates of 60 per cent or more has almost doubled to over half a million as a result of the 1986 Act (House of Commons Debates, 1987c and 1988). Moreover the use of net income to calculate entitlement, whilst removing the worst excesses of the poverty trap, creates a new tax trap for the poor: a tax cut now has virtually no effect at all on the income of someone claiming means-tested benefits. Other more recently identified problems are associated with the distribution of resources within families to women and children and the position of those immigrants whose right to stay in the country is dependent on not having 'recourse to public funds' which are defined as means-tested benefits.

(vii) A provisional balance sheet. The Fowler Review, for all its ideological hype and individually damaging elements which have resulted in more losers than gainers, did not constitute the radical break with the past hoped for by the New Right – with the important exception of the social fund.

Indeed, there was a fundamental contradiction in a review that strived for simplification, improved incentives and greater self-reliance, while at the same time prioritising mean-tested benefits which are inimical to these objectives. And the philosophy of targeting help on those in greatest need was created on a very narrow conception of need, unrelated to any examination of how far social security benefits actually meet needs. Furthermore, the review was doomed from the outset by the Treasury remit which excluded consideration of the parallel fiscal welfare state of tax allowances and reliefs and which imposed not just a nil-cost constraint (as it had with the previous Labour review) but also demanded cuts (although Norman Fowler succeeded in containing these to some extent). The *Financial Times* in 1988 predicted that 'historians are likely to regard the "Fowler" social security reforms as little more than a penny-pinching stop gap'.

The outcome of the Review also has to be set against the overall record since 1979. The Government is able to point to £12½ billion or 39 per cent real growth in social security spending over its first two terms. This, however, conceals cumulative savings of over £11 billion according to the House of Commons Library. Moreover, two-thirds of the growth in spending is explained by an increase in the number of claimants, in particular unemployed supplementary benefit claimants. Nor is all of the other third attributable to an increase in the real value of benefits. There has been some increase in benefit rates for adults, although, with the exception of cheaper benefits such as mobility allowance, this has been more by accident than by design. There has also been a real improvement in means-tested support for children in contrast to that provided through the national insurance scheme and child benefit, which has been cut significantly. Child benefit was worth nearly 7 per cent less in 1988 than in 1979.

Whether many claimants have experienced a real improvement in benefits as such is debatable when the retail price index against which their value is measured tends to underestimate the impact of price increases on the poor. Families on supplementary benefit who have relied on single payments to eke out their benefit in the past have been particularly hard hit, notwithstanding an improvement in some of the children's scale rates in 1980.

Claimants can also see what is happening in the rest of society. At a time of a considerable growth in the real living standards of the working community (other than the low paid), gilded with generous tax cuts, even those benefits that have improved in real terms are falling further and further behind average living standards.

2   Into the 1990s

The 1987 manifesto made clear the context for the development of future social security policy, with the promise of further tax cuts combined with the aim 'that public expenditure takes a steadily smaller share of our national income'. Discussion of social security itself was largely confined to those policies already in the pipeline and reassuring noises about safeguarding 'the living standards of those who have to depend on the community'. The main exception was the promise of an improved framework of benefits for people with disabilities (already signalled back in the 1979 manifesto). This was expected following an OPCS survey, but John Major (then Social Security minister) made clear in an interview with the journal *Poverty* just before the election that there was no commitment to more resources.

It has been suggested that Phase 3 of the 'Thatcher Revolution' would mark a 'radically new approach to social issues' (*Daily Express,* 1987). In the social security field the ink was hardly dry on Mr Fowler's review, which it was promised would deliver a system 'capable of meeting the demands into the next century' (DHSS, 1985, vol.1, para. 1.4.), than his successor Mr Moore began to make the case for continual revolution in the DHSS. He outlined as the key tasks, first 'to change the climate of opinion' around welfare, and second 'to change the policies which have done so much to create the attitudes' (Moore, 1987).

Cuts and more cuts

The commitment to further tax cuts and the containment of public expenditure means that social security continues to be vulnerable, as the first uprating under the third term made clear. According to *The Guardian,* the April 1988 cuts signalled the start of a new round of reductions promised to the Prime Minister by the Social Services Secretary. Apart from pensions and the linked long-term benefits, there was no commitment to maintain the real value of any benefit. Even pensions, it must be remembered, are likely to fall further and further behind average wages during the 1990s as a consequence of the 1980 Act.

There are two danger signals already clearly visible. The first concerns housing benefit. The Explanatory and Financial

Memorandum to the Housing Bill stated that it would 'result in higher rents for new tenancies granted by private landlords and housing associations and this will in turn lead to some increase in housing benefit expenditure'. Some estimates have put the increase as high as £3 billion. The White Paper, *Housing, the Government's Proposals,* made clear, however, that the Government would do what it could to restrict this increase. The White Paper points out that local authorities' discretion to restrict benefit on unreasonable rents is already being strengthened as part of the April 1988 housing benefit changes. There is more to come however: 'The Government proposes in addition to require rent officers to scrutinise the level of rents which are being met by housing benefit. Where a rent is excessive, the subsidy to the local authority will be restricted to an appropriate market rent for the dwelling in question. The Government is prepared if necessary to place direct limits on housing benefits rather than on subsidy' (Department of Environment, 1987a, para.3.18). Pressure will also be placed on the housing benefit budget with the introduction of the poll tax, which it is officially estimated will increase the housing benefit caseload significantly.

The combined pressure of higher rents and the poll tax could mean a re-run of the story of housing benefit in the 1980s: a steady rise in housing benefit expenditure, due primarily to increased local authority rents (which were justified partly on the grounds that the poor would be protected by housing benefit) led to the successive cuts in the benefit, which, it was claimed, was now going to too many people.

The other likely target is child benefit. It is widely understood that, as the Conservative MP, Sir George Young, observed, the 1988 freeze means that 'the Party, is at the moment marking time, before deciding in which direction it should move'. He went on to say, 'it should think long and hard before abandoning the family – there is more than 30p at stake' (Young, 1987). What is not clear is whether the outcome of the internal review conducted in 1988 will be long-term erosion, more radical restructuring or even abolition (see below).

Targeting revisited

John Moore has emphasised that sharper targeting on those in greatest need is 'crucial as part of the longer term effort to change the climate of opinion in welfare' (Moore, 1987). It is generally believed that the most significant extension of means-testing is likely to be in the area of child support, although probably not until after the next Election because of the 1987 manifesto pledge that child benefit 'will continue to be paid as now'. When questioned at the time of the uprating statement, Mr Moore responded, 'I have no specific proposals at present to change the nature of child benefit but . . . in view of its cost and its ill-targeted nature, there is clearly a need to keep it constantly under review' (House of Commons Debates, 1987).

If child benefit were abolished, subjected to means-testing or even simply eroded in favour of means-tested family credit, ironically this could make family credit itself more vulnerable to cuts. To quote Richard Berthoud:

A policy heavily reliant on income-related benefit is unlikely to remain stable . . . When there is already a heavy investment in benefits or subsidies paid universally, it appears possible to offer a generous income-related benefit and still save money. Once the latter has replaced the former, however, the concept of a public share in family responsibilities gives way to that of special help to the needy; it would then easily appear that the income related benefit was excessively generous. That is what happened with housing benefit.

If greater reliance were placed on family credit at the expense of child benefit, he argues, 'as sure as eggs is eggs, it would be only a few years before it was judged to be excessively generous' (Berthoud, 1985, p.84). The fact that family credit now goes considerably higher up the income scale than housing benefit itself adds considerable weight to Berthoud's argument.

The abolition of the universal child benefit would also remove a major political obstacle to a more thorough going selective negative income tax type scheme, as advocated for many years by right-wing economists. However, although such schemes continue to be advocated, it does appear as though the tide of political support for them is receding. The Green Paper on the reform of personal taxation argued that integration of tax and benefits of the kind proposed by the Institute for Fiscal Studies or traditionally associated with negative income tax schemes was unlikely. In the US it is no longer on the serious political agenda; the Right has moved on to the issue of welfare dependency, as we see below.

The extension of means-testing is also likely as a by-product of other policies. In both local government and the health service, it is clear that charges will be increased and extended. More and higher charges inevitably mean more means-testing as even the most hard-hearted government recognises that the poorest cannot pay such charges without help.

On the way to workfare?

Even more than targeting, the main thrust of Mr Moore's first major speech as Social Services Secretary lay in its hymn to the virtues of personal independence. 'A welfare state worthy of the name,' he claimed, 'while accepting its obligation to care for the distressed and needy, also works to encourage the resourcefulness and enterprise that are the true foundations of both personal and national success' (Moore, 1987). Melanie Phillips suggested that 'If Mr Moore's speech means anything concrete, Workfare-type schemes seem most likely to top the agenda' (Phillips, 1987 – see also chapter 5). These could have implications both for unemployed claimants and for lone parents, two groups causing concern to the Right. Already the withdrawal of the right to benefit from most 16–17 year olds has been heralded as a 'youth workfare system without question' (Burton, 1988).

A 1988 BBC radio "File on Four" programme provided a fascinating insight into current Right-wing thinking in this area. The presenter, David Levy, observed that 'the agenda for the welfare revolution is ambitious. The aim is to change our attitudes to work and to benefits. The ideas behind the new attack on the benefit culture are rooted in Victorian notions of self-help, but the language of the new welfare theorists is largely American . . . The American insistence on the language of obligation rather than of entitlement has fallen on fertile soil over here.' David Willetts, once a member of Mrs Thatcher's Policy Unit, explained that the US is now concerned with 'the real world questions: issues like how much is right to spend on helping poor people; if there's a problem of welfare dependency . . . and we in Britain I think are now ourselves beginning to learn that these are the real, meaty, interesting questions in welfare reform'.

Shedding responsibilities

A further theme of Mr Moore's speech was the need 'to inject some long overdue modesty into government's attitude towards its own role in welfare'. There are a number of ways in which the Government's role in welfare is likely to be narrowed still further in the 1990s. Every encouragement will be given to the spread of private personal pensions bolstered by 'substantial tax concessions' (Conservative Party, 1987) as SERPS is cut back as part of the Fowler reforms. At the same time the downgrading of universal state benefits is likely to encourage greater reliance on employer-based schemes more generally among those in the 'core' of the labour market. This would mean that the 'dual labour market would be reflected in provisions for security' (ILO, 1984, para.47).

It has already been noted that the social fund is likely to result in a growing number of claimants forced to turn to social service departments and charities for help with meeting their basic needs. The more social services departments get involved in operating their own financial safety net beneath the social fund, the greater the danger that they might find themselves pinned down with responsibility for it. The likely transfer of responsibility to social services departments for the income maintenance of those in private residential care following the Firth and Griffiths reports could similarly pave the way. DHSS officials were reported already to have floated the idea informally that the fund might be passed over to local authorities (*Social Services Insight*, 1987; *The Times*, 1987). A further straw in the wind is Griffiths' recommendation that the funds earmarked for the community care grant element of the social fund should be transferred to social services authorities. Whether or not the fund is transferred, it is difficult to believe that it will not have to undergo significant modification in the light of the experience of its operation.

Finally, there has been some speculation that the restructured DSS might be preparing to shed its responsibility for the administration of much of the social security scheme by contracting it out to the private sector. The computerisation of the system would be the vehicle for such a move. The full computerisation of the system is due to be completed by the 1990s. How far claimants benefit from computerisation will depend largely on whether or not staff savings are ploughed back into the system to provide the adequately staffed scheme that is currently lacking. The actual administration of benefit is likely to go the way of that of unemployment benefit which is being hived off into a new Employment Service run by a chief executive.

A residual welfare state

As the 1990s progress we can see the probability, in the words of Malcolm Wicks, of a 'move towards a residual welfare state, characterized by increasing inequality, deepening poverty, greater reliance on the means test, a growing role for the private market and consequently social division and conflict' (Wicks, 1987, p.9). The model is that provided by the United States in contrast to the Continental model of social security which emphasises security and protection for all citizens (however imperfectly this is achieved).

3   An alternative scenario

It has been argued above that if such social security policies are pursued into the 1990s, the UK will become an increasingly divided society. At the same time economic and demographic trends, if not countered with different kinds of policies, are themselves a force for greater division. A transformation in the UK labour force has been identified as growing numbers are found either among the unemployed or in the 'periphery' of part-time and/or flexible jobs which provide neither employment nor welfare security (Leadbeater, 1987). Inequalities during working life will be reflected in old age, condemning a minority among the growing pensioner population to 'live out their final years in poverty' (Wicks, 1987, p.159).

The purpose of social security

If the social security scheme is to play a role as part of the solution to a divided society rather than as part of the problem, it must be regarded 'as a force which helps to integrate individuals and groups in society' (ILO, 1984, para. 26). A key concept is that of 'social citizenship', coined by T.H. Marshall, who wrote of 'progress from the right to a modicum of economic welfare and security to the right to share to the full in the social heritage and to live the life of a civilized being according to the standards prevailing in the society' (Marshall, 1963, p.11).

What is at issue is not mere technical argument about the best way to deliver social security but more fundamental questions about the purpose of a social security scheme. At present we appear to be heading for a social security scheme which aims merely to relieve the worst poverty. This, of course, is one function of a social security scheme but if it is treated as the only one, it serves to isolate and marginalise those in poverty. Other functions include collective insurance against risk; the transfer of income between generations and over the individual lifestyle; societal sharing of responsibility for the care of children and other dependants. These functions are the more important at a time of social change.

Alternative models

Different models of social security can be viewed as a crude continuum according to the narrowness or breadth of the eligibility criteria applied as shown in Table 4.1.

Table 4.1   *Social security models*

	Eligibility		
Narrow			*Wide*
Means-testing	Beveridge – contributory benefits	Beyond Beveridge – non-contributory contingency benefits	Basic income or social dividend

On another axis, they can be grouped according to the extent to which benefit is conditional or contingent upon belonging to certain categories and it is this which is the primary distinguishing feature between the models to be found towards the 'wide eligibility' end of the continuum.

There is growing support across the political spectrum for some kind of basic income scheme which, in its pure form, would provide without any conditions attached a tax-free cash payment to each individual citizen in place of existing benefits. In practice, supporters of basic income have conceded that modifications would have to be made to reduce its cost which, in turn, would sacrifice some of the simplicity and freedom from conditions which are the scheme's main attractions.

The scheme is, indeed, an attractive one. In particular, by treating those in and out of work alike it would end the categorisation of different groups and would not require special rules for the growing number of part-time workers. But is it a realistic scheme for the 1990s? The answer depends very much on how one perceives the future of work, for a basic income challenges the centrality of the wages system as a means of distributing income. For all the current changes in the labour market, our political and economic culture is still imbued with the work ethic and the Poor Law 'less eligibility' principle. As David Piachaud argues, 'the notion that it will in the next decade be accepted that able-bodied people should be free to choose guaranteed income at a decent level without satisfying any conditions about availability for work seems very remote. It seems politically inevitable that either the income guarantee would be very low or tests of eligibility would be applied' (Piachaud, 1987b, p.48).

An attempt to use the social security system to achieve the more fundamental social changes upon which a successful basic income scheme would be contingent is likely to backfire if public attitudes are not ready for such changes. Thus while a basic income scheme remains a possible and attractive option for the future, it would be premature to attempt to introduce it in the early 1990s. In the meantime, an alternative model for the early 1990s should be compatible with any eventual move to such a scheme.

Beyond Beveridge

One model which could represent a step towards an eventual basic income scheme would be that known as 'Beyond Beveridge'. This model builds on the present system but goes beyond the Beveridge contribution-based scheme by extending the scope of eligibility for non-means-tested benefits. Eligibility would still be conditional on meeting certain contingencies but these contingencies would be widened by phasing out contribution tests and time limits and by ending differential basic benefit rates currently applied to different groups. Thus the long-term unemployed, one-parent families and people with disabilities would have the same entitlement to non-means-tested benefits as those groups currently covered by the national insurance scheme.

Implicit in this model is the principle of non-discrimination between different claimant groups. It also embraces the principle of non-discrimination on grounds of gender, race, marital status or sexual orientation. More positively, it would seek to provide benefit on an individual rather than a couple basis in recognition of the right to autonomy of individual adults, particularly women, and of the fact that 'gender inequality is a major cause of income inequality' (Piachaud, 1987b, p.52), not least because income is not always shared fairly within the family (Glendenning and Millar, 1987). There is also a 'need for a rigorous examination of possible ethnocentrism in all aspects of the social security system' and for the DSS 'to make the clearest and most unequivocal statement of intent to root out racism, conscious or not, overt or not, from the social security system' (Gordon and Newnham, 1985, p.74).

There are a number of other issues which need to be dealt with if we are to achieve a social security system consistent with the notion of social citizenship and able to provide genuine security at a time of social change. First, is the question of adequacy. The concept of social citizenship involves that of enabling full participation in society. If this is to be realised, the assessment of need for social security purposes must take account of social and cultural as well as basic physical needs, in the development of what Professor Peter Townsend has called a 'participation standard'. Such a standard cannot be achieved overnight but its development could provide a goal to be reached in stages.

Another important issue to be addressed – and debated – is how far society should share the costs of children, through a decent child benefit scheme, and the cost of caring for children. Linked to this is how the social security system can help parents combine caring responsibilities with paid employment and, more broadly, how social security can come to terms with the spread of part-time work. A number of other European countries have been attempting to tackle these questions and there may well be lessons to be learned from their experience, one example being the Swedish parental insurance and temporary parental benefit schemes (Hurstfield, 1987).

Finally, in terms of respecting the dignity of recipients, how the social security system is administered can be as important as the benefits administered. Any social security system must provide clear rights to benefit and be administered efficiently and courteously. As Judy McKnight, has noted, 'new technology could provide a golden opportunity for major improvements in the administration of the social security system' (McKnight, 1985, p.37). This opportunity must be grasped so that instead of providing an excuse for cuts, staff resources can be diverted to provide a better, more helpful service to the public. More, better trained staff, in pleasanter offices with decent facilities would be a first step.

More fundamentally, there are, as Nicholas Deakin has argued, problems in relying on an unpopular institution such as the DSS to deliver the kind of social security system envisaged. Deakin sees the solution as lying in the development of the value of democracy: 'a social policy based on democracy would have something important to contribute about institutions and their responsiveness to the needs of their customers . . . Accountability would become a key virtue in such a reformed system' (Deakin,

1987, p.188). How to achieve a social security system more accountable to its users represents a major challenge.

A wider strategy for redistribution

While social security has a crucial role to play in healing the growing divisions in our society (7 out of 10 people live in families receiving some form of social benefit), it cannot do so on its own. The Beyond Beveridge model therefore has to be viewed as part of a broader strategy.

First, the underlying inequalities in the distribution of primary incomes, and therefore the distribution of paid and unpaid work, have to be tackled directly rather than leaving it to the social security and tax systems to pick up all the pieces. This means, on the one hand, a policy to deal with low pay. As Joan Brown has commented, 'the existence of a low paid sector in the labour force has always had a strong influence on social security. Its pivotal influence has now been fully recognised, but the attempt to deal with its consequences almost entirely through social security measures has introduced distortions into the social security system and has created problems for which, in turn, solutions have to be found' (Brown, 1987, p.143).

On the other hand, it points to employment policies which must, *inter alia*, take account of and try to facilitate the relationship between paid employment and unpaid caring responsibilities. The development of adequate child care facilities and other services to support those caring for dependants is crucial here.

Social security policy must also deal with the 'social division of welfare', i.e. the parallel occupational and fiscal welfare states identified by Richard Titmuss back in the 1960s. In particular, progress cannot be made on the development of a coherent housing benefit scheme so long as the present distorting tax subsidies for owner-occupation are treated as sacrosanct.

Whether or not the alternative scenario sketched out here has any hope of being adopted in the 1990s depends not just on which political party is in power but on that party being prepared to commit itself to a redistributive fiscal and social strategy and to the integration of social with economic policy.

Conclusion

Two dangers arise from the Government's success in shifting the boundaries between the politically thinkable and the unthinkable. After years of the oppositional politics of the finger in the dyke, it is easy to become pathetically grateful for the maintenance of inadequate benefit levels or for a cut that turns out not to be as bad as earlier kite-flying had intimated. At the same time, exaggerated claims about the dismantling of the welfare state can be brushed aside, thereby diverting attention from the more subtle processes which are slowly undermining its foundations. The first and second sections of this chapter have attempted to steer a path between these two dangers in recording past and likely future developments in social security policy.

Second, one of the most potentially damaging legacies of the shifting of the political boundaries and of key policy developments such as the social fund and the growing restrictions on the entitlement to benefits of unemployed people is the insidious impact it has on expectations. The repeated theme of the 'File on Four' programme mentioned earlier was that 'attitudes to welfare are entering a new phase where obligation will replace rights' ('File on Four', 1988). As the Right raises the flag of the US-inspired 'welfare revolution', it is crucial that the debate about the kind of alternative strategies outlined in the third section, which are based on principles of social citizenship and cohesion, is kept alive. In the words of Peter Golding, 'the triumph of Thatcherism has been to make the unthinkable appear irresistible. If this is not to become the irreversible, a major task remains in recreating an alternative common sense about social policy and poverty' (Golding, 1983, p.12).

Notes

1. The 'unemployment trap' refers to the situation in which some low paid workers can be worse off or little better off in work than on benefit. The 'poverty trap' describes the situation of those low paid workers who gain nothing or very little for each extra £ that they earn and who can in some cases

even be worse off. The last situation though possible in theory was rare in practice. Under the Social Security Act 1986 it is no longer possible even in theory for full-time workers.

2. Operation Major was an anti-fraud exercise in which DHSS fraud investigators aided by Thames Valley Police rounded up 203 claimants in a blaze of publicity and inflated claims about the extent of the fraud involved. A detailed account can be found in *Poor Law* (Franey, 1983)

Acknowledgements

The author would like to thank Fran Bennett and Michael McCarthy for their helpful comments on the first draft of this chapter.

5

Employment

MOLLY MEACHER

'The dispute between wet and dry does not only concern economic policy, but – just as important – the balance between economic policy and social policy. To insist that unemployment is an urgent social problem in need of immediate and imaginative attention may or may not require a new economic policy but it undoubtedly requires a sympathetic social policy.' (Francis Pym *The Politics of Consent*, 1985.)

1 The recent past

In the 1980s mass unemployment became an accepted feature of British life. Full employment has by the same token become an unrealistic objective to many or, even, to some, an undesirable one.

To what extent is it possible to find the seeds of these movements of opinion in the 1970s? How permanent are the changes to perception and policy? What are the implications for the future either under a succession of Conservative governments or in the hands of a new Labour or Democrat administration? This chapter will explore these questions.

Lessons from the 1970s

Only in the context of our 1970s experience can Britain's acceptance of the mass unemployment of the 1980s be understood. Perhaps the

Figure 5.1   *Whole economy – actual and trend labour costs 1971–86*

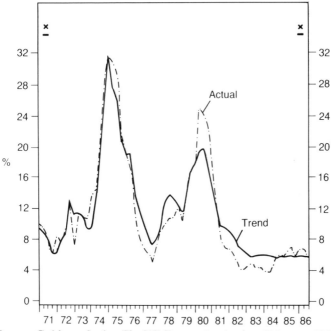

Source: Goldman Sachs, *The UK Economics Analyst*, February 1987,
London.

oil crisis of November 1973 is as good a starting point as any for this
discussion. The oil price increase nudged the retail price index up
by about 2 per cent and commodity price increases added another
3 per cent to the RPI. Strong government action was needed to
contain the situation. Instead the Labour Government returned in
the Spring of 1974 had a majority of only 4. Fears of a showdown
with the trade union movement before another election could be
held and the majority increased inhibited Harold Wilson and his
team from doing what they knew they needed to do – make clear
to everyone that a small temporary fall in the standard of living was
necessary in order to absorb the oil price increase. Instead, a social
contract was attempted. The stronger unions took the opportunity
to improve their members' positions and a free-for-all resulted,
with wages and inflation topping 30 per cent within two years.

An incomes policy was imposed in August 1975, ten months
after a further general election had secured a slightly larger

Figure 5.2   *UK unemployment rates 1855–1986*

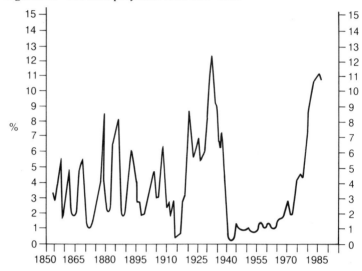

Source: R. Layard, *How to Beat Unemployment*, Campaign for Work
Pamphlet no. 1, London.

Figure 5.3   *Public sector debt as a percentage of GDP at market prices
1958–1986*

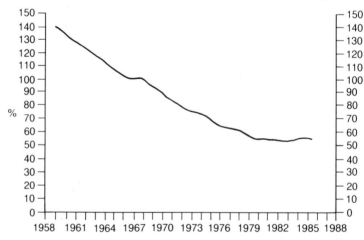

Source: R. Layard, *How to Beat Unemployment*, Campaign for Work
Pamphlet, no. 1, London.

majority. Within a period of two years wages were back under control. The Labour Government of the time was convinced of the value of a permanent incomes policy as an essential ingredient of a full employment strategy. In can be assumed that, had a Labour Government been returned in 1979 an incomes policy would have been retained, the value of the pound would have been kept in check and the unemployment of the 1980s would have been more in line with that of the 1960's and 1970's.

Turning economic policy on its head

The Conservative Government, returned in 1979, had to deal immediately with the second oil price increase, and their response effectively ended the post-war all-party commitment to full employment. It is worth noting that an alternative was presented to them. The Keynesian economists at the time recommended a package of policies to absorb the impact of the oil price rise on prices generally – a sharp increase in taxes on the oil producers which would be paid out of their increased profits and which would be used to finance a cut in VAT, thus *reducing* prices to counteract the RPI effect of the oil price increase. Such a package would have prevented the price and wage spiral of 1979–80. Instead the Government increased VAT from 8 per cent to 15 per cent, thus fuelling price and wage inflation. At the same time a tight money policy with high interest rates forced up the value of the pound, choking off exports and putting whole tracts of Britain's industrial heartland to waste.

Mass unemployment became the central weapon with which to tackle inflation. As Nigel Lawson explained in his Mais lecture (HM Treasury) macroeconomic policy was to be turned on its head. In the past macroeconomic policy, monetary policy and fiscal policy had been used to control unemployment by sustaining sufficient demand in the economy. Microeconomic policy – in particular incomes policies – had been used to control inflation. In future, said Nigel Lawson, economic policy would be used in quite opposite ways. Macroeconomic policy would be used to control inflation. Money supply would be controlled through lower government spending and a reduced budget deficit. Such policies would tend to reduce the volume of spending and would therefore limit price inflation. In reality, however, such contractionary policies operate through reducing the level of *real* demand in the economy and thus *increasing* unemployment. The effects of the contractionary fiscal and monetary policies of 1979–81 can be seen in Figure 5.2. Unemployment soared to within half a percentage point of the highest level in the 1930s.

Mrs Thatcher argued persuasively that Britain had no alternative to mass unemployment; that as a nation we could not spend more than we earned. What the Prime Minister failed to point out was that, unlike a housewife who has no control over the value of the pound in her pocket, the British Government could control the value of the pound and thus the competitiveness of British products and our capacity to sell exports. Secondly, the value of Britain's public sector debt was lower in 1979–81 than it had been for the previous twenty years and more (Figure 5.3). It had fallen steadily as a percentage of GDP since 1958, irrespective of the political party in power. The Government's claim that previous Labour Governments had been profligate does not hold water.

A short-term increase in the public debt to maintain employment would have been entirely sound, so long as the Government had been willing to use policies other than mass unemployment to control inflation. But Mrs Thatcher was not prepared to risk a re-run of the 'Winter of Discontent' suffered by her predecessor, James Callaghan. More particularly, the British people appeared willing to accept mass unemployment as an acceptable price to pay for a reduction in trade union power. The Government had won the argument and felt free to sustain mass unemployment and to use microeconomic policies to respond to the social consequences of mass idleness.

The microeconomic response reducing the unemployment figures

Instead of reflating the economy and creating real jobs as had been done in the 1930s the Government decided to leave the number of real jobs unchanged while taking steps to cut the unemployment figures and to cut the level of wages acceptable to unemployed people.

The Community Programme was established in October 1982. The aim of the new programme was to provide *temporary*

Table 5.1 *The effect of adminstrative and policy changes on the registered number of unemployed 1981–6*

Date	Change	Estimated reduction in monthly count
February 1981	First published estimate of register	−370,000
	Effect of special employment measures (increase from 250,000 participants at start of 1979)	−558,782 (by 1989)
July 1981	Unemployed men aged 60 and above drawing supplementary benefit for a year or more given option of long-term rate in return for not registering for work	−30,000 (by May 1982)
October 1982	Change in definition and compilation of monthly unemployment figures from a clerical count of people registered for work to a computer count of benefit claimants	−180,000
	Effects of these changes on number of school leavers recorded.	−26,000
October 1982	Monthly publication of number of unemployed people seeking part-time work discontinued	−52,204
April 1983	Men aged 60 and over and not entitled to benefit no longer required to sign on at benefit offices in order to get NI credits	−107,400 (by June 1983)
June 1983	All men aged 60 and over allowed long term rate of supplementary benefit	−54,400 (by August 1983)
June 1983	School-leavers are missed from the monthly figures for June, July and August each year	−100,000 to 200,000
June 1983	Change in CP eligibility rules. Entry now limited to unemployment benefit claimants only	−29,000

Table cont. overleaf

Table 5.1   *cont.*

March 1986	Introduction of two week delay in publication of the monthly count.	−50,000
June 1986	New method of calculating unemployment rate	1.4% or −42,000 in 1987
October 1986	Abolition of right to half and three-quarter unemployment benefit for people with insufficient NI contributions to qualify for full rate	−30,000
October 1986	Introduction of tighter Availability for Work tests	−120,000
	Approximate total effect of changes amounts to a *reduction* in number of registered unemployed of	1,379,786

employment for as many people as possible at a strictly limited cost. Anyone over 18 years old and unemployed for at least a year qualified for a place. Tight control over the average weekly wage in each CP project (an average wage of no more than £67 per week in 1986–7) ensured that the scheme was predominantly part time and did not create any upward pressure on wages: 'The Programme has generally been managed to ensure a basic level of quality and not to maximise the benefits to individuals and the community. This has been particularly so in the last year when all the attention has focused on getting and filling the places which will enable the 230,000 target to be met' (Normington *et al.*, 1986).

This major initiative, despite inadequate funding for training has been greatly preferable to total idleness for most of those involved. From the Government's point of view one of the major achievements of the CP was that it has kept 230,000 unemployed people out of the unemployment count. Alongside the CP, however, have been a series of administrative and policy changes which have, in almost every case, reduced rather than increased the unemployment figures while doing nothing to affect the numbers of people finding real jobs (*Unemployment Bulletin*, Winter 1986). The most significant of the changes are summarised in Table 5.1. The figures reveal that using the definitions of unemployment applied in the 1960s and 1970s, the underlying unemployment rate in May 1988 was *above four million* rather than 2.7 million as the Government claimed.

2   The current position

Recent policies have, then, forced a very substantial number of people to depend upon the state against their will. Most find their situation intolerable. Some develop psychiatric disorders (Smith, R., 1985), others become physically ill or opt to take their own lives (Platt, S., 1984). In all, Scott Samuel calculated that in 1984 unemployment caused 3,000 deaths per year in Britain (Scott Samuel, 1984). Inevitably, however, a proportion of unemployed people adjust to their new life, particularly those who see no prospect of ever working again.

The Government has focused attention upon those who have adjusted. Punitive policies have been applied to unemployed people in general as if all had lost the will to work. Having created dependency on an unprecedented scale, the Government has castigated what it calls the dependency culture. Having created an underclass of unemployed people whose confidence has been shattered by hundreds of unsuccessful job applications, when those people cease applying for jobs they are labelled 'work-shy'. Benefit reductions, tough availability for work tests and Restart interviews are used to victimise the victims of a single-minded drive for economic efficiency.

Reducing the wage levels acceptable to unemployed people

Lower benefit levels, Restart interviews and tighter availability for work tests have an economic function too. They are designed to adjust downwards people's expectations and the type of job and level of pay they are willing to accept.

Restart

Introduced in 1986, Restart is a programme of compulsory interviews for long-term unemployed people. It involves an 'invitation' to an interview which, if turned down without good reason, may lead to a loss of benefit. The interview may last for a few minutes or up to an hour and involves going through the menu of options available as alternatives to the dole. The options described in detail in 'Action for Jobs', the Government's booklet, may be summarised as follows:

Jobclubs

Probably the most successful and popular of the 1980s initiatives have been the jobclubs, introduced in 1985 and expected to cater for 200,000 entrants a year. Entrants are required to attend four half-day sessions each week and to follow up at least ten job leads a day. On that basis they can continue attending a jobclub for as long as necessary. If a member remains in the job club for a lengthy period without finding work then he will be introduced to options such as a CP or training course.

There is no doubt that jobclubs have helped to break down the isolation of unemployment, to give individual claimants valuable feedback on their approach to job hunting and provide them with the materials to make far more applications and to follow more leads than they could afford to do otherwise (Unemployment Unit, 1987).

Job Training Scheme (1987) and the Employment Training Scheme (1988)

The original Job Training Scheme was launched in April 1987, and provided the basis for the much more extensive training scheme to take the place of the Community Programme in 1988. The key features of the original scheme were

- a)   its temporary nature – trainees spent an average of six months on the scheme.
- b)   a minimal training input – six hours per week.
- c)   the working-for-benefit principle.

The 1988 Employment Training Scheme adopted all three key principles. The average length of training was to be six months; the training input was to be increased to 40 per cent but has remained at a low level due to the limited funding of the scheme; and the working-for-benefit principle has been carried through to the wider scheme. The 1988 scheme, however, catered for the whole age range 18–59 with priority given to 18–24 year olds who have been out of work for more than six months; and to people aged 25–49 who have been out of work for more than two years. The training allowance has a small premium above the income support level to ensure that on average the income received by trainees is £1 per week above the benefit plus the small earnings (£5 in 1988) allowed for people receiving Income support.

In terms of the Government's objective of reducing the wage levels acceptable to unemployed people, the Job Training

Scheme and subsequent Employment Training Scheme have an important role to play. For the under-25s who had until 1986 been the main participants on the CP the 1988 training scheme offers about half the pay for double the work (full-time under the training scheme instead of part-time under the CP scheme).

Restart Courses

These are one to two week courses designed 'to help people assess what they are good at and to show them how to look for jobs more effectively' (Action for Jobs, Department of Employment 1987). Practical help with interview techniques and the preparation of a CV are supplemented with group sessions designed, at least in some cases, to 'bring job expectations in line with reality', and to help participants to adjust to a low income. The courses have been widely criticised for requiring people to adjust to artificially low incomes. If demand were stimulated and full employment restored, higher incomes could and would be paid by employers.

New Workers Scheme

This pays employers a £15 weekly subsidy for engaging 18 and 19 year olds on wages less than £55 a week (or £65 for 20 year olds). Only 18,000 people had taken up this option in 1987 but the elimination of the CP option for younger people and its replacement by a full-time 'Work for Benefit' programme greatly increased the attractions of a wage of £40–£50 per week for young people.

Jobstart Allowance

A jobstart allowance of £20 per week may be paid for up to six months to long-term unemployed people of 18 years or more if they accept a job with a wage of less than £80 per week. The young person must be successful in getting the job *before* applying for the allowance. Again the emphasis has been upon acceptance of low wages with a temporary bonus to entice long-term unemployed people back into work with little or no financial reward beyond an initial period.

Other options which may be available at a restart interview include training courses. However, TOPS courses and Skill Centres have been cut in order to free up the funds for the Job Training Scheme. Places on vocational schemes are therefore limited, and waiting lists long. Secondly, many courses do not

142   *Employment*

Table 5.2   *Results of Restart interviews*

	Great Britain		London	
Interviewed	779,051	(100%)	95,883	(100%)
Submitted to jobs	5,478	(0.7%)	568	(0.6%)
Submitted to CP	19,916	(2.6%)	1,689	(1.8%)
Submitted to job clubs	6,489	(0.8%)	970	(1.0%)
Offered EAS	1,760	(0.2%)	332	(0.3%)
Offered training on new JTS	12,598	(1.6%)	1,350	(1.4%)
Offered Restart courses	66,968	(8.6%)	6,282	(6.5%)
Offered VPP	1,375	(0.2%)	166	(0.2%)
All above options		14.7%		11.8%
No placement		85.3%		88.2%

Source: Trial by Restart, Unemployment Unit, July 1987, p. 4.

qualify the trainee for financial support. Finally, Restart interviews are intended to direct people into real jobs, but only 0.7 per cent of people interviewed are successfully placed in work.

The failure of Restart interviews to place people in work or training despite the underlying threat to deny benefit to the claimant makes clear the limitations of microeconomic policies to deal with a macroeconomic problem. Table 5.2 sums up the outcome.

Finally, the tightening of the 'availability for work' test has undermined the right of unemployed people to a job compatible with their skills and experience. All new unemployed claimants now have to fill in a form ('Are you available for Work' – UB671) to 'test' whether they are genuinely available for work. The answers to the following three questions, for example, need to imply a sufficient degree of flexibility if benefit is to continue:

What job do you normally do?
What job are you looking for?
Are you willing to consider any other jobs? If no, please give your reason.

Similarly, answers to the following two questions should not suggest excessive expectations:

What was your weekly wage or salary in your last job?
What is the minimum weekly wage or salary you are willing to take?

The Government's measures to achieve the first two of their objectives have been summarised: to reduce the unemployment figures and to reduce the wage levels acceptable to unemployed people. A third important ideological theme of the Thatcher Governments has been the promotion of self-employment and individual enterprise. Mrs Thatcher has argued that a major fall in unemployment will come about 'When our people, instead of relying on subsidies, set out to create more small businesses themselves'. To that end, income taxes have been cut, planning controls relaxed, employment protection and wage-fixing legislation eroded.

Between 1979 and 1984 the number of self-employed people increased by 873,000 or 48 per cent. The 1985 Labour Force Survey found, however, that nearly half the increase was of people who had been employees (46 per cent). The increase in self-employment had occurred at a time of recession and mass redundancies. Firms in financial difficulties had actively encouraged employees to leave the firm but to continue their work on a self-employed basis in order to cut the firm's costs. At the same time people made redundant and unable to find a permanent job turned to self-employment as an alternative to the dole. Far from reflecting a new enterprise culture the shift from regular employment into self-employment in the 1980s may reflect the sluggishness of the economy under excessive monetary controls.

How has the Enterprise Allowance Scheme affected the level of self-employment? The Scheme introduced nationally in August 1983 was designed to promote self-employment amongst unemployed people. The EAS provides a weekly allowance to support unemployed people who want to become self-employed or to start their own business. The only conditions are that an applicant has been out of work for at least eight weeks and is receiving unemployment or supplementary benefit. Secondly, that he/she has £1,000 to invest in the business – or is able to raise a loan or overdraft of that sum.

The EAS appears to have been moderately successful within its own terms, MSC surveys of EAS participants suggest that 70 per cent of people who join EAS are still trading 15 months later. However, the job creation potential of EAS has been limited. At 15 months, the MSC has estimated that, for every 100 EAS entrants, a total of 124 new job opportunities will exist, made up of 53 EAS survivors and 52 additional jobs (26 full-time and 26 part-time). The scheme has just under 100,000 participants each year so that, on the basis of the above figures, a similar number of unemployed people each year will be successfully launched into self-employment.

At the end of the day, however, the money supply and consequent overall level of demand will substantially determine the number of jobs so that the benefits of such 'numbers policies' will be more apparent than real in the economy. Most economists would argue that 100,000 jobs created through EAS will simply take the place of 100,000 others which would have been sustainable in the absence of EAS. If the level of demand created by the Government gives rise to a real unemployment level of 4 million, as at present, microeconomic policies can determine the allocation of jobs; the level of benefits; the training input to government schemes and the length of unemployment before a person is required to take steps to become actively involved in a scheme. Only if these policies affect the relationship between the level of inflation and the level of unemployment will the overall level of unemployment be affected.

To what extent will the policies of the 1980s affect the relationship between the levels of inflation and unemployment?

There are at least three ways in which the Government plans to alter the key relationship between inflation and unemployment in the longer term: first, by reducing the level of benefits and thus the level of wages acceptable to unskilled workers; second, by improving the skills of unemployed people, and third, by reducing the power of the trade union movement. These policies will be discussed in turn.

The social security and employment legislation of 1986 and 1988 respectively introduced benefit reductions and related changes of quite a different order from those of the past. The employment legislation, in particular, will usher out the welfare principle and will establish, probably permanently, new employment and self-help principles which will transform the experience of unemployment in this country.

16 and 17 year olds
Young people leaving school at 16 or 17 will no longer be able to draw the dole and pursue part time studies or other voluntary activities. In future 16 and 17 year olds will be guaranteed a place on a YTS scheme and will be expected to remain on a scheme for two years unless they find a job or move into full-time study. The only exceptions will be a bridging allowance to cover a short break if a scheme proves unsatisfactory; and child benefit extensions for a limited period while school-leavers await a YTS place.

YTS is an employment-based scheme with a requirement of 20 weeks of off-the-job training. The training allowance (£28.50 and £35 for the first and second years respectively in 1987) can be topped up by employers but the state's responsibilities for 16 and 17 year olds will in future be strictly limited and will be tied to a willingness to work and train. Young people in families living in poverty understandably feel under pressure to leave school at 16 in order to supplement the family income. Many opted to continue their studies on a part-time basis (under the 21-hour rule) while drawing benefit. With this option ruled out, some young people for whom the YTS does not offer an appropriate training will settle for unskilled work. As is so often the case one of the effects of Government policy will be precisely the opposite of that intended.

18–50 year olds
The Government will move towards a situation where no one in this age group can remain unemployed for more than six months without being involved on the Employment Training Scheme or other activity (HMSO, 1988). Norman Fowler, the Secretary of State for Employment, announcing the new scheme to the House of Commons in 1987, claimed that the new programme would offer up to 12 months training to anyone who had been out of work for more than six months (Hansard, 1987). Entry to the programme is through Restart interviews and Jobclubs. Each person's individual needs will be assessed and a suitable programme will be provided. In 1988 the Government hoped that 600,000 trainees would pass through the ET scheme a year at a cost of £1.6 billion.

Until 1988, unemployed people could remain on the dole until a suitable job became available. Following the mass redundancies of 1979, many learned to live from hand to mouth eking out their dole money with the help of undeclared odd jobs. Although illegal,

Table 5.3   *Unemployment and vacancies, September 1987*

	Unemployment (thousands)	Job Centre vacancies (thousands)	Total vacancies estimate (thousands)
South East	653	96	288
Greater London	355	39	117
East Anglia	67	8	24
South West	168	20	60
West Midlands	299	24	72
East Midlands	178	14	42
Yorkshire and Humberside	280	17	51
North West	396	26	78
North	211	13	39
Wales	155	12	36
Scotland	333	20	60
Great Britain	2,775	250	750

Source: Employment Gazette, November 1987.

such activities came to be widely regarded as an understandable response to a hopeless situation. From 1988 this was no longer an option beyond the initial six-month period. Compulsory Restart interviews pick up every individual at the end of the initial six-month period of unemployment. But whereas in 1988 88.2 per cent of interviewees had no placement at the end of the interview, the guarantee of places now makes possible the implementation of the Workfare principle. The changes introduced during the 1980s – the harsher availability for work test, the combining of job centres with unemployment benefit offices, together with Restart courses and Jobclubs, have all played their part in ensuring that continued benefit entitlement is dependent upon a willingness to work and train.

The incentive for people to return to 'real' work is greatly enhanced by two factors – first, the elimination of the rate for the job on MSC schemes and its replacement by the payment of 'benefit plus expenses' for full-time work and training. The training scheme introduced in 1988 will effectively remove the possibility of employers topping up the pay of participants to an acceptable level. (Any top-up payment would be offset by a loss of benefit.) The second major factor is the replacement of part-time work on the Community Programme by a full-time work commitment under the unified training scheme, thus effectively ruling out the

Figure 5.4 *Skills mismatch.*

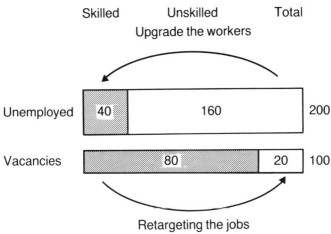

NB The numbers used in the diagram are illustrative only.

Source: R. Layard, How to Beat Unemployment, Oxford University Press, p. 120.

possibility of an additional part-time job within a normal working week to supplement the income from the scheme. In contrast with the Community Programme, the status of participants' income under the new arrangements means that any earnings from an evening job, for example, have to be declared and, if more than £5 per week, must be offset by a benefit reduction.

There can be little doubt that a number of young single people who might otherwise opt for the dole do prefer a 'real' job, however poorly paid and however poor the conditions of work, to compulsory enrolment on a training scheme which may be of poor quality and unsuited to their interests and aptitudes and which involves a level of pay barely higher than his or her dole entitlement. It might therefore be expected that the employment legislation of 1988 will lead to a permanent fall in unemployment at any given rate of inflation. The extent of such a shift depends upon a matching of vacancies and unemployed people in total numbers, geographical spread and in terms of skills.

Table 5.3 shows that there are nearly four times the number of unemployed people as there are vacancies. If every vacancy were filled by an unemployed person there would still be about 2 million people out of work. Table 5.3 also shows the regional imbalance of vacancies which will inhibit even that degree of improvement.

Table 5.4   *Percentage of the relevant age group in the population gaining higher education qualifications 1979[1]*

	Below degree standard	At degree standard	At both standards	At post-graduate level
West Germany	12	8	20	1
US (1981)	10	22	32	9
Japan	12	25	37	1
UK (1981)	4	14	18	4

[1] DES estimates (unpublished) based on normal age-range of new entrants in higher education.
Source: Competence and Competition, MSC, London, 1984, p. 82, Table 6.2.

Table 5.5   *Proportion of 16–18 year olds in full-time education*

	%
USA	79
Japan	69
France	58
Germany	45
UK	32

Source: R. Layard, *How to Beat Unemployment*, Oxford University Press, 1986.

In the north of England, for example, the unemployment and vacancy ratio is 5:1; in the East Midlands 4:1; and in the South-East a little over 2:1.

Improving the skills of unemployed people

The second problem is the mismatch between the skills of unemployed people and the skills needed by employers with vacancies. Figure 5.4 illustrates the approach needed when a relatively small proportion of vacancies are for unskilled people while the majority of unemployed people are unskilled. At the same time, many skilled unemployed people have redundant skills or live in a region where their skills cannot be used. Compulsion and benefit reductions are therefore likely to have a limited effect in reducing unemployment at a given inflation rate. Taking the imbalance between vacancies and unemployment, both national and regional, together with skills mismatch, the maximum unemployment reduction at a given rate of inflation in the absence of policies to rectify these problems is likely to be in the region of 0.5 per cent.

The contribution of training
The UK has a poor record in preparing young people for work. Mathematical ability is central to much economic activity and yet only a quarter of pupils achieved 'O' level mathematics at the time of the introduction of the GCSE in 1987. Twice as many achieve the equivalent in West Germany. At the graduate level too, we do badly compared with the US and Japan though much the same as West Germany.

Our real failure, however, is at the sub-degree level. In Germany 60 per cent of the labour force have sub-degree level qualifications including completed apprenticeships. Only 30 per cent of people in Britain have comparable qualifications. Part of the problem lies in the exceptionally small proportion of young people remaining in full time education from 16–18 in the UK, as shown in Table 5.5.

To move into the same league as its competitors the UK would have to enable at least 80 per cent of young people to enter the labour market with a relevant qualification from either school, college or the YTS. The decline in apprenticeships since 1979 has created a substantial shortage of suitable people for supervisory and technicians, posts and a severe skills shortage in marketing, selling, production, financial services, personnel services and administration, engineering and building. A CBI survey of 2,000 companies in 1984 suggested that firms had little confidence in the YTS as a solution to the problem. Seventy-one per cent of companies saw in-company training as the best solution (CBI, 1984). The Government appears to agree with this view.

In discussing the contribution of YTS to skills development the *Employment Gazette* (October 1987) painted a gloomy picture. It maintained that 'where the alternative to YTS is unemployment, young people would not acquire the habits of working, and for some of them their prospects for employment would be permanently impaired. This effect of YTS – to *prevent a deterioration* in the employment prospects of young people – will have long-term

Table 5.6   *Unemployment 1988–90 (millions) – leading forecasts**

	*1988**	*1989*	*1990*
London Business School	2.9	2.9	2.8
National Institute of Economic and Social Research	2.7	2.7	2.7
Goldman Sachs	2.7	2.8	2.9

Note: The seasonally adjusted figure *October 1988* excluding school leavers was 2·16 million.
Source: Phillips & Drew – *Sunday Times*, 4 Dec. 1988.

consequences for employment'. Far from enhancing the skills of young people we were told that the main effect of the scheme is to prevent a deterioration of skills in response to unemployment.

The new adult training scheme can be expected to achieve less than YTS in terms of skills enhancement. Although the scheme will double the number of places available for 18–50 year olds and increase the hours worked from part-to full-time, no additional resources are available to provide enhanced training (Hansard, 1987). The training content is scheduled to involve most of the trainees' time but the quality of training is believed by those closely involved to be minimal.

In conclusion to this section there is no evidence to suggest that the training policies of the 1980s have improved the level of employment at any given rate of inflation. The only significant change has been in the official unemployment figures which fall to the extent that people are coerced to join training schemes.

3   Employment prospects for the 1990s

Most economists would argue that the only inhibition to a return to full employment is the fear of a return to the high inflation rates of the 1970s. If the British people decided that a return to full employment should be regarded as the first priority, could this be achieved while maintaining a stable inflation rate? Indeed could it be achieved *at all* given the recent rate of technological change?

To answer the second question first, we need to look again at the level of unemployment over the last century (Figure 5.2).

Figure 5.5 *The 'output gap' 1975–87*

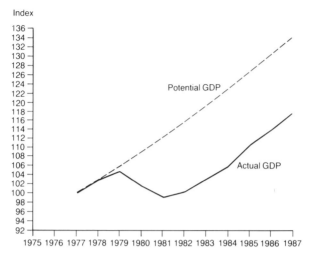

Source: R. Layard, *How to Beat Unemployment*, Campaign for Work, 1988, London.

If technological change caused higher unemployment, we would expect periods of high productivity growth to coincide with periods of high unemployment, and unemployment would have increased significantly over the past hundred years with the introduction of plastics, electric motors, telephones, typewriters, and so forth. In fact the opposite has been true. In Britain, productivity growth was unusually high in the 1960s as in the last five years. In the 1950s and 1960s it caused little or no unemployment. Unemployment in the 1950s was considerably lower than it had been 100 years earlier. On the contrary, it was when productivity fell in the 1970s that unemployment increased. If we look at other countries we find that the major country with the lowest unemployment is the one with the highest productivity – Japan (Layard R., 1988).

Why then did we have high productivity growth and high unemployment in the UK in the 1980s? The answer lies in the catastrophic fall in output in 1980–1. Over the centuries output has risen in line with productivity growth. This relationship was broken in 1980–1 as shown in Figure 5.5. below. The top line is a trend line for potential output, assuming this to grow from 1979 onwards at 3 per cent ($2\frac{1}{2}$ per cent for labour force growth and $\frac{1}{2}$ per cent for productivity). The bottom line is actual output. This fell catastrophically in 1980–1 and the resulting output gap has never been closed. Britain is some £50 billion poorer than the country would be without the gap. It is important to note that since 1981 output has grown in line with productivity growth.

Having established that a return to full employment is entirely consistent with rapid technological change, we now have to wonder how it will be achieved without an inflation explosion. To answer this question a reference to the Swedish experience will be helpful.

In Sweden registered unemployment peaked at 4.1 per cent in 1983 but held at about 3 per cent throughout the 1980s, despite the effects upon the Swedish economy of the restrictive polices of other countries in Western Europe. Unlike the UK, *'full* employment has remained the primary objective of Swedish economic policy throughout the postwar period and has enjoyed broad support among the different political parties in Sweden' (Jangenes, B., 1986). In 1980, while in the UK policies were being pursued which inevitably destroyed work opportunities, the non-socialist coalition government in Sweden was passing an Act of Parliament reaffirming that 'the crucial feature of employment policy is that those people who want a job should have a genuine opportunity to find a job'. Good quality training was geared to the needs of the economy and the Government played a major role in creating jobs as well as training.

Between 5 per cent and 8 per cent of the State budget and 2 per cent of the Swedish GNP is devoted to labour market policy. The Swedes spend twice as much as Britain per person on training schemes for unemployed people; they provide recruitment subsidies of 50 per cent of wage costs for the long-term unemployed compared with the UK £20 per week payment to people accepting very low paid jobs. The total spending of Sweden on unemployment and training programmes for unemployed people amounts to sixteen times the sum spent in the UK per unemployed person.

Despite the level of government spending the Swedish inflation rate in 1987 was identical to that in the UK at 4.7 per cent and over the entire period 1979-84 inflation in Sweden was only 0.1 per cent higher than in Britain. Likewise the growth rate was comparable in the two countries at an average of 1.7 per cent from 1979–87, though Sweden was pessimistic about its future growth potential should the heavily restrictive policies of so many European countries persist.

Conclusion

The end of the 1980s saw important and possibly irreversible changes in the employment field. The welfare principle and provision of indefinite benefit to unemployed people until they find a job has ended and it will be difficult for any government to restore that principle. In its place a form of workfare has been introduced under which all unemployed people are required to work or train in order to qualify for benefit. The numbers of unemployed people make it difficult for the Government to ensure activity throughout the unemployment period, but this is undoubtedly the target. If real work or good quality training were provided, many would agree that activity is greatly preferable to forced idleness. The major criticisms will continue to concern the quality of provision and income, and the non-availability of real jobs.

In the 1990s unskilled rates of pay can be expected to fall as a result of measures to coerce people into work or training at subsistence rates of pay. The most serious consequences of Conservative policies in the 1980s include a continuing mismatch between the skills of those out of work and the skills needed by employers. Secondly, we can observe a further widening of the North-South divide. As a result of those two problems and the lack of priority given to solving mass unemployment, the number of people without a paid job remains unacceptably high and the black economy continues to grow.

In the 1990s the only hope for a significant shift towards full employment will be: either a) an influx of foreign companies attracted by low wages and the availability of unskilled workers, willing to invest in their own training programmes to achieve a satisfactory range of skills; or b) significant policy reversals to include: (i) increased government borrowing to finance a major job creation programme, (ii) training levy on firms with a poor training performance to provide the resources for training subsidies for these companies willing to provide an above average level of training; (iii) mobility incentives to encourage firms to move into high unemployment areas and unskilled people to move from depressed areas to those with job possibilities; and (iv) introduction of an education maintenance allowance to encourage a higher proportion of adults to develop educational and vocational skills.

6

Education

MIRIAM E. DAVID

> 'The Act of 1944, in common with its predecessors of
> 1870, 1902 and 1918, affords a classic example of what
> Dicey called "our inveterate prejudice for fragmentary
> and gradual legislation". It did not, as some would have
> wished, sweep the board clean of existing institutions in
> order to start afresh . . .. Henceforth every child would
> have a right to free secondary education and in order
> that those secondary courses should become a full reality,
> they were to last for at least four and eventually five years.
> It was, however, equally important to ensure that a stigma
> of inferiority did not attach itself to those in secondary
> institutions . . .. Even so equality of opportunity would
> remain something of an empty phrase if children entered
> the period of compulsory schooling from conditons of
> family deprivation, or left it to pursue what Churchill
> called blind-alley occupations.' (R.A. Butler, *The Art of
> the Possible: Memoirs*, Landan, Hamish Hamilton, 1971.)

This chapter evaluates educational policy as it has developed
during Mrs Thatcher's period of office and it anticipates some
of the likely implications of the educational reforms proposed by
the Conservatives in the 1980s. The great Educational Reform Bill,
nicknamed GERBIL (now ERA), is the main focus of attention.

Of central concern is whether the Education Reform Act
(ERA) heralds a new era of education, making mammoth rather
than minute reforms in existing educational provision. The title,
of both the Bill and the Act, clearly implies a wide remit
and indeed its clauses cover the range of educational provi-

sion from compulsory schooling through to higher education. The only apparent exclusions are early childhood, and adult, education and yet these are implicated in the major part to be afforded to parents and the community in reforms.

Indeed, the Act is probably unique in the history of educational legislation in its coverage of both schools and higher education. Even the 1944 Education Act, which has always been hailed as the major cornerstone of post-war educational policy, was centrally concerned with the school system, and not with higher education. No previous Education Act took both together.

It is useful, therefore, to focus on the Conservatives' intentions for, and the likely effects on, peoples' lives – on children in the privacy of the family and on adults both in the privacy of the family (as parents) and also in the public sphere of the labour market and community. This also has, as we shall see, implications for class, gender and race divisions.

The great Educational Reform Bill was published on 20 November 1987, having been presaged by several consultative papers to parents and schools and a major White Paper on higher education. In some senses its timing was peculiar, coming more than eight years after Mrs Thatcher came into office. Its lateness might be due to its relative unimportance on the Conservative policy agenda or, conversely, to its relative difficulty given its major importance. In other words, given that it is unique in the history of educational policy it may have required considerable time to gestate, or for other social and economic changes to occur first.

1 Educational policy and resources

The first two Thatcher administrations, 1979–87, were not by any means neglectful of educational issues. Both schools and higher education were tackled, though not in a systematic fashion. Changes focused chiefly on issues of resources, finance and economy rather than the reform of institutions and access to them. In other words, the changes in how educational institutions from schools through to universities and polytechnics were run were achieved through reductions in the finances available to the institutions themselves and through limitations imposed upon salary negotiations. In particular, in higher education the chief funding bodies – the University Grants Committee (UGC) and the National Advisory Board (NAB) – achieved economies in funding by means of rigorous selective criteria, in terms both of disciplines or subjects and of students. The conditions of change were, therefore, largely negative.

Similarly, at the school level the majority of changes were of a negative kind – the result, largely, of limitations of resources. Indeed, the effects of these constrictions have been extremely well documented by HMI in a series of reports on the effects of public expenditure cutbacks on the operation of the schools (DES, 1984; 1985; 1987).

Resources were also diverted away from the state education system to a range of private and independent schools through the development of the Assisted Places Scheme. This scheme in part replaced the system of direct grants from central government to independent schools, which had been started at the turn of the century, codified during the Second World War and phased out by the Labour Government from 1976. The latter argued that the system maintained a form of privilege for a minority of children and worked against comprehensive education. The Assisted Places Scheme aimed to extend grants to individual pupils, on a test of parental means, to a wider variety of public schools than had been the case under the direct grant schools' scheme.

There were, too, changes in the balance of the curriculum, particularly in secondary education, in an attempt to tie what schools offer more clearly to the perceived needs of a changing economy. A range of developments in personal and social skills, in vocational courses (CPVE was introduced in 1984), work experience and the injection of specifically technical courses through both TVEI (launched in 1983) and changes in post-school activities through the YTS Scheme were initiated. Furthermore, the system of examining has been radically overhauled in an attempt to develop assessment criteria and profiles that will be more clearly understood by employers in industry and commerce. Teacher training and qualifications were also modified to ensure greater compatibility with changes in courses and curricula.

Thus far the chief changes in how the education system operates have been as a result of Conservative notions of who the consumers of education are. Consumers were seen to be the *employers* in the market place as well as the pupils and students.

Yet the pupils themselves have not been canvassed about their needs or interests. Their views have instead been channelled through their parents, through a new system of representation and accountability that enhances parent power. The changes were foreshadowed by the Labour Government (David, 1980).

The Conservatives have tried to broaden the basis of school government, particularly through the introduction of parent governors, as advocated by the Taylor Committee (1976). These ideas have been developed (Education Act, 1980) and modified (Education Act, 1986). In addition, schools have been required to provide more regular information on curricular offer and examination results to their clientele.

In a slow but clear fashion, the education institutions have taken on the characteristics of business rather than professional organisations for the pursuit of teaching and learning. They are now generally more concerned with both financial and educational accountability to the full range of their 'consumers', than was routinely the case under previous governments.

Social welfare policies and the Conservative reaction

These changes may be variously accounted for. Mrs Thatcher came to power in 1979, with the Conservatives firmly committed to restoring Britain's competitive edge in the world economy, and reversing Britain's economic decline. The Conservative vision, at that stage, was to ensure that education, efficiently and economically, supplied the appropriately skilled personnel. Indeed, the previous Labour administrations were blamed first for presiding over Britain's economic decline and second for developing a programme of social policy measures, (including education) which directly contributed to such decline (David, 1983). A chief concern of the first Thatcher Government, therefore, was to break what was then seen to be the prevailing political consensus of welfare capitalism and especially the commitment to equality of opportunity.

The 'bipartisan' policy of post-war Conservative and Labour governments had hitherto sought to ensure the viability of industrial capitalism through the provision of a range of public services to industry and through the welfare state (Mishra, 1984). There were political disagreements about the means of ensuring a healthy mixed economy, but Left and Right alike agreed that at least minimal state intervention was necessary to ensure the smooth running of the 'mixed' economy.

In Britain, one of the cornerstones of that policy was the 1944 Education Act, passed by the wartime coalition Government. Both Conservative and Labour were committed to the necessity of providing equality of opportunity, through educational means, to ensure a viable economy. However, what equality of educational opportunity came to mean in the post-war years differed considerably between the political parties. The Labour governments of the 1960s transformed the concept from that of individual access to educational institutions, on the basis of intellectual ability, to a stronger notion, to borrow Crosland's memorable phrase (Crosland, 1956), of achieving preferred 'educational outcomes'. Both of these notions were about how to tap 'pools of ability' from amongst different social class groupings in society, apparently regardless of gender differences (Halsey, 1972). Indeed, the subsequent efforts of the Labour Government were to try to provide educational opportunities for all children, without regard to their home backgrounds or socioeconomic status (David, 1977). These attempts not only included moves to provide state comprehensive secondary education (launched in 1965) but also positive discrimination in both state primary and secondary schools, through the Educational Priority Area and Urban Aid projects, launched in 1967. There were similar attempts to extend educational opportunities in higher education, through Crosland's binary policy (1966), as well as the creation of new universities in the 1950s and 1960s.

By the early 1970s, resources devoted to state education at all levels had far outgrown the initial intentions. This mammoth increase in public expenditure on education and other social policies was quickly and readily scapegoated in the early 1970s as Britain's economic growth began, first, to slow down and, then, by the late 1970s, to go into decline (Gough, 1979).

However, the Conservative Party had not, at this stage, developed an agreed or coherent philosophy for education. Some members of the Conservative Party were still committed to some form of equality of educational opportunity and public spending for educational provision. Others had become more critical of the so-called liberal-Conservative approach and, indeed, from the 1950s there had been a strand of traditional Conservative thinking committed to both 'excellence in education' and the 'promotion of standards'. Some of these ideas were articulated by Conservative lobbyists and philosophers in reaction to various policy measures. For example, in the late 1960s, a group of intellectuals and educationalists put together their criticisms of educational developments in a series of so-called Black Papers, published between 1969 and 1977 (Cox and Dyson, 1969; 1970; 1971; Cox and Boyson, 1975,1977). Their criticisms focused on the effects on educational standards of comprehensive education and the expansion of universities. Together, they tried to argue for a return to 'excellence in education' and attacked what they called, derogatorily, 'egalitarianism', or the commitment to social and economic equality through education.

However, these ideas remained embryonic in the Conservative Party, despite Mrs Thatcher's close association with the Black Paperites when she was Secretary of State for Education between 1970 and 1973. Nothing that was achieved by the Conservatives during the Heath administration (1970–4) amounted to a full-scale attack on this bipartisan policy of equality of opportunity, although the stronger concepts were eroded and diluted.

The chief plank of the Conservative programme, launched in 1979, was to reverse Britain's economic decline by reducing public spending and specifically by the application of monetarist principles in controlling the flow of money into the economy. The concern was with the economic efficacy of both public and private sector organisations, hence they were relatively starved of resources, and forced to make radical changes to accommodate their impecuniousness. This form of resource constraint was applied not only to educational institutions, but also to the local authorities that administered them (through changes to the legislation on rates and the Exchequer's Rate Support Grant) and to other social welfare institutions, such as hospitals and homes for the elderly and handicappped.

These initial changes in the welfare state were to reduce access to social and educational services by means of limited finance. Such policies did, indeed, provide a much reduced state set of services and increased the reliance on voluntary and family-based schemes. 'Self-help' became a clarion call and volunteers were drafted in to furnish services hitherto provided by the state (see Finch, 1985). For example, schemes for parental involvement in the primary school classroom, as well as with homework, developed apace. These schemes reflected other similar developments taking place in the personal social services with pre-school home visitors and family aides (David, 1985).

The second plank of the Conservative programme, launched after Mrs Thatcher's re-election in May 1983, was to be as Peregrine Worsthorne had predicted it would be immediately before:

> Thatcherism Mark 2 is going to be very much more deeply controversial than the Mark 1 variety. Wanting to dismantle the welfare state was controversial enough but the raw nerves touched by the ideal will be as nothing to those frayed to tatters by the attempts to build up what will amount to a Tory welfare state (Worsthorne, 1983).

This was the attempt positively to transform the welfare state by putting into place a Conservative programme. This programme rested chiefly on the principle of 'giving power back to the people' and transforming social institutions. In order to achieve this, the 'culture' of the liberal-social democratic political consensus of the post-war era had to be fully dismantled and a new culture of populism put in its place. The idea that every citizen should have equality of opportunity which, at its minimum, means equality of access to participate fully as citizens regardless of socioeconomic circumstance, had to be turned on its head. In its place the idea of a market place for social and educational provision had to be popularised, with consumer choice its chief selling point. Stuart Hall argued, in 1983, that this process began to happen in the early 1980s:

> The right have temporarily defined the terms and won the struggle because they are willing to engage. For a brief period in the 1960s and 1970s the involvement of parents with the school was the left's most democratic trump card. The dismantling of this into 'parental choice' and its expropriation by the right is one of their most significant victories. They stole an idea designed to increase popular power in education and transformed it into an idea of an *educational supermarket* (1983, p.1) (my emphasis).

However, at this stage the 'supermarket' continued to refer only to state education. To extend the idea to all institutions and to create a consumer culture, the Conservatives first tackled some old rankling issues in the debate with Labour, rather than approach education. They tackled both trade union powers and the powers of local authorities in a series of major public confrontations – specifically the miners' strike of 1984 and issues with various Labour councils, including the abolition of the Greater London Council (GLC) in 1986. In this latter, an attempt was made to make a *cause célèbre* of the unique education authority – the Inner London Education Authority (ILEA) – but a cautious approach was advised instead, given the local opposition apparently roused by proposed abolition.

Thus by 1987 the Conservatives had set in place a completely new approach to social and education policy. In place of the commitment to ensuring equality of social and economic opportunity for all was a new culture committed to ensuring that all citizens were able to compete in the market place and choose the goods and services to their taste. Organisations committed to providing goods and services would have to ensure that they met the tastes, choices and pocket of their consumers as efficiently and economically as possible.

It remains, however, a puzzle that major education reform was not enacted in this second stage of the Conservative programme. One answer is that the proposals for educational reform were insufficiently coherent to be placed in one single policy package. Sir Keith Joseph, the Secretary of State for Education from September 1981 and for much of Mrs Thatcher's second term of office until his resignation in June 1986, attempted to set in place a single unitary new educational policy, heralded at the 1983 General Election as 'The Pursuit of Excellence'. Many of his aims were set out in his White Paper *Better Schools* in 1984 and covered the issues pressed upon him by an increasingly vocal, articulate and coherent Conservative educational lobby. Indeed, Sir Keith Joseph represented what Angus Maude has called the 'Conservative Educationalists' (Knight, 1988). He tried to develop a comprehensive educational philosophy, capable of being translated into policy. However, his philosophy of 'educational excellence' was not, during his term of office, ever fully or coherently translated into such. There was, nevertheless, some *ad hoc* success. He was responsible for the major review of examinations and forms of assessment, now put into practice, particularly through the GCSE, which commenced in the autumn of

1987. Joseph was also responsible for initiating and taking forward the debate on the content of the school curriculum, rather than continuing the discussion of education purely in terms of forms of educational institution. However, he was initially responsible for *stitching up* the existing system of state education, by not returning to a system of selective secondary education. Instead, he sought to develop a system of selection on the basis of merit within schools, through the emphasis on a grammar school curriculum for those academically able pupils or vocational skills for those deemed to be less able. The merit scheme was also to be applied to teachers by developing first a more selective and specialist system of teacher education and second through trying to develop selective schemes of teacher pay, based on merit. His proposals, however, to lessen the control on the education system through implementing a system of education vouchers foundered.

One reason that the new Conservative educational philosophy was not put into effect in the Joseph years was because of the paradox of attempting to return to a selective system of education, based on the pursuit of excellence, within a system which had recognised the injustices of such forms and was fully accepting of the meritocratic arguments for equality of educational opportunity. It could only be by breaking that mould that a complete system of parental choice and accountability could begin to flower. The attempts to pursue even one of those twin goals failed and left the way open for a much more explicit strategy of selectivity in individual access to state and private schools and between institutions to blossom.

By the end of Mrs Thatcher's second term of office in June 1987, it had already become clear that a new Conservative philosophy was in the ascendance and that this would inform future policy developments. The notion of state or public provision of social and educational services, in order to ensure the full and active participation of *all* citizens in political life, had finally been laid to rest. In education, in particular, there had been a number of *causes célèbres* which had proved that such notions were dead and buried.

For example, Ray Honeyford, a headteacher of a middle school in Bradford, had written a series of articles which attacked the concept of multiracial education. He sought to develop the argument for a Eurocentric education in state schools, given the paucity that he perceived of the Asian culture of his pupils. His school, in fact, comprised children 95 per cent of whom had Asian home backgrounds. Although the parents, who organised a Parents' Action Committee, and many of the governors of his school objected to the sensationalist terms in which he raised the issue, his ideas were taken up by one of the main organs of Conservative philosophical debate, *The Salisbury Review*, as well as being addressed in the press through the *TES and the Guardian*. He was eventually invited to a meeting of a Conservative educational think-tank, in the Cabinet Office, when he had been suspended by the Labour-held local authority and an inquiry instituted. In the resolution of the political dispute, he was awarded a large financial settlement on his eventual resignation. The significance of this issue was that the commitment to equal treatment had finally given place, in Conservative reality as well as rhetoric, to a notion of academic standards which were, it was alleged, to be found only in a Eurocentric, rather than an Asian and, by implication, any other culture, signalled by parental or home background.

A later débâcle in the adjacent local authority of Dewsbury served to underline the extent to which monocultural notions of academic excellence were being given continuing Conservative political support. In this case the parents of 36 white pupils objected to the local authority's allocation of their children to a middle school with a predominantly Asian intake. They refused to allow their children to attend this school and appealed to the Secretary of State to alter the decision and allow the children to enter the school equidistant from their homes with a predominantly white clientele. The Secretary of State felt unable to intervene but, on the other hand, did not try to cajole the parents into sending their children to state schools. From September 1987 until March 1988, ironically, the children were taught in a room in a public house by an untrained teacher, paid for by the parents' voluntary contributions. The outcome of their appeal to the law about whether the local authority has acted unreasonably in trying to force them to send their children to a school they did not choose was in their favour.

Both these issues illustrate the extent to which vocalisations of academic standards, which are divisive on grounds of race or culture, have become a normal part of Conservative rhetoric. Moreover, the implied support for an expression of parental choice, which runs counter to the reasonable use of public

expenditure on schools, as is currently part of educational legislation, indicates the changes afoot.

2   The Conservative Government and educational reform

GERBIL, viewed in this context, seems to be more than a
rubber stamp or ratification of past changes. It aims to go well
beyond these piecemeal changes, and usher in an entirely new era
of education, ultimately oriented to individual choice, rather than
to any form of equality of opportunity. Seen alongside changes
in local government legislation – namely the community charge
(nicknamed the poll tax) to replace the rates; the introduction of
clause 28 to prevent the promotion of homosexuality through local
education authorities and the amendment of GERBIL to abolish
the unitary Inner London Educational Authority – it is clear that
the aims of the current Conservative Government are to promote a
narrow and particularistic sense of individuality. Chances to develop individuality are limited to particular classes of citizens; to those
who are fortunate in their access to socioeconomic resources; to
those who define their sexuality conventionally; to those who, by
reason of gender, are able to be freely involved in the labour market; to those who, by chance and racial background, reside outside
the ILEA, and to a myriad of other such privileged individuals.

The changes in local government revenue, through the abolition
of the rates and their replacement by a community charge (or poll
tax), will have a major impact on the characteristics and quality
of local education authority (LEA) provision of schools. The
significance of the community charge to higher education will
be minimal, because of GERBIL's proposals to give to all
public sector higher education institutions corporate status, and
independence from local authorities. Given that, historically, local
government finance contributed over 50 per cent to the finance of
state education (the rest being found from the Exchequer) the
effects of the change from rates to community charge cannot but
affect local authority educational decision-making.

The Educational Reform Bill contained a relatively simple
set of educational ideas, the kernels of which are to be found
in traditional Conservative educational philosophy – namely the
pursuit of educational excellence through an academic curriculum

and the setting of particular standards for achievement, the fostering of social inequality through educational access and parental privilege and the notion of economic accountability. All of these notions have a long pedigree stretching well beyond the post-war period. Mostly they are to be found in the emergence of capitalism and industrialisation and are particularly associated with the early Victorian era. Indeed, they hark back to times before the introduction of mass, universal, compulsory education. Kenneth Baker, Secretary of State for Education, opened the debate on the Second Reading of the Bill, in the House of Commons with the declaration that:

> This Bill will create a new framework, which will raise standards, extend choice and produce a better-educated Britain . . .. We must give consumers of education a central part in decision making. That means freeing schools and colleges to deliver the standards that parents and employers want (House of Commons, 1 December 1987, col. 771–2).

The above quotation identifies a key objective of the Government in the Bill which is to raise standards through the exercise of parental choice. In this respect, the Bill is informed by the central tenets of Conservative educational policy. Indeed, Baker sums it up in these terms: 'I would sum up the Bill's 169 pages in three words – standards, freedom and choice' (ibid. col.780).

Specifically, the GERBIL has two sets of clauses – one about schools, the other about higher education. To deal with schools first, the bill provides for : i) a new *national curriculum* and set of educational *standards*, tested according to the age of pupil; ii) *parental choice* through both *open enrollment* to schools up to their physical capacity; iii) an extended system of parental governors having a greater *financial and curricular control* of schools; and iv) the choice, by school governing body, for state maintained schools to opt out of local authority control and become directly *grant-maintained* by the central government.

The national curriculum is to be prescribed only for those schools currently in state control, namely the state maintained and voluntary-aided schools. It is assumed that the current private, independent or public schools are teaching to a standard equivalent to or above that of the state system. The national curriculum draws on the debates about the core and common core curriculum as developed by Sir Keith Joseph during his period of office as Secretary of State. It also draws on longer-standing debates about the range of the curriculum, initiated by the Labour Prime Minister, James Callaghan, in 1976, entitled the Great Debate on education (David, 1980). However, that debate, which was eventually orchestrated by the then Labour Secretary of State for Education, Shirley Williams, considered not only curriculum questions but also issues about parental and community control. The current Conservative argument is concerned less with the processes of decision-making and more with the *content* of the curriculum. This is, indeed, a new phenomenon of the post-war era, since legislation in this period has not touched on the question of the content of schooling but has generally focused on its form. In the nineteenth and early twentieth century, however, the Government did try to specify, through Codes and Regulations, the curriculum especially in terms of core courses and specialised subjects for the receipt of grants, in both the then elementary and higher or high schools (David, 1980).

There is a clear sense in which the specifications for the new National Curriculum hark back to those days. The three core subjects are proposed as Maths, English and Science; and the seven foundation subjects are stipulated as History, Geography, Technology, Music, Art, Physical Education and a modern foreign language. As a late addendum to the core subjects, Welsh has been added for those schools, in Wales, which teach in the native language. It has also been added as a modern foreign language to be taught in those Welsh schools where Welsh is not the language of the curriculum. This gives some indication of the kinds of foreign languages deemed acceptable. Although the classics – Latin and Greek – do not figure in this new curriculum, nor do their modern equivalents as the languages of some of the minority ethnic groups in Britain. Indeed, minority ethnic languages such as Urdu or Gujerati are not included in the list of modern foreign languages. The presumption appears to be that the languages normally to be taught will be French, German or Spanish; languages associated with a modern Eurocentric culture, confirming some of the suspicions of the approaches to a multiracial and multicultural society and the question of bilingual education of minority ethnic groups. Indeed, this question was raised in the huge Swann Report, published by the Government in 1985, entitled, disarmingly, *Education for All*, and concerned with questions of multiracial education.

That report dismissed bilingual education or minority language maintenance as practically impossible and educationally unsound. It is perhaps no surprise that such modern foreign languages have found no supporters in the new National Curriculum.

What is also notable about the new National Curriculum is that, with the exception of classics and gender-specific curricula such as Domestic Science or Home Economics and Craftwork, it signals a return to a strict subject-based curriculum as prevailed before the Second World War. All the integrative and interdisciplinary subjects developed in the post-war period, but particularly with the self-conscious research and involvement of teachers in the discussions about the process of learning, have been lost (CCCS, 1981). Even the more philosophical approaches which developed through religious education into moral, health, social and personal education are now absent from the agenda (David, 1983). It is, indeed, a curiosity that religious education or instruction was originally missing from the Bill. However, during the committee stage, as a result of some political pressure and lobbying, the Secretary of State introduced an amendment to include religious education in the foundation subjects. An attempt by the House of Lords to ensure Christian acts of worship and teaching, initially , failed (17 May, 1988) but was later included.

It is also puzzling that the vocational 'subjects' developed especially for those pupils seen as less able such as child care and parenting or social and life skills are absent. This signals a more rigid, traditional approach both to teaching and learning, and a downgrading of these subjects, to marginal areas of the curriculum.

This approach is also signalled by the new proposals for 'testing' of all pupils at the ages of 7, 11, 14 and at the school-leaving age. Although there is some lack of clarity about whether the tests are to be norm- or criterion-referenced, there are some indications that attainment targets, programmes of study and methods of assessment are to be clearly spelled out. This was the traditional approach in the system that became known, in the nineteenth century, as payment-by-results (David, 1980). Through the Re-revised Code of 1861, teachers' pay became tied to the test results of their pupils in a series of annual, age-specific, subject-based examinations. Although there have been some discussions about changing the basis of teachers' pay and introducing a system of merit awards, these issues are not clearly linked in GERBIL. Negotiations about teachers' pay have, since the early twentieth century been separated from other education questions and although the Conservative Government revised and circumscribed these procedures in 1986, it has not tied them back to pupil performance.

The second set of school-based changes signalled by GERBIL are to do, again, with the form rather than the content of schooling. In this case, each school, through both its headteacher and its governing body, is to be afforded more autonomy from the local authority in exchange for more financial and administrative accountability to the consumers. The revisions made to the constitutions of governing bodies, giving a majority of parent governors over local political, community or employer governors, now extend powers of decision-making to governing bodies. These newly constituted parental governing bodies will have stronger powers, through financial delegation, to hire-and-fire staff, to maintain the physical and emotional fabric of the school and to determine curricular and disciplinary issues. In another curious twist of history, the constitutional position will be more like that of the traditional managing bodies of primary or elementary schools. They will be required to manage schools and ensure their accountability to their clientele. They will also have more flexibility through the new system of open enrollments, whereby numbers cannot be artificially limited by the LEA.

These powers may become even stronger for those governing bodies which choose (as they will be given permission to do) to 'opt out' of the system of local government control and become grant-maintained schools. In other words, GERBIL allows for school governing bodies to choose whether to receive their 'grants' for maintenance from the local or central government. The choice will be made by a simple majority of parents at *one* ballot, after consideration by the school governing body, at a meeting. This decision will have long-term, irreversible effects. Indeed, one Conservative MP, Keith Hampson, tried to move an amendment to make the decision more rigorous by allowing for a secret ballot and a two-thirds majority. This amendment was not accepted. However, the House of Lords, on 12 May, 1988, approved an amendment, brought by the Bishop of London, making opting out more rigorous by insisting on a majority of all parents eligible to vote. The Government, however, may try to rescind this.

The decision does indeed spell major changes for decision-making not only about schools but also over local government finance, since the notion of 'grant-maintained' is very clear. The DES will have the power to precept on local authorities for the per capita funding for the grant-maintained schools. This will mean that the resources, through the community charge, at the local authority's disposal will be limited by the amount they will be obliged to give over to the grant-maintained schools, in their areas. In other words, they may have fewer resources left for their remaining state-maintained schools.

They may also have limited choices over the kinds of pupils and ways of teaching in the state-maintained schools, since governing bodies which 'opt-out' will be able to restrict their own intakes to pupils of their choice. This may not leave a 'comprehensive' intake for the state-maintained schools. The only limitation on governors' choice of status is size of school. Primary schools with less than 300 pupils will not be eligible for grant-maintained status. However, open enrolment may reduce the numbers of ineligible schools to 'unpopular' ones. Once schools have 'opted-out', local education authorities will be further limited in their resource-base as they will be required to 'hand over' the buildings and staff contracts to the grant-maintained schools, without receiving any compensation.

The challenge to ILEA

The situation in Inner London promises to be even more complex, since an amendment was recently introduced by the Secretary of State for Education, to abolish the local authority itself. Hitherto, the plan was to allow both boroughs and/or schools to 'opt-out' of the local authority. The Inner London Education Authority (ILEA) is unique, being the only 'single-issue' local government in the country. It is directly elected to deal with educational policy for the 13 inner London boroughs. The new proposal will make the 13 inner London boroughs equivalent to the outer London boroughs and metropolitan districts having responsibility for a range of social services. The reasons given for this proposed change are that the ILEA is 'profligate' and, given its excessive expenditure, did not achieve its purposes, having the lowest rate of examination successes in the country. However, these arguments may well be spurious, since the costs of living in central London are far higher than any other inner city area. The Metropolitan police, also uniquely a police force for London, costs far more than the police force of any other inner city, too. Secondly, the range and spread of social and economic difficulties for the children in inner London have to be set against the examination results. In fact, given these disadvantages, ILEA's results are not remarkably bad, all things considered. However, these arguments may not be the reason but only the rationale for ILEA's proposed abolition. For the last decade, ILEA has been run by elected Labour councillors and its entire range of policies runs counter to those of the Conservative government. In particular, ILEA has been fully committed to pursuing equal opportunities not only on the grounds of class or home background, but also for racial or ethnic minorities and for gender. It is the positive pursuit of these policies that has aroused the ire of the Conservative Government. It proposes, therefore, to recreate 13 metropolitan boroughs, each with powers to run their own education service. However, the option of schools within each of the 13 boroughs to receive grant-maintained status will still apply. A large minority of the 13 are at present Conservative-held local authorities and it is assumed that at least boroughs such as Westminster and Wandsworth will be committed to these new Conservative notions of social inequality. Both have already advertised for education officers. However, a ballot of ILEA parents, held in April 1988, and run by the Electoral Reform Society, found 94 per cent of the parents who voted (being 54 per cent of the electorate) against abolition. With this success, ILEA's leader tried to get the House of Lords to set up a review board before deciding on abolition. This amendment was defeated (17 May 1988).

Higher education

The higher education provisions of GERBIL follow neatly on from these school provisions. New funding mechanisms are to be established for both the polytechnics and the universities, and with that new forms of control over the kinds of subjects to be offered by the educational institutions. Hitherto, the binary system meant that public sector higher education was funded and controlled by the individual local authorities responsible for particular Polytechnics in concert with the National Advisory

Body for Higher Education (NAB) and the CNAA. The CNAA was established as a body of academics to provide peer review of the workings of individual academic institutions and to maintain universal standards of courses and their resulting degrees. Indeed, individual polytechnics have not routinely given degrees but have had to have them ratified by the CNAA. The CNAA's role is now reduced to that of, in the short-term, giving accreditation to individual polytechnics, and in the longer term, advice and setting standards for quality assurance. Under GERBIL, polytechnics will also be afforded financial independence and autonomy from their individual LEAs, by receiving corporate status. Their finances will come from 'grants' from a new central government body, entitled the Polytechnic and Colleges Funding Council (PCFC).

This new system of finance will also apply to the Universities. In place of the University Grants Committee, established in 1919, as a body made up of academics to provide advice on the distribution of government funds to the various academic institutions, will be the Universities Funding Council (UFC). Both the UFC and PCFC will be made up of industrialists and financial advisors, rather than academics, and will be charged with making strictly economic decisions about the disbursement of grants in the two sets of academic institutions. The grants will be related to contracts won for teaching certain subject areas. Institutions will be expected to bid for subject-based teaching contracts.

In addition, academic institutions will not only be differentiated by status in terms of polytechnics and universities, but also by level of funding for teaching and research and by the range of subjects offered. Some academic institutions will be offered full research status whereas others will be expected only to provide teaching. However, institutions will be free to bid for contracts for both teaching and research from organisations other than the PCFC and UFC. The governmental funding offered to academic institutions will be a minimum amount. Some consideration is also being given to the idea of changing to a differentiated form of student finance.

However, academic institutions, like schools, will be expected to develop new management systems of financial and academic accountability. To this end, the system of academic tenure which was the standard in the majority of universities is also to be abandoned. Teaching contracts will become more closely related to the financial viability and popularity of the appropriate academic disciplines. Moreover, academic freedom by this means, is no longer guaranteed. But the House of Lords, in its committee stage, did agree an amendment to ensure that a definition of academic freedom is included in the bill, which would not be guaranteed implicitly with the loss of tenure. Dismissal, in other words, cannot be on the grounds of unpopular or minority values and beliefs (19 May 1988).

A review of the implications of educational reform

There are common threads running through the apparently complex sections of the Education Reform Act. The main thread is to achieve greater institutional financial accountability by means of devolving funds and responsibility down to the institutional level of management. Tighter systems of management appraisal of performance and effectiveness, on traditional business organisation lines are to be set in place. These replace notions of public bureaucracies whereby commitment to the objectives of scholarship and learning took pride of place. Forms of measurement of performance, in terms of cost-effectiveness, replace the more elusive measure of academic achievement which were not conventionally tied to cost.

This system of measurement and accountability also puts a premium on subjects, disciplines and courses which admit readily of quantification. It also militates against forms of teaching and learning which are multi-disciplinary, which attempt to be discursive and integrative. In other words, although no national curriculum is laid down for higher education, the principles underlying forms of financial accountability will ensure a premium placed on similar types and forms of subject in higher education. Throughout the education system the more philosophically-based subjects will be marginalised and the more rigidly structured subjects will become the norm.

The second thread that runs through ERA is the increasing centralisation of resource control, through the distribution of grants or funds to academic institutions and to grant-maintained schools. Furthermore, taking the terms of ERA together with changes in local government finances implies greater central control not only of grant-maintained schools but also the state-maintained schools. By implication, the local authorities will have less room for manoeuvre (as noted above). Local authorities are, too, losing any form of control over the polytechnics and colleges, which fall under the remit of PCFC. The abolition of the ILEA and its replacement by 13 local authorities, all of them further subject to financial restrictions from central government, also indicates an additional centralising tendency.

Indeed, commensurate with the tendency towards centralisation is the reduction in LEA control and powers over decision-making. In place of local democracy is the tendency towards institutional forms of control and government. Each academic institution and each school will acquire a new governing body, composed largely of its clientele or consumers as 'representative' of the broader community. At the level of higher education these will chiefly be industrialists, employers in commerce and industry, and professionals, chosen because of their expertise and position rather than because of their political values or commitment. Similarly, at the school level governing bodies will be composed chiefly of parents. Here parents will be eligible to run for office on their own individual merits, rather than party political involvement. Given that the governing body will have greater financial responsibilities and control, business acumen may well become a major criterion for election. Clearly the task of being a parent governor will be very different from being a member of a governing body in the past: it will not be to represent the interests of the children as a collectivity in issues of curriculum and learning but will range over the financial viability of the educational institution. Moreover, for governors at all levels of education there will be a further responsibility to ensure not only that the public funds disbursed from either central or local government are spent in a cost-effective way but also that alternate sources of finance from industry or commerce, through parental contributions or other means are carefully maintained. In sum, governing bodies will become the financial heart of the educational institutions. On the other hand, opportunities for institutional diversity such as single sex schools, schools for ethnic minorities on the lines of Jewish schools, may begin to proliferate.

3   Heralding a new era?

By transforming the form and characteristics of educational institutions so that they become business organisations in the educational marketplace, the nature of education itself will be transformed. Individualism and competitiveness as root values replace notions of academic community and scholarship. They also replace notions of education as creating forms of social cohesion and solidarity and tending towards social equality.

These new ideas are signalled, too, in the forms of curriculum and its individualistic forms of assessment. By the development of overt forms of individual testing at four ages of compulsory schooling individual competition becomes a major criterion of educational outcomes and success. Although this has remained a criterion of educational achievement throughout the post-war period, it has not been afforded the key place it now appears to be given. Indeed, most forms of pedagogy, especially at the primary school level, have in recent years suggested that educational achievement ultimately is best attained by means of cooperative forms of learning and teaching.

Yet another implication, however, of this is that parents become more concerned about their own children's progress at the expense of other children. The democratic role of parent governor as representative of the collectivity of parents becomes far more difficult to sustain in such an environment. Moreover, it allows for parents to make decisions about types of schooling for their own children purely on selfish reasons, rather than seeing schools as contributing to the well-being of the community, and creating forms of social solidarity.

Indeed, the initial system of parental choice will, apparently, be very complex – weighing the choices between opting in or opting out, the effects of the community charge on local resources, the likely voluntary parental contributions through cash, in kind or by covenanting. This means that parental energies will be so devoted to concerns about individual children and their potential successes in different kinds of school that there will be little room for more cooperative endeavours.

In the longer run, the effects on social and educational inequalities may be even more dramatic. State schools in inner-city areas may be pressed for resources because of the pincer effect of these various decisions about grant-maintained schools and the burden of the community charge. Moreover, the effect of the testing on the subjects of the national curriculum may lead to pupils in these schools reaching only lower age-standards by the school leaving age. Dr Rhodes Boyson, himself a former headmaster of an inner-city comprehensive school and a Conservative Minister of State for Education, has already expressed a desire for the Government to emulate the American system of criterion-referenced pupil assessment. By this scheme, pupils would be kept in a class pursuing an age-specific standard until the test was successfully accomplished. This could have the effect of either limiting a child's educational experience or reducing the standard of the test to such a level that the majority of pupils in grant-maintained or private, independent schools achieve their passes prematurely. Either way, inequalities between pupils, between schools, between areas become accentuated and exacerbated. Centralising tendencies in resource control do not imply centralising tendencies in standards of achievement for different types of pupil. Indeed, the Chair of the Society of Education Officers has already predicted that this could spell the demise of state education. It certainly twists the concept of universal, mass, compulsory education. Educational provision will by these means become increasingly differentiated.

Similarly, at the level of higher education the prospects of the centralising tendencies in terms of resource control spell a return to a more uniform system of relatively privileged access to higher education. The quest to develop wider forms of access – for mature students, for students with unusual and unconventional backgrounds, with interests cross-cutting subject boundaries – will be severely curtailed by the imperative to seek out and maintain regular financial support. Only courses and subjects with proven financial viability will initially succeed. Furthermore, ILEA has been at the forefront as a pioneer of access courses to ensure equality of opportunity for mature women students, particularly from minority ethnic backgrounds. These schemes will be severely curtailed by the moves to abolish ILEA. The further education system developed to sustain these courses crossed borough boundaries and as yet no system has been proposed to ensure the continuation of this commitment.

Reactionary educational reform: back to the future?

The effects of the Conservative educational reforms are likely to be far-reaching. They will transform all our lives and identities

– as pupils, as parents, as students, and as teachers, whether in schools or in higher education.

Children in schools, whether boys or girls, white or from black or minority ethnic groups, will learn the essence of individuality, of difference, of hierarchy and of competition. Through schemes of testing and assessment, questions of ability rather than sociability will be paramount. Despite the apparently cohesive form of a national curriculum, school differences will reinforce forms of social, sexual and racial differentiation. On the other hand, the possibilities for this differentiation at the level of educational institution seriously enter the political agenda. Parent-run, grant-maintained schools allow for the possibility of single-sex or separate ethnic or religious schools, or even schools concentrating on music or art as specialisms. Similarly, students in higher education are to be introduced to notions of academic hierarchy rather than collegium, to differentiation by specialisation and subject and institutional status. Gender-specific curricula and subjects may become revitalised by such measures, with both positive and negative connotations (Spender, 1981).

Equally, for parents – whether of pupils in schools or as students in higher education – difference is reinvoked, individualistic choices, achievements and successes rewarded. As parents, the cohesive effects of participatory democracy through local government, through parental involvement, become a distant notion as choices are continuously requested on an individualistic basis.

Finally as teachers, professional identities are transformed from ensuring social learning and group cohesion and collegium to pressing for individual initiative, effort and success through forms of learning and assessments.

The impact on the society in which we live of these reforms promises to be the recreation of the identities of a bygone era. By forging new freedoms of choice, of individual success, by breaking down old forms of cooperation through local government and local community democracy we are returned to a world of Victorian values of elitism and excellence. Education, through ERA, will teach us all to conserve a world we considered we had vanquished in an attempt to create an equal citizenry. The future promises not the chance to participate but to compete for scarce resources. By this measure, education will not be liberatory but truly conservative.

Acknowledgements

Thanks are due to the following for help with preparing this paper. First, Jackie West and Will Guy, of the Bristol University Nursery Parents' Association (UNPA). Students and staff in Women's Studies at Bradford and Kent Universities, especially Claire Callender, Clare Ungerson, Sheila Allen, Jalna Hamner, Kum Kum Bavnani and Peter Taylor-Gooby. I should also like to thank Judy Allsop, Norman Ginsburg, Phil McGeevor and Pauline Perry for comments on the first draft of the paper.

7

Criminal Justice

ROD MORGAN

'The Conservative view of law is, I have suggested, clear, consistent and, through being in harmony with normal feelings, at variance with received ideas. As the will of the state, the law must enact the will of society. The idea of 'individual freedom' cannot suffice to generate laws that will be either acceptable to the normal conscience or compatible with normal administrative needs. Nor is it cogent to claim that law derives its legitimacy solely through preserving the individual from 'harm'. Legitimacy arises from the civil bond alone. Such an attitude to law necessitates a corresponding attitude to punishment. This attitude, which may seem harsh when initially stated, is in reality as humane as its liberal competitors.' (Roger Scruton, *The Meaning of Conservatism*, Harmonds worth, Pelican, 1980.)

Criminal justice issues have traditionally been subject to a broadly bipartsan approach in Britain. As a result, specific criminal justice policies have rarely been mentioned, let alone had a prominent place, in political party manifestoes. There are fundamental disagreements about the degree to which the state should provide such services as health, education, housing, etc., but politicians of Left and Right are agreed that it is the principal rationale for and first duty of the state to provide for the security of citizens by means of law and law enforcement. As a consequence it is doubtful whether a visitor, unaware of the political complexion of successive governments, could readily detect which party has been responsible for introducing the criminal justice initiatives of recent decades. There are exceptions to this rule. But, generally speaking, policy has been the product of exigencies within the criminal justice system and has followed the recommendations of official working parties. Seldom have ministers brought to office criminal justice programmes worked out by their party apparatus while in opposition.

In this sense the 1979 Conservative manifesto constituted a radical departure. Restoring 'the rule of law' was one of five objectives the Party set itself and in a chapter devoted to the topic several specific policy undertakings were made. Moreover, the Government's criminal justice programme has excited considerable acrimony. The question is whether this is because new policy directions have been taken or because criminal justice has been affected by broader strains and changes taking place in British life? Before considering this question and the likely course of policy during the Government's third term of office and beyond, we need first to review the major developments and issues during the period 1979–88.

1   The 1979 manifesto

'Law and order' has traditionally been a Conservative phrase. In 1979 it was loudly trumpeted. Surrounding the central manifesto message of a minimalist vision of the state was an emphasis on law. Individual freedom and welfare would best be assured by getting government off the backs of the people. By reducing public expenditure people would be left with more of *their* money in their pockets, enterprise would be promoted and the resulting prosperity would better enable the state to provide *necessary* services. The most necessary of these was said to be law enforcement, 'for the rule of law is the basis of a free and civilised life' (Conservative Party, 1979, p.19). In Conservative ideology 'law and order' is implicitly about enforcing the rules which 'naturally' govern a free consumer market place. Ensuring order is primarily about what the police and courts do to back up the chosen customs of the people (Aughey and Norton, 1984). It means providing the police and judiciary with the wherewithal, the powers and resources, to do the job.

The Party gave high priority 'to the fight against crime' and was prepared to 'spend more on fighting crime while we economise elsewhere'. On the hustings this tough stance became a central plank in the Election strategy. The then Labour administration was attacked for being soft on crime, for adopting dangerously exculpatory policies, and for undermining respect for law and the morale of the police. By contrast the Conservatives promised simple, direct and precise solutions. They would 'implement in full the recommendations of the Edmund Davies Committee', a substantial police pay package the Labour Government was prepared to implement only in stages. This would enable 'Chief Constables to recruit up to necessary establishment levels' and, as the Home Secretary Mr Whitelaw explained to a press conference in April 1979, 'raise the standing of the police in our society'.

Second, the Party would trust the courts by removing restraints on sentencing powers. In a concerted attack on Labour's juvenile justice record they would amend the terms of the Children and Young Persons Act 1969 'to give magistrates the power to make residential and secure care orders on juveniles'. They would also repeal section 3 of the Criminal Justice Act 1961 which restricted courts' ability to imprison young adults eligible for borstal. Further, they would provide for 'more effective sentencing' by making 'a wider variety of sentences available to the courts'. There were two messages about sentencing generally. 'For violent criminals and thugs really tough sentences are essential . . . but in other cases long prison terms are not always the best deterrent'. The manifesto went on to give examples of both. More 'compulsory attendance sentences for hooligans', an 'experiment with a tougher regime as a short, sharp shock for young criminals', 'greater use of community service orders' and intermediate treatment. But it was toughness which was stressed on the hustings. Thus with reference to the most commonly used non-custodial sanction the Party argued that 'unpaid fines and compensation orders are ineffective . . . fines should be assessed to punish the offender within his means and then be backed by effective sanctions for non-payment'.

Policy initiatives 1979–88

All the specific manifesto criminal justice undertakings have been honoured to the letter. The Edmund Davies police pay award was implemented the day after the Election and has been added to with further inflation-related increases almost unmatched in the public sector. It has become customary for other public service workers adversely to compare their financial standing relative to the police. It is also clear that total 'law and order' spending has increased substantially. Though analysis of public expenditure since 1979 suggests that the Government's commitment, or ability, to cut public spending has been less than their rhetoric suggests, and though detailed scrutiny of costs within services is necessary before conclusions can be drawn from total supply figures (O'Higgins, 1983; Robinson, 1986), it is apparent that 'law and order' departments have benefitted more than almost all others. Indeed the Government boasts the fact (Home Office, 1986). The most recent Expenditure White Paper (January 1988) indicates that 'law and order' spending has risen by 56 per cent in real terms since May 1979, a figure exceeded only by the Manpower Service Commission's training and employment programmes.

The question begged by these figures, however, is whether law and order services have improved at the point of delivery or whether, as the Opposition maintains (Labour Party, 1986), the Government has inflamed lawlessness and presided over a period of disorder without equal in recent history. In which case, as the police and the Prison Department are wont to argue, the extra spending has scarcely kept pace with increased demands made on key services. This is a question to which I shall return.

As far as sentencing is concerned the Government has introduced a formidable array of legislation. The Criminal Justice Act 1982 has, *inter alia*: removed both of the sentencing restrictions cited in the manifesto; replaced borstal training (the custodial duration of which the courts could not determine) with youth custody (which they could) for offenders under 21 years; given effect to and amended the provision under the Criminal Law Act 1977 whereby courts could impose partly suspended sentences of imprisonment; provided for shorter detention centre orders (to accompany the 'sharp shock' regimes which the Prison Department had by then begun to implement); amended the provisions for attendance centres (the number of which the Government has expanded); and increased maximum fines. Since which time various classes of 'offending' behaviour have been addressed by specific statutes: football hooliganism by the Sporting Events (Control of Alcohol etc.) Act 1985; drug trading by the Drug Trafficking Offences Act 1986; protesting and trespassing by the

182   *Criminal Justice*

Public Order Act 1986; and the possession of guns by the Firearms
Act 1988. The Government has shown itself willing to introduce
legislation quickly, following particular incidents giving offence,
to restrict behaviour and give additional powers to the police and
courts. In all these statutory provisions it has remained faithful to
the position taken in the manifesto of providing the courts with
broad powers, leaving sentencers with considerable discretion.

This doctrine is summed up in the statement that 'the sentence
to be passed on an individual is and must remain entirely a
matter for the courts subject to the maximum penalty enacted
by Parliament for each offence' (Home Office, 1986, p.21). Few
critics would take exception to the first part of the statement.
The question is whether the discretion exercised by sentencers
is too broad? Should Parliament continue merely to set maximum
penalities representing worst conceivable cases? Or should it
more precisely instruct the courts on how particular classes of
offenders within offence categories should be punished, or create
mechanisms to achieve that object by providing sentencers with
more detailed guidance? There is no constitutional reason why
either should not be done, and no shortage of methods for doing
so (Ashworth, 1983). But to date the Government has rejected this
approach. Its public stance has been to argue that if sentences fail
to reflect public feeling, then exhortation and additional disposals
will serve to close the gap, a doctrine appealing to the judiciary
and magistracy. The logical extension of this approach is that if
the courts commit increasing numbers of offenders to prison, or
indeed any other disposal, it is for the government to provide
sufficient places to accommodate them. It is this approach which
has led the Government to introduce the largest prison building
programme since the mid-nineteenth century.

The two criminal justice initiatives which are arguably the
most important introduced during the Government's first two
terms of office had their origin in a policy review set in train by the
previous Labour administration. Police powers and complaints,
and the responsibility for bringing prosecutions, would have been
the subject of new legislation whatever the political composition of
the government, though the detail of the legislation would almost
certainly have been very different had Labour been in power.

Following the Report of the Royal Commission on Criminal
Procedure (Cmnd 8092, 1981, though not all the recommendations),

the controversial Police and Criminal Evidence Act 1984 (PCEA) covered all the major police powers of arrest, stop and search, detention and interrogation. According to the Government the PCEA clarified existing police powers and removed anomalies. Moreover the new powers were accompanied by procedural devices – recording, explaining, justifying or corroborating decisions – which, the Government maintained, safeguard individuals against abuse of police powers. Further, the Act introduced a new Police Complaints Authority (PCA), an independent agency which, together with the requirement that police authorities introduce local arrangements for consulting people about the policing of their area, the Government argued were 'designed to increase police openness and accountability and so to promote public confidence in the nature and extent of police powers and the way in which they are used' (Home Office, 1986, p.11).

Most of these measures were vigorously attacked during prolonged Parliamentary debate, in the course of which Labour committed itself to repealing the PCEA. The Government's critics argued that: the legislation greatly increased police powers; the alleged safeguards were inadequate; the new powers would permit further oppression of minorities and promote 'policing by coercion'; the PCA would have no credibility because it failed to provide for independent investigation; and the consultative arrangements constituted a con-trick which failed to make for any form of police accountability worthy of the name (Christian, 1983; Spencer, 1985; Baxter and Koffman, 1985).

The Royal Commission recommended that one vital responsibility, that of prosecution, should be removed from the police. This proposal, which was given effect by the Prosecution of Offences Act 1985, enjoyed substantial cross-party support. Though there were differences of opinion about the appropriate administrative structure for the new service, most commentators agreed with the Royal Commission that, in the interests of impartiality, decisions to prosecute should not be made by persons responsible for investigating offences. It was also agreed that the existing hotch-potch of local police arrangements made for inconsistency, inefficiency and too little accountability. Thus in 1986 prosecution decisions were transferred to a national Crown Prosecution Service (CPS), a development of potentially great significance for controlling the workload of the courts.

Before considering events which forced themselves on the attention of the Government we need to mention one further policy initiative not peculiar to criminal justice. The Financial Management Initiative (FMI), whereby those services which remain within the public sector are required to state objectives, devise means for measuring performance, and devolve to managers control of those resources which determine their capacity to set and attain objectives, has been applied to the police, courts and penal agencies in common with all other public sector services (Prime Minister, 1982). As elsewhere the three Es – Effectiveness, Efficiency and Economy – performance indicators, and the rest of the FMI baggage train permeates the work of every department. However, there are important differences in the penetration achieved by the FMI. The CPS, for example, is the only government department created since the FMI. As a consequence it has been designed so that key activities can be costed and performance indicators built into its operation (CPS, 1987). These attributes could well have an important bearing on future prosecution policy.

The FMI is also having a major influence on prisons because, uniquely among criminal justice agencies, prisons are the sole, undivided administrative and financial responsibility of a central government Prison Department. As recently as 1979 an official inquiry into prisons criticised the Department for its failure to cost activities and institutions (May Committee 1979). Today the work of the Department is dominated by cost centres, 'accountable regimes', overtime budgets and staffing ratios. It is difficult to gauge the degree to which the use of this language is superficial but the signs are that the conflict-ridden 'Fresh Start' negotiations, whereby prison officers agree to phase out their considerable overtime in return for higher minimum wages and more flexible shift arrangements, is a by-product of the FMI. Insofar as the difficulties surrounding 'Fresh Start' have precipitated the exploration of contracted-out prison services (Home Affairs Committee, 1987) the FMI can be said to have had far-reaching consequences.

As far as policing is concerned the Home Office has issued guidance on effectiveness and efficiency to chief constables (HO Circular, 114/1983), there is a vogue for 'policing by objectives' (Butler, 1984), Her Majesty's Inspectorate of Constabulary is beginning to collect and analyse financially-related activity and resources data on a routine basis (HMIC, 1984) and the hunt is on for policing output measures (Sinclair and Miller, 1984; Horton and Smith, 1988). However, the devolved constitutional organisation of policing in Britain, its diffuse mandate and reactive character, appear to make policing relatively FMI-impenetrable. Certainly the official reviews of progress provide no evidence that policing has been greatly affected (HCCPA, 1986; NAO, 1986). Yet there is some evidence that the mere fact the police are collecting and making available more data on aspects of their work has implications for the degree to which politicians, locally and nationally, are able to scrutinise their activities (Loveday, 1985).

Unplanned events 1979–88

The Government's fight against crime has by any standard not been a conspicuous success. Recorded crime has continued to rise, as it has done steadily since the early 1950s, by approximately 5–6 per cent per annum. It is well recognised that changes in recorded crime do not necessarily correspond with changes in the incidence of crime (Hough and Mayhew, 1985) and most analysts are profoundly sceptical that aggregate crime levels are in the short term susceptible to changes in criminal justice policy. Nevertheless whereas there were just under 2.4 million notified offences in 1978, by 1986 there were just over 3.6 million.

More important perhaps, has been the incidence of public disorder. It seems probable that the 1980s will be remembered as a litany of places that were the scene of fire and tumult and televised pictures of groups of citizens locked in battles of unprecedented ferocity with the police. Most serious were the riots in the inner cities. These began in St Paul's, Bristol, in 1980, assumed alarming proportions in Brixton and many other cities in 1981, and have periodically erupted since, most seriously in Handsworth and the Broadwater Farm Estate, Tottenham, in 1985. In most major cities much police effort is now routinely devoted to anticipating and responding to large-scale physical challenges to their authority.

Police involvement in major industrial disputes is not without recent precedent: it occurred regularly throughout the 1970s. However the struggles between pickets and police during the miners' dispute of 1984–5, and at the Wapping newspaper plant during 1985–6, were prolonged, bloody and intensely bitter. Moreover, the methods employed by the police nationally to coordinate their efforts and prevent public assembly aroused widespread concern both professional and lay. Indeed, when violence exploded in 1986 near Stonehenge, until then the ultimate rural symbol of peaceful mysticism, the scale of the transition in British policing methods became vividly apparent. These issues were in part addressed by Lord Scarman in his seminal Report following the Brixton disturbances in 1981, and from which the Government drew the proposal, now incorporated in the PCEA, that there be statutory consultation about policing with people locally. Ultimately, the issue at stake is whether the Government's package serves to bolster public confidence that the police, as the Government claims, 'police by consent' (Morgan, 1988).

One consequence of the disorders has been to put additional strain on police resources, already overburdened, according to the police, as a result of new legislation. The police contend that the procedural safeguards in the PCEA *are* onerous, that they make it more difficult to bring offenders to book and are submerging officers in a rising tide of paperwork (Oxford, 1986; Curtis, 1986). The repercussions have been continued pressure for further resources which the Government now seems intent on stemming.

By far the largest slice of law and order spending, some £3.2 billion in 1987–8, is on the police. The bulk of the police budget, 85 per cent, is taken up with staffing costs. It follows that a major part of the increase in the total law and order budget has been swallowed up by the substantial police pay increases. These have undoubtedly aided the quantity and quality of police recruitment and most forces are now up to authorised establishment. The Home Secretary has also approved *increases* in force establishments. Between 1978–9 and 1987–8 the number of police officers and civilian support staff rose from 151,050 to 169,464, an increase of 8.9 per cent. There are now 2.47 officers per 100,000 population compared to 2.3 in 1979 and the civilianisation of administrative and communications posts has ostensibly released regular officers for other tasks, such as foot patrol, for which there is a demonstrable public demand.

Despite these staffing increases the proportion of crimes cleared up by the police fell dramatically from 41.6 per cent in 1978 to 31.6 per cent in 1986. In the same way that recorded crime is an inaccurate guide to crime committed, so clear-up rates are not a good indicator of police efficiency (Bottomley and Pease, 1986). The vast majority of offences are known to the police only because members of the public choose to tell them: likewise most crimes are cleared up because citizens inform the police 'whodunnit'. Yet, in the absence of other indicators, recorded crime and police clear-up figures exert a powerful influence in arguments about resources. If both statistics are related to the number of police officers and civilian support staff, there were 15.8 offences recorded and 6.6 cleared up per police employee in 1978 compared to 21.6 and 6.8 respectively in 1986. The police claim this is indicative of resources failing to match increased demands, yet proof of continued effectiveness.

The Government, increasingly intent on resisting police demands, has paid close attention to the research evidence, much of it collected by the Home Office Research and Planning Unit, that employing more police officers is unlikely to prevent or clear up a higher proportion of crime (Clarke and Hough, 1984). Ministers have detected some resonance between their general commitment to a market approach and cuts in public spending and the evidence about effective policing: namely that most policing, considered broadly, is undertaken not by the police but by people and organisations informally and privately. Recourse to the criminal justice system is for most people a last resort. Much policing is of course already privatised in the form of a security industry which already employs more personnel than there are police officers (Draper, 1978). While no government can afford to encourage the privatisation of law enforcement as such, the Government never-theless appears to see considerable scope for the voluntarisation of aspects of policing: getting the community itself to shoulder a larger part of the protection, prevention and surveillance parts of the policing mandate. Considerable effort has therefore been put into the promotion of 'neighbourhood watch' and similar schemes (Home Office 1986) and we may expect this to continue.

The criminal justice system has a tendency to backfire on the best laid government plans for the simple reason that it is not a system. It is neither administratively combined nor rationally co-ordinated. It is a loose federation of decision making arenas, each substantially autonomous, separately financed, subject to different authorities and operated by professionals exercising a large discretion more or less resistant to bureaucratic control. The result is that decisions taken in one arena – police, prosecutors, sentencers, prison administrators – are likely to structure, in an *ad hoc* way, the burden placed on another. There are also considerable cost overspills. Defenders of the system refer to its dispersed powers and checks and balances: critics talk of its incoherence and inefficiency. The best illustration of this theme since 1979 has been the continuing problem of prisons.

Prisons: matching supply and demand

Prisons, as we have noted, are administered in England and Wales by the Prison Department for which the Home Secretary is fully answerable to Parliament. During the last decade prisons have almost continuously occupied an urgent place in the Minister's in-tray. The problems have been various: prisoner disturbances; interventions by the domestic and European courts to condemn Prison Department practices; decaying plant; and, above all, industrial disputes with prison staff. At the root of all these problems – either precipitating them or constraining the Department's scope for action – has been prison overcrowding. The simple fact is that the Department is routinely required to house many more prisoners than it has places available. Yet, crucially, the Prison Department has no direct control over the demand on its services. The courts determine the use of prisons.

Prison overcrowding is not new. But it has grown in scale. In the 1950s the prison population exceeded places available by on average 0.5 per cent. The overload increased to 5.4 per cent in the 1960s and 8.5 per cent in the 1970s (Morgan 1983). In the 1980s overcrowding exploded. In 1979 there were on average 42,160 prisoners occupying 38,494 places. In March 1988 there were some 50,500 prisoners in a system certified capable of housing approximately 42,800, an overload of 18 per cent: over 1,500 of these prisoners were housed in police cells. The Government's response to this increasingly critical situation has been to set in train a massive prison building programme providing a planned increase of 24,000 extra places to be available by 1995, 14,300 of them in 26 new prisons. At first the Government maintained the building programme would mean the end of overcrowding by the early 1990s. However, to date the number of new places coming on

stream has been unable to keep pace with the surge in the population and it is now widely recognised that unless the Government
is able in some way to stem the upward population trend, there is
no prospect of overcrowding ending during the 1990s (Stern, 1987).

Critics have always argued that increasing the supply of prison
places runs the risk of stimulating demand and may therefore
be self-defeating (King and Morgan, 1980; Rutherford, 1986).
Moreover, the perpetual pressure on the system that overcrowding represents makes it extremely difficult to tackle the
long-recognised deficiencies of the prison estate, regimes and
staff practices. In a revealing paper presented to a bicenten-
nial penal policy conference in Australia in January 1988, the
Permanent Secretary at the Home Office, Sir Brian Cubbon,
admitted that the building policy was not a complete solution and
wondered whether the Government might 'contemplate inserting
mechanisms of demand management into the sentencing process,
so that the volume of demand for imprisonment can be more
closely tied to the available supply' (*Guardian*, 25 January).
Were the Government to entertain such an approach, long
advocated by its critics, it would represent a radical departure
from the sentencing stance set out in the 1979 manifesto.

Prospects for change

The problem for the Government is that imprisonment is the
centrepiece of the sentencing system. An enormous range of
offences, many of them by any standard trivial, are imprisonable.
During court proceedings, defendants are repeatedly reminded
that if they fail to comply with court orders – to surrender to
bail, pay a fine, keep the peace, etc. – they will be liable
to imprisonment. Non-custodial sentences are referred to as
alternatives to prison, as if the latter was the natural disposal.
Thus though only a minority of offenders are sentenced to
imprisonment the prison nevertheless dominates the system,
a position which has arguably been encouraged (in spite of
successive Home Secretaries' periodic exhortations of justices
to use imprisonment only when no other sentence will suffice)
by the Government's tough law and order talk.

Britain now has more people in prison relative to population
than any other country in Western Europe: in 1986 there were

Table 7.1   *Patterns of sentencing (all courts) 1978–86*

	17–21 years		over 21 years	
	1978	*1986*	*1978*	*1986*
Absolute and conditional discharge	7	10	8	10
Fine	55	41	54	41
Probation	7	12	5	7
Community Service Order	7	14	2	7
Detention Centre	6	5	–	–
Borstal or Youth Custody	7	16	–	–
Suspended Imprisonment	4	–	13	12
Immediate Imprisonment	5	–	17	21
Others	2	2	1	1
	100	100	100	100

[Sources of these and other crime and sentencing figures quoted in this chapter are the Home Office annually published *Criminal Statistics England and Wales*.

95.3 prisoners per 100,000 population in the United Kingdom compared, for example, to 52.4 in Eire and 34.0 in Holland (Council of Europe, 1987). Moreover, whereas the proportionate use of custody has declined during most of this century, in the last decade it has risen. The changing pattern of sentencing for indictable offenders between 1978 and 1986 in all courts is shown in Table 7.1.

The dramatic change during the period has been the decline of the fine. The fine is the most parsimonious of disposals. Besides being the simplest, most flexible, straightforwardly punitive and effective of sentences, it is uniquely revenue-generating. All other sentences are relatively costly, imprisonment immensely so. Reduced use of the fine from 54 to 41 per cent, a trend almost entirely attributable to high unemployment and the impecunious position of many offenders, has been a penal disaster not sought by the Government. Virtually all other sentences, non-custodial and custodial, have been the beneficiaries. But the serious consequence has been the proportionate increase in immediate sentences of imprisonment for adults from 17 to 21 per cent. Given the rising number of defendants brought before the courts this trend has swelled the number of committals to prison and whereas the length of custodial sentences passed by magistrates' courts has marginally decreased, crown court sentences have lengthened.

Clearly, this shift in sentencing policy is partly attributable to changes in offending and offender characteristics as well as the Government's law and order chickens coming home to roost. But whatever the cause, the Government has been forced by circumstance to try to 'manage' the prison population behind the scenes. Two developments are noteworthy. First, set against Mr Brittan's tough announcement to the Conservative Party Conference in autumn 1983 that prisoners serving more than five years for offences of violence or drug trafficking would only exceptionally be released on parole, has been the lowering of the parole minimum qualifying period from twelve to six months (Criminal Justice Act, 1982, Section 32) and Mr Hurd's 1987 increase in remission from one third to one half for prisoners serving twelve months or less. This represents a twin-track approach: loudly keeping a small number of serious offenders in prison longer, whilst quietly letting out earlier a much larger number of run-of-the-mill petty offenders. The majority of prisoners, approximately 75 per cent, are recidivist petty offenders and almost 50 per cent of all prison receptions are serving sentences of eighteen months or less. By these means the Home Secretary has temporarily managed to stem what would otherwise have been a catastrophic rise in the prison population.

These measures provide only a temporary solution, however. They run the risk of further widening the gap between sentences passed and sentences served. It is for this reason that, after much tampering, the increasingly complicated and arbitrary nature of the parole system was to be subject to a thoroughgoing review by a committee under the chairmanship of Mr Mark Carlisle. The Government asked the committee to report by autumn 1988. Whatever parole changes the Carlisle Committee presage, however, they are unlikely to provide a complete solution to the Government's imprisonment/sentencing problem.

2   1987: *The Next Moves Forward*

The 1987 Conservative manifesto, *The Next Moves Forward*, was a much more tentative document than that of 1979. The Party stood by its criminal justice guns but no longer 'underrated the challenge'. It pointed out almost defensively that 'crime has been rising steadily over the years; not just in Britain but in most other countries, too. The origins of crime lie deep in society' (1987, p.55). The Government's record – more law, more police officers, more prisons – was listed as if, rhetorically, these measures themselves represented a more law-abiding society. There was no reference to the crime and police statistics, the riots and the overflowing prisons. There was instead the confession that 'Government *alone* cannot tackle such deep-rooted problems easily or quickly'.

The Government's message, therefore, had changed. No longer a promise to spend much more on law and order services (the Expenditure White Paper of January 1988 announced real growth of only 1 per cent over the next financial year) but rather an emphasis on partnership with the public, 'encouraging local communities to prevent crime and to help the police detect it'. The Government has led the way, made the right symbolic 'law and order' gestures, demonstrated its tough-mindedness. Now voluntary effort is the underlying theme: 'we will go further in drawing on that (public) support by promoting crime prevention'. There is reference to the 'more than 29,000 Neighbourhood Watch Schemes' which have sprung up since the last Election, a popular movement on which the Party intends to build by 'establishing a national organisation to promote the best practices in local crime prevention initiatives'. Significantly, there is also a promise to 'seek ways to strengthen the special constabulary' (unpaid volunteer police officers who undertake patrol and other peripheral duties in uniform for a few hours each month). In matters of law enforcement there was no mention of privatisation (though, as we shall see, that is not ruled out of court) but there is to be voluntarisation.

The second message is detectable largely by its absence. There was no longer any reference to extending the range of sentences available to the courts. Instead toughness was signified via a measure to curb sentencers' abuse of their wide discretion, namely the controversial proposal (currently before Parliament in the Criminal Justice Bill) that Crown Prosecutors be able to refer to the Court of Appeal sentences they consider excessively lenient. There was, however, a minor reference to 'managing' the system in the shape of experiments with laying down time limits by which the cases of those defendants held in custody must be heard.

The evidence suggests criminal justice 'new realism' on the Right as well as the Left. Labour Party post-Election revisionism, which appears to involve,' *inter alia*, drawing back from plans (Labour Party, 1986) to bring policing policy under local police authority control, is paralleled by Conservative ministers seeking now to manage the criminal justice system, rein in its budget, damp down unrealistic public expectations and promote community self-help. The interesting question concerns the degree to which Conservative Home Office Ministers will be hoist by their Government's earlier rhetorical petards. This question is best explored by looking in detail at some of the issues which continue to confront the Government during its third term and possibly beyond.

The way ahead

The Government has built up a substantial stock of credibility with the police and possibly the general public over policing. Numbers are up and the tripartite arrangements (chief constables, local police authorities and the Home Secretary) for the governance of the police under the Police Act 1964 seem to have been bolstered by a blend of initiatives – the FMI and 'policing by objectives', the police community consultative committees, lay visitors to police stations, inter-agency crime prevention schemes, etc. – which have made for greater openness about day-to-day policy. Moreover the fears of civil libertarian critics about the use of new police powers under the PCEA have so far not been realised. The statistical returns (which may greatly underestimate 'voluntary' submission to police attentions) show a modest use of stop and search, prolonged detention and other police powers (Home Office, 1987). Further, the shocking events at Broadwater Farm in October 1985 have not been repeated: protesting groups have successfully been marginalised through processes demonstrating, however spuriously, that there is 'policing by consent' (Morgan, 1987a, 1989).

The degree to which the Government is able to restrain the police budget is contingent on broader aspects of Government policy and public reaction to it. If events similar to the miners' dispute of 1984–5 were to occur, or there were to be a resurgence of social unrest, police spending would inevitably rise. Precedents suggest the Government would not stint chief constables under such circumstances. However, it is doubtful whether the national crime prevention agency, which the Government launched in 1988 to co-ordinate 'neighbourhood watch' and other initiatives, will permit cuts in police spending. Nor is it likely that the Government will risk the wrath of the Police Federation by greatly increasing the recruitment or extending 'the range of duties of Special Constables' (Home Office, 1986, Section 18). Voluntary effort may supplement the amount of policing that takes place but it will not displace the police.

Through a mixture of financial controls over local government spending, the abolition of the metropolitan counties and increasing use of authoritative advice by Home Office circular, direction of policing policy has shifted even more to the centre (Morgan, 1987b). But this centralisation has been balanced by local administrative devices which emphasise the idea of partnership between professional officers and community leaders. *De facto* we have moved several steps closer to a national policing system, but the legal fiction of local authority accountability has been preserved. Police autonomy has been maintained within a framework of tighter corporate Home Office management without conceding formal political accountability either to local police authorities or Parliament. Yet however neat the trick of reinforcing police autonomy while ostensibly maintaining a high measure of public consent (Brogden, 1982) the legal position remains that chief constables alone are responsible for the 'direction and control' of the 43 forces in England and Wales (Lustgarten, 1986). And the police are the gatekeepers to the criminal justice system. Some chief constables are and will remain resistant to the wishes of the present and future Home Secretaries that they control the input to the courts. It seems likely, therefore, that the Government will look increasingly to the newly established CPS in an attempt to manage the court workload.

The CPS is a national service which incorporates the Directorate of Public Prosecutions to which the police were previously obliged to refer certain serious or publicly sensitive cases. In law the powers and functions of the DPP are now exercisable by all Crown Prosecutors in the 31 areas in which the Service is organised. Following the Royal Commission recommendation that 'there should be agreed and consistent criteria for the exercise of the discretion to prosecute' (1981, para. 9.10) the CPS, as required by Section 10 of the Prosecution of Offenders Act 1985, has published a *Code for Crown Prosecutors* (CPS 1986). Prosecution policies have two elements – whether there is sufficient evidence and whether it is in the 'public interest' to prosecute. It is the latter element which is likely to prove important. Because Prosecutors have the power to discontinue cases referred to them by the police with a view to prosecution, their decisions will undoubtedly influence police decisions to refer, or alternatively to caution. Indeed the *Code* requires (para.8) that Prosecutors 'ensure that the spirit of the Home Office Cautioning Guide lines (HO Circular, 14/1985) is observed'. Thus, though the decision to caution remains with the police, it will be surprising if the considerable disparities in the proportions of offenders cautioned by different police forces are not reduced in future by levelling upwards.

Noteworthy among the factors which prosecutors are required to assess when deciding 'whether the public interest requires a prosecution' (para 7) are: whether, if a prosecution results, the penalty imposed is likely to be 'purely nominal'; and how 'the likely penalty' weighs with the 'likely length and cost of the proceedings' (para.8 (i)). Thus, in addition to the considerations which decision makers have previously been advised to take into account – the complainant's viewpoint, the seriousness and staleness of the offence, the youth, old age or infirmity of the offender, etc. – prosecutors are now to have regard to sentencing and cost criteria. The implication is that the CPS will closely monitor these cost factors so that they can be built into the general calculation as to whether a prosecution, with all that that entails, is likely to achieve crime control gains.

To date the CPS has had a bad press and this was freely acknowledged in its first annual report (CPS, 1987). The Service has had considerable teething problems, the result of dramatic staff shortages and inexperience. However, the CPS is being remarkably secretive about those aspects of its operation which in the long-term are likely to be of great importance. There is no published information on the cost of different proceedings nor the proportions of cases discontinued. Moreover the CPS manuals for *Policy* and *Practice and Procedure* are 'restricted documents'. All of which suggests that the Government is sensitive about discussing in public a control aspect of criminal justice policy which may not command the support of referring agencies or may fit ill with the tough-minded image they have previously cultivated.

At the other end of the criminal justice system the prison building programme will go ahead roughly as planned, though loss of accommodation due to prisoner disturbances and exhausted or uneconomic plant will mean that overall capacity will not be increased by the figure currently predicted. There will almost certainly be overcrowding throughout the 1990s (NAO, 1985; HAC, 1987a). The Government is likely to pursue two initiatives in an attempt to solve the festering prisons crisis. First, the development of the 'electronic prison' concept both to release more prisoners earlier or as a bail condition and alternative sentence to persuade sentencers to commit fewer people to prison. Second, there are likely to be experiments in contracting out aspects of prison services in an attempt to cut costs and bring the Prison Officers Association to heel.

The 'electronic prison' could take a variety of forms – radio beacons, electronic tags, or random logged telephone calls to offenders' addresses – but its essence will be enhanced surveillance of offenders' activities and whereabouts while in the community. Electronic surveillance could be made a condition of bail (the rise in the number of trial and remand prisoners has been larger than in any other category of prisoners) or early release from prison. Willingness to submit to closer surveillance might also be made one of the conditions of a toughened probation or community service order designed to appeal to sentencers as a more credible non-custodial alternative to prison. These proposals will not be welcomed by the Probation Service and will be attacked by the Opposition and penal pressure groups on the grounds that past experience suggests that new non-custodial disposals displace other non-custodial sentences as much as custody (Ashworth 1983). However, the Government will gain support for the idea where, as in the case of early release, immediate displacement of custody is virtually certain. Moreover, the task of surveillance is likely to be given to the prison service or police, or even contracted security services, rather than the probation service.

Whatever form any new sentence or conditional release scheme takes it is doubtful whether the Government will resort to those measures urged on it by its critics to curb the broad discretionary powers currently exercised by the courts. Any attempt at reducing maximum sentences or introducing sentencing guidelines would almost certainly be interpreted by the tabloid press as an abandonment of the Government's 1979 manifesto commitment. The last official recommendation on these lines – the Advisory Council on the Penal System's 1978 Report *Sentences of Imprisonment* – was ignored by a Labour administration on precisely these grounds. The Government's hope must be that declining unemployment will mean sentencers judging an increasing proportion of defendants to be in a position to pay financial penalities. The Home Office may encourage such a trend by devising ways of encouraging greater use of means-related fines possibly by permitting the courts directly to attach the transfer payments of impecunious defaulters. Such a move would almost certainly do more to reduce the prison population than the introduction of any new sentence.

Contracting-out of prison services, as recommended by the House of Commons Home Affairs Committee (1987b), is unlikely to take the form of whole institutions being run by private security firms. Such an arrangement would be complex to organise legally, would be unlikely to produce major savings and might precipitate a major industrial dispute with prison staff. It is more likely that the Government will contract out particular services – laundry, food, prison workshops, classes, etc. – in prisons generally. There is no reason why the contracting agencies should not be voluntary as well as profit making and such an approach might command the support of those penal pressure groups who have complained of the intransigent opposition of prison officers to regime reforms over the years. Such a development would assist the 'normalisation' of the prison, and might stimulate far-reaching changes and savings (Morgan and King, 1987).

3 Alternative future and conclusion

The orderliness of any society is determined by a welter of factors. The evidence suggests that particular criminal justice polices – the number of police officers, the methods the police employ, prosecution policy, the sentences handed down by the courts, etc. – have at best only a marginal impact on crime rates. This is not to suggest a 'nothing works' pessimistic approach to criminal justice. But it is to argue that the maintenance of a law abiding society depends as much on the distribution of a variety of market and public sector services as on anything the police or the courts do. The corollary is that it is extraordinarily difficult to measure the effectiveness of criminal justice policies, which is why there is a tendency within the system to concentrate on intermediate tests of efficiency.

Criminal justice is largely about transmitting symbolic messages. Ideally, the presence of the police both reassures and deters; the due process of the courts suggests an impartial application of the rules; sentences denounce; and prison walls signal both social obloquy and public protection. The messages are part of civic socialisation. To be effective they must reinforce what is taught and learnt in the home, the school and the workplace. If they do not it is unlikely that their minor amendment will greatly alter behaviour. Most people, most of the time, obey the law not for fear of legal punishment – if reporting and clear-up rates are taken into account, the likelihood of that occuring is relatively small – but because they accept as legitimate the authority represented by the criminal law and are morally committed to the general rules of right conduct which underpin the law. If that legitimacy is lacking – then the system of criminal justice logically bears the strain.

If we accept these propositions it becomes sensible to adopt a damage limitation and minimalist approach to criminal justice. Resort to the criminal law beyond that required to reinforce agreed rules of right conduct is financially costly and runs the risk of exacerbating – through labelling, social conflict and alienation – that which it is designed to counteract. The criminal law ought to be a last resort.

Let us begin with the deep end of the system, the use of imprisonment. The reason why the British prison system is so large is not because the courts commit to prison a much higher proportion of offenders than other countries in Europe (whose crime levels appear to be similar to our own), but because they commit them for longer. Were the average recidivist thief or burglar (who make up approximately two thirds of prison receptions) to receive sentences reduced in length by 20–25 per cent, there would be no prison overcrowding. There is no evidence that reducing sentences of 18 months to 14, 12 to 9, or 4 to 3, would be less effective in deterring would-be offenders or those sentenced (Brody, 1976). Further, such a policy would make it possible largely to abandon the enormous and costly building programme of new prisons and permit instead concentration on upgrading the Victorian local prisons which are, and will continue to be, the bedrock of the system.

How might the courts be persuaded to adjust their sentencing tariffs downwards? The adoption of reduced statutory maxima for each offence would involve lengthy and controversial deliberation which would draw politically unacceptable attention to the issue. Moreover the exercise would be of doubtful value. Most offenders receive sentences well below the maxima. What the courts require is more precise guidance as to appropriate sentences for types of offender *within* offence categories. In theory, this is the present function of the Court of Appeal. However, as critics have observed (Ashworth, 1983) the corpus of Court of Appeal decisions lack coherence and downwards penetration: few decisions, for example, are relevant to magistrates' courts. There is need for a Sentencing Council to develop and promulgate systematic setencing guidelines.

Little benefit will accrue from creating new non-custodial sentences. Rather the credibility of existing non-custodial penalties has to be enhanced and measures adopted to ensure that they are truly non-custodial in the sense that non-compliance does not lead to a back-stairs route to prison. Fine default provides the most glaring current illustration of this process. Over 20,000 fine defaulters are committed to prison each year. Fine default might be reduced were sentencers offered more precise guidance as to how fines should be related to offenders' means and enforcement procedures made more efficient. However, the widespread practice of enforcing fines by imposing suspended prison sentences (an understandable practice given that failure to ensure compliance by this means costs the court budget nothing) will be eliminated only by removing the provision and providing an effective substitute. The best remedy would be to allow courts to impose Attachment of Income Orders: at present only earnings may be attached. Attachment of Income Orders (state benefits, unearned income, etc.) would have to be accompanied by protected income limits which would ensure that fines were better means-related.

The introduction of the CPS is a welcome development. Experience and improved resources should gradually improve the reputation of the Service. Nevertheless, it has to be recognised that diversion from prosecution in the public interest

– for which there is substantial scope particularly for minor adult offenders – is a controversial proposition. If the policies of the CPS are to command public understanding and respect the Service will have to be less secretive about how many and which offenders are not prosecuted and why.

The application of the FMI to policing has begun to open up forces to greater public scrutiny. Nevertheless policing has become more centralised since 1979. Given the politicisation of policing policy there is now a good case for undertaking a fundamental review, possibly by means of a Royal Commission, of the constitutional arrangements for the governance of the police. We have to choose. If we are to recognise *de jure* that we have a national police force the Home Secretary must be fully accountable for it to Parliament. If we are to retain local forces – the proposition which continues to command most support – then forces must be genuinely accountable locally. On these grounds there are powerful arguments for: providing London with a locally elected police authority; hiving off truly national policing functions (protection of the Royal Family, members of the Government, foreign embassy staff, etc.) to a small national force responsible to the Home Secretary; removing unelected and unaccountable magistrates from police authorities (as recommended by the Widdicombe Committee, 1986, paras 5.92–5.106); and empowering police authorities (subject to their obligation to uphold the law) to make general policing policy. Vague talk of 'policing by consent' needs to be substantiated by visible political mechanisms for conferring consent.

Few of the ingredients in this programme are likely to be implemented. It used to be argued that in matters of criminal justice Conservative administrations typically have more reforming room for manouevre than Labour governments. Labour tends to attribute problems of crime and disorder to social deprivation and injustice. Labour programmes for tackling crime generally stress collective social welfare as much if not more than criminal justice policy. Thus Labour is easily made to look soft on crime and has difficulties generating support among law and order personnel. The result, it is argued, is that Labour Home Secretaries are often more conservative than their Conservative counterparts.

This account has now to be balanced by the possibility that a Conservative administration, by stressing a legal as opposed to a social concept of justice may, through deference to the autonomy and independence of criminal justice decision makers, find it difficult to control the criminal justice machine and may stir up public antagonism to the law itself. A tough 'law and order' stance may turn out to be the Conservatives' Achilles' spear *and* heel. The Conservative approach is vulnerable in two respects. It depends on congruence between the policies of enforcement personnel and the customs of the people. This is manifest, *inter alia,* in the ability of the police to enforce the rule of law with minimal force and command the active co-operation of most members of the community. It relies on the 'dependable' behaviour of lay magistrates and juries, and on those persons condemned by the law suffering also the moral opprobrium of the people. If enforcement personnel grow unreliable, if the police encounter community resistance, or if offenders are feted, the 'naturalness' of the law, and its rule, is called into question: the relationship between social and legal justice, between the laws approved by Parliament and citizens' rights, becomes suspect.

The second difficulty is associated with the first. If rigorous enforcement of the law fails to deliver substantial compliance, expenditure on criminal justice services begins to run away with itself and cannot easily be brought to heel. Conservative administrations cannot readily question the judgements of enforcement personnel because the tough postures with which they have wooed the electorate cannot be seen to be compromised. Nor can the Government support stances which suggest that environments resulting from their broad socioeconomic policies are criminogenic. The net result is that in adverse circumstances law and order services can become bottomless expenditure pits dangerously immune to control.

In the years since Mrs Thatcher first came to power Conservative law and order policy has been precariously balanced. Britain has undergone fundamental social and economic change with unprecedented levels of unemployment, industrial decline and urban decay. Whether the Government's policies have exacerbated the social tensions which inevitably attend such change is beyond the scope of this essay, but the period since 1979 has not been orderly. Fear of crime and disorder is now a blight in many urban areas (Kinsey, 1985; Jones, Maclean and Young, 1986) and the changes in the policies of the police have been profound. The unarmed bobby walking the street is still the familiar face of

British policing. But it is shadowed now by NATO helmets and flameproof suits, reinforced vans and long shields, CS gas and plastic bullets. In the long term it may be that the British public will judge these developments to be the necessary concommitants of the rule of law for which, *inter alia*, they voted in 1979 and demonstrated further confidence in 1983 and 1987. However, a rule of law represented by too ready or frequent use of force may come to be regarded as inimical to individual rights and liberties, an order more threatening than protecting.

8

Community Care

ALAN WALKER

'All of us can need support or care at some time in our lives, for example in old age or illness. It comes from many quarters and takes many forms. For most of us who are fortunate to have them the first line of support will always be families and friends. But partly as a result of changes in social structure increasing importance has to be attached to local mutual help groups; other voluntary bodies, local and national; privately provided services such as residential and nursing homes; and the wide ranging social services provided by local authorities. The government believe that this partnership in the provision of the personal social services offers the right way forward. It provides for choice, for sensitivity to individual needs and wishes, and for involvement of the community in a way that is traditional in this country.' (Malcolm Rifkind MP, Secretary of State for Scotland, in a speech on the 'Boundaries of Care' to first UK Social Services Conference, September 1987.)

'In the past, poor quality selective services for poor people, were the product of a society which saw "welfare" as a residual, as a public burden.' (Titmuss, 1968, p.129).

1 The precarious consensus

Signs that the post-war consensus on community care policy was about to be destroyed became apparent soon after the election of the first Thatcher Government in 1979. The Government's first public expenditure White Paper (Treasury, 1979) combined with a speech by the Secretary of State for Social Services (Jenkin, 1979) marked a radical break with the past – ending of protected status for personal social services spending, abandonment of the coordination and monitoring of local service provision and increasing reliance on non-statutory forms of welfare (Webb and Wistow, 1982; Walker, 1986) – confirmed subsequently by a series of official reports and statements over the past nine years. The most significant landmark so far in the Government's strategy, that has redefined both the meaning of community care and the state's role in promoting it, has been Sir Roy Griffiths's (1988) report to the Secretary of State for Social Services. While the Griffiths Report cannot be said to represent the zenith of this strategy it was certainly an advance camp with a clear view of the summit.

The purpose of this chapter is to record the main developments in the shift in the official community care policy since 1979 and to look forward to the implications of the continuation of present trends. It is argued that the principle strategy being pursued by the Government is the 'residualisation' of the role of social services departments in the provision of community care services. Thus, the main thrust of policy in this field has been towards reducing the role of local authorities as service providers while encouraging the growth of informal, voluntary and private welfare, often under the guise of promoting a 'mixed economy of welfare'. The politics of community care in the 1980s, therefore, may be regarded as a specific illustration of four of the main manifestations of the neo-liberal philosophy that has dominated the Thatcher governments since 1979: antagonism towards public expenditure on the welfare state (Walker, 1982), increasing emphasis on self-help and family support (Wilson, 1982), extension of the market and commodification of social relations (Le Grand and Robinson, 1984; Offe, 1984), and the general breakdown of the social democratic consensus (Gamble, 1987). In retrospect, what is remarkable is not that there was a sharp change of policy but that the cosy consensus on community care had survived unscathed for the whole of the post-war period. It is important then to examine the basis of this consensus if we are to fully understand why the government was able to set a radical new course.

The post-war consensus on community care existed largely at the level of political rhetoric and provides a good example of the symbolic use of language in public policy: 'words that succeed and policies that fail' (Edelman, 1977). Underlying this precarious consensus was, on the one hand, ambiguity and uncertainty of purpose and, on the other, a power struggle between competing institutional and community interests.

The policy of community care had its origins in the early part of the century, developing as a reaction to criticisms of institutional forms of care. It was confirmed in the field of child care in the late 1940s and mental health in the late 1950s. But it was the *Hospital Plan* (Ministry of Health, Cmnd 1604, 1962) and its sister report *Health and Welfare* (Ministry of Health, Cmnd 1973, 1963; the 'community care blue book') that firmly established the policy by coupling the planned contraction of hospital provision, for elderly people, people with mental illnesses and physical and mental handicaps, with the planned expansion of local authority services (Walker, 1982b, p. 14). However, the policy was characterised by ambiguity from the outset (Walker, 1982b, 1983). Community care was never clearly and consistently defined and the political will, in the form of policy-making and planning machinery and especially resource allocation and re-allocation, were never mobilised to achieve it.

In theory, the term community care implies that help is provided by ordinary members of local communities: friends, neighbours, volunteers. According to Abrams (1977, p. 125) it is the 'provision of help, support and protection to others by lay members of societies acting in everyday domestic and occupational settings.' The development of community care policy, however, stressed care *in* rather than *by* the community. In practice, therefore, community care became help and support given to individuals – children, people with physical and mental disabilities and elderly people – by professional and quasi-professional staff in non-institutional settings. Thus the delivery of formal domiciliary services, primarily by local authorities, was the main focus of community care policy in the 1950s, 1960s and 1970s. Beyond this general support for a concept that is overladen with idealistic values and connotations, but ill-defined (Titmuss, 1968; Walker, 1986), there was no real consensus. For example, there was no agreement about the precise amount of formal provision required to enable severely disabled people to live in their own homes, or about how it might be achieved. There was and remains a wide divergence between local authorities in their provision of domiciliary services. The question of how to ensure local compliance with national minimum service guidelines has never been faced squarely.

There is no doubt that the appealing term, as well as the policy's lack of clarity, were significant reasons for their survival and widespread political support. But underlying this support for an ideal was profound disagreement between different professional groups in the health and social services and between their administrative representatives in the policy-making process. So, for example, when the official definition of community care was extended by the DHSS, in the mid-1970s, to include hospitals, hostels, day hospitals, residential homes and day centres, as well as domiciliary support (DHSS, 1977, p.78), this was not just indicative of confusion about the aim of community care policy and lack of commitment to thorough implementation of even the minimalist form of the policy; it was a clear manifestation of a power struggle over resources and, ultimately, the meaning and form of social care. (A later example is the proposal of the Wagner Report, 1988, to include residential care as part of a continuum of community care). This is a battle for ascendancy that has been going on within both the NHS and social services departments over the last forty years, between those favouring institutional and those favouring community-based forms of care. It is a struggle in which, overall, the institutionally-orientated interests in the medical profession and, to a lesser extent, in the social services professions, have reigned supreme.

A succession of measures, such as the 1959 Mental Health Act and the White Papers on services for the mentally disabled and mentally ill (DHSS, Cmnd 4683 1971, and Cmnd 6233 1975), encouraged a shift in the general balance of services towards local authority domiciliary care but failed to provide clear planning targets to achieve this and left the bulk of resources with the hospital service (Walker, 1987a, p. 4). Within the social services, too, over the whole of the post-war period, residential care took a much larger proportion of their budgets than community care and continues to do so. Thus a recent study of health and local authority spending on the elderly and people with physical and mental disabilities found that, excluding acute medicine and primary health care, institutional facilities took on average 73 per cent compared with only 18 per cent for community services (Gray, Whelan and Normand, 1988). This failure to change the allocation of resources in line with political rhetoric demonstrates not simply the 'inertia factor' (Klein, 1983, p. 130) but also the continuing strength of the institutional lobby in the health and personal social services.

So, at the end of the 1970s, the policy of community care attracted support across the political spectrum but was, none-theless, precarious. It was characterised by confusion, ambiguity, inconsistency and lack of political determination to translate even a minimalist policy into common practice. As a result of this long-term failure to implement community care policy, there was a growing 'care gap' between the need for care and the provision of local services to meet that need (Walker, 1985).

2 The new politics of community care

New ideologically inspired pressures arising in the late 1970s and early 1980s – budgetary and resource constraints and the cost-effectiveness imperative – combined with a major expansion of need for care, particularly among very elderly people, produced the political will to overcome both inertia and sectional interests. But the policy itself departed significantly from the, albeit weak, consensus that had existed for the previous forty years. Thus, the emphasis in policy has shifted away from care *in* the community by local authority personnel towards an even more confusing mixture of care *by* the community itself and private care, regardless of whether in domiciliary or institutional settings.

Promoting the private sector

While the primary intention of community care policy over the past nine years appears to have been the negative one of reducing the role of health and social services authorities in the provision of care, the 1980s also witnessed for the first time the active official encouragement of the private sector. This new policy direction was signalled early on in the life of the first Thatcher government when, soon after coming to power, the DHSS moved to encourage a switch in the provision of residential care from the public sector to the private sector.

It did so, first of all, by reducing the resources available to local authorities, by 4.7 per cent in 1979–80 and 6.7 per cent in 1980–1 (Walker, 1986, p. 17). Although cuts in PSS expenditure were carried out in the mid-1970s these fell particularly on capital, with some limited protection (2 per cent real growth per annum) being offered to current spending. In fact what happened in practice was that many local authorities took steps to protect their PSS spending, that is until the introduction of the block grant in 1981–2 and the subsequent imposition of ratecapping considerably reduced their room for manoeuvre (Walker, 1985, p. 27).

Secondly, while the public sector received the stick the private sector was given the carrot. The DHSS agreed not only to meet the full cost of care in private residential and nursing homes for those on income support (then supplementary benefit) but it also allowed local offices to set limits on such board and lodging payments deemed appropriate for their area. As a result the number of residential places in private rest homes for the elderly and physically and mentally disabled nearly doubled (97 per cent) between 1979 and 1984, with expenditure on both residential and nursing homes increasing from £6 million in 1978 to £460 million in 1986. The proportion of people in private residential homes receiving help with their fees through income support payments increased from 14 per cent in 1979, to 35 per cent in 1984 and, by 1987, had reached 54 per cent (Bradshaw and Gibbs, 1988, p. 4).

Since this growth in spending conflicted with the government's policy of reducing public expenditure, the DHSS acted to stem the flow of resources first by freezing local limits in September 1984 and then in April 1985 imposing national limits for board and lodging payments. These limits, reviewed three times since their introduction, were in 1988 £130 for residential and £185 for nursing homes for the elderly and £160 and £200 respectively for homes for people with mental disabilities and, therefore, still continue to provide a substantial subsidy to the private sector. In addition, many local authorities use private homes on an agency basis to house some of their residents. The picture sometimes painted of DHSS ministers being taken by surprise by the unplanned expansion of the private residential sector sits rather uneasily with the purposeful encouragement given to it and the governments antagonism towards local authority spending.

Some policy analysts (see for example Day and Klein, 1987) have mistakenly viewed the growth of the private sector of residential care as beneficial in terms of increasing choice in an expanding 'mixed economy of welfare'. Indeed, the appeal to increased choice has proved an important source of popular legitimation for the fast expansion of the private sector. However, while it is true that there has been a rapid multiplication of private homes – estimated by the Audit Commission in 1986 to be doubling in size each year – genuine choice requires a range of alternatives: public sector homes, day care, the chance to remain in an ordinary home with community support. But, ironically, this choice has been restricted by the 'perverse' incentive' (Audit Commission, 1986) provided by social security. Furthermore, when it comes to entering a residential home the concept of 'choice' is rarely appropriate. The need for residential care usually arises because of a crisis of care in the informal sector, leaving little time to 'shop around'. Thus, as Bradshaw (1988) has confirmed, the promise of choice held out by the supporters of the private sector is illusory.

A study of the private sector by the Centre for Policy on Ageing found that only a quarter of residents exercised any choice about the home they were admitted to, while nearly a quarter said that their admission resulted from unsolicited arrangements by a third party (Bradshaw, 1988, p. 18). Choice between private homes is severely restricted by factors such as geographical area, waiting lists and ability to pay. There is, for example, a clear North-South divide in the public/private mix of welfare. Private nursing home beds in the South-West outnumber those in the Northern region by seven times. In two regions, South-East and South-West Thames, the private sector already provides more than half the total unit health care for elderly people (Larder, Day and Klein,1986). According to the Audit Commission (1986) a more equitable distribution of resources for health and social services, sought through RAWP and GREA calculations, has been offset by board and lodging payments for private care.

Within local areas choice is restricted by the admission criteria applied by private homes, often excluding demented people or those who are difficult to control. Thus an ADSS (1986) survey found a tendency for private rest homes to select the less severely disabled elderly people, leaving the more severely disabled for the public sector. Also private homes often levy charges above the income support limits, requiring top-up payments, or make supplementary charges for single rooms or items such as laundry.

Once inside a private home residents cannot exercise much choice either. A recent study of homes in North Yorkshire found that 21 per cent had undergone a change of ownership in the previous 18 months (Bradshaw, 1988, p. 19). Residents have no say in such changes and are not always informed before they happen, nor do they have any choice about other changes in the character of their home.

> Residents entering small homely homes may find them enlarged. Residents have no control over the mix of residents or who shares their bedroom. As charges move ahead of (income support) limits residents may find themselves shifted into double or treble rooms, required to commit their pocket money to supplement the (income support) allowance or being subsidised by relatives – often without their knowledge (Bradshaw, 1988, pp. 19–20).

Questions have been raised not only about the distributional consequences of the Government's policy of promoting the private sector; considerable doubts have also been raised about the quality of the care provided. As the private residential sector has mushroomed, evidence has mounted of abuse, misuse of drugs, fraud, lack of hygiene and fire hazards in some homes (Harman and Lowe, 1986; Holmes and Johnson, 1988). Some of the worst cases of abuse have been documented by the media, such as Yorkshire Television's 1987 programme *The Granny Business*. Evidence of abuse in the private sector inevitably invites comparison with the public sector and there are similar instances of ill-treatment to be found there (see for example Gibbs, Evans and Rodway, 1987). However, concentrating on this sort of comparison of rogues diverts attention from the key issues: the operation of power in a residential setting, regardless of whether it is publicly or privately run, and which of the two sectors can be sufficiently regulated to ensure that no abuse of power occurs, issues we return to later.

Care in the community

At the same time as imposing severe resource constraint on local authorities and encouraging the rapid growth of the private residential and nursing home sector, the Government had embarked on a radical programme of mental health hospital closure. The policy of hospital rundown, particularly of mental illness facilities, dates back to the *Hospital Plan* of 1962. However, prior to 1987 no major hospital had been closed (Social Services Committee, 1985, p. xix).

There has been a steady decline in the number of patients in both mental illness and mental handicap hospitals. For example, in the ten years to 1986 the average number of daily occupied beds in mental illness hospitals fell from 109,000 to 82,500 and in mental handicap hospitals from 59,000 to 42,500. But the decline accelerated in the 1980s as the Government's discharge programme took effect.

The 1981 Care in the Community initiative (DHSS, 1981a, 1983) was specifically intended to promote the discharge of long-stay hospital patients by enabling district health authorities to transfer their funds (above and beyond joint finance) to local authorities and voluntary organisations in order to support ex-patients in the community. In addition the DHSS has exerted considerable pressure on health authorities to close hospitals within specified time limits (Social Services Committee, 1985, p. xxi). This contrasts with the earlier consensus period of community care policy as exemplified by the 1976 DHSS document on priorities in the health and social services: 'The closure of mental illness hospitals is *not* in itself an objective of Government policy, and the White Paper stresses that hospitals should not encourage patients to leave unless there are satisfactory arrangements for their support' (DHSS, 1976, p. 55).

Although the radical Conservative welfare policy has succeeded where previous consensus policies had failed in overcoming institutional inertia and professional interests in the promotion of community care, the main motivation for doing so is cost-efficiency with the effectiveness of care received in the community taking second place. This was the main thrust of the trenchant critique of the Government's community care policy towards people with mental disabilities by the House of Commons Social Services Committee (1985), one of the most authoritative among several similarly critical reports in recent years.

The Social Services Committee focused attention on the disaster course that had been set by forcing a closure programme without sufficient planning preparation and consultation and, furthermore, without any agreed understanding of what the intended community care would actually entail. It was especially mindful of the danger that community care is perceived as a cheap option. In the Committee's own words: 'A decent community-based service for mentally ill or mentally handicapped people cannot be provided at the same overall cost as present services. The proposition that community care could be cost-neutral is untenable . . . . We are at the moment providing a mental disability service which is underfinanced and understaffed in its health and social aspects' (Social Services Committee, 1985, p. xiv).

The official rhetoric surrounding the Government's policy may be community care, but the reality is decanting and de-hospitalisation coupled with an increase in both public and private residential placements. For example, between 1976 and 1985 there was an increase of 70 per cent in the numbers of mentally handicapped people in local authority staffed homes and 154 per cent in private homes. The bulk of the increase (133 per cent) in the numbers in private homes occurred between 1981 and 1985 while most of the increase (47 per cent) among those in public sector homes took place between 1976 and 1981. So, the result of hurried de-hospitalisation in the face of the underfunding of community-based services is that many people with mental disabilities have merely been shifted from one institution to another. People are ending up in residential homes when they do not need to because there is no realistic alternative and private sector places are subsidised by social security.

The Social Services Committee summed up the irresponsible nature of the Government's care in the community policy in its now famous sentence: 'Any fool can close a long-stay hospital: it takes more time and trouble to do it properly and compassionately' (Social Services Committee, 1985, p. xxii). In trying to bring some sense to bear the Committee attempted to establish the basic principle of a community care policy and insisted that the statutory health and social services are central to the provision of community care, both of which harked back to the pre-1980s consensus.

Residualising the social services

A series of what seemed as they occurred to be separate policy developments over the last decade or so may, with the benefit of hindsight, be seen as part of an evolving government strategy aimed at turning local authority social services from the main providers of formal care into something far more limited: the provider of those residual services which no one else could or would take on.

In 1980, in a speech to directors of social services departments, the then Secretary of State, Patrick Jenkin, outlined a supportive and decidedly residual role for the social services: 'a long stop for the very special needs going beyond the range of voluntary services' (Jenkin, 1980). In 1981 the White Paper on services for the elderly asserted, in a widely quoted phrase, 'care in the community must increasingly mean care *by* the community' (DHSS, 1981, p.3). The previous year, when giving evidence before the House of Commons Social Services Committee, Jenkin had justified the cuts in PSS expenditure and the closure of long-stay hospitals (outlined above) on the, unsubstantiated, assumption that the non-formal sector would expand: 'When one is comparing where one can make savings one protects the Health Service because there is no alternative, whereas in personal social services there is a substantial possibility and, indeed, probability of continuing growth in the amount of voluntary care, of neighbourhood care, of self help' (Social Services Committee, 1980, pp. 99–100). This aim of placing greater reliance on quasi-formal voluntary help and informal support was reflected in the Care in the Community (1981) and the Helping the Community to Care (1984) initiatives.

But it was Jenkin's successor as Secretary of State, Norman Fowler, in a speech to the 1984 Joint Social Services Conference in Buxton, who provided the clearest and most detailed outline of the new residual role proposed for social services. He argued that there are 'three paramount responsibilities' of social services departments: to take a comprehensive strategic view of all the sources of care available in the area; to recognise that the direct provision of services is only part of the local pattern and that in many cases other forms of provision are available, to see a major part of their function as promoting and supporting the fullest possible participation of the other different sources of care. The fundamental role of the state, according to Fowler, is 'to back up and develop the assistance which is given by the private and voluntary support' (Fowler, 1984, p. 13).

The Audit Commission's inquiry into community care came to the same conclusion as countless previous independent studies: 'Joint planning and community care policies are in some disarray.

The result is poor value for money. Too many people are cared for in settings costing over £200 a week when they would receive a more appropriate care in the community at a total cost to public funds of £100–£130 a week. Conversely, people in the community may not be getting the support they need' (Audit Commission, 1986, p. 3).

The Audit Commission proposed various organisational changes aimed primarily at clarifying the overlapping responsibilities of health and social services authorities. In the case of the physically and mentally disabled, local authorities were to be given lead responsibility and made responsible for their long-term care in the community, except for the most severely disabled who would be the responsibility of the NHS. The long-term care of the elderly people in the community would be financed from a single budget established by contributions from the NHS and local authorities. The budget would be under the control of a single manager who would purchase services from the appropriate public or private agency. Health authorities were to be given lead responsibility for the care of the mentally ill in the community (Audit Commission, 1986, p. 4).

The Audit Commission's critical report was much more influential with the Government than any previous one had been, including the authoritative analysis by the House of Commons Social Services Committee. The Secretary of State had been promising, for two years, the publication of a Green Paper on the personal social services. This did not materialise and, instead, in response to the debate following the Audit Commission report, Sir Roy Griffiths was appointed, in March 1987, to examine problems in the arrangements for community care between the NHS and local authorities and to explore the option of putting the whole service for elderly people 'under the control of a manager who will purchase from whichever public or private agency is appropriate'. (Sir Roy Griffiths had conducted a similar inquiry into the management of the NHS in 1983, which led to the appointment of general managers at district level.) The report of the Griffiths inquiry was published in March 1988.

Together these policy developments, taken with those reviewed earlier, suggest a strategy aimed at residualising the social services. The issue of how far the Griffiths Report itself chimes with this strategy will be discussed in the next section. The three main dimensions to the policy of residualisation may be summarised.

In the first place, the provision of community care is being deliberately *fragmented*. Though sometimes presented as promoting a more mixed economy of welfare, the main motivations here are to curtail the monopoly role of local authorities in the delivery of formal care – an aim that, as we have seen, has already been achieved in several parts of the country with regard to the residential care of elderly people – and to encourage the growth of cheaper sources of informal and quasi-formal care. Sir Kenneth Stowe, the former permanent secretary of the DHSS, described this new approach as 'letting a hundred flowers bloom'.

The first of the Thatcher Secretaries of State for Social Services, Patrick Jenkin, had hoped for the expansion of voluntary help, self-help and informal care (see above) and, to encourage the development of these alternative forms of provision a series of special initiatives, including the Care in the Community and the Helping the Community to Care programmes, have been introduced. Indeed, with the DoE so effectively controlling local authority expenditure by means of the block grant, the main influence exerted by the DHSS over community care has been the promotion of these initiatives and the targetting of research resources on projects designed to extend informal and voluntary help, such as the Kent Community Care Scheme. One result of this policy of fragmentation has been the advent of a wide range of precarious, often short-life, projects relying on grant aid and Training Commission special schemes. Thus, in September 1986, there were some 66,459 community programme workers engaged in providing direct services to social welfare clients.

Secondly, there is *marketisation*. As we have seen, while finances for local authority services have been tightly controlled the private sector has been encouraged to expand by the open-ended provision of social security board and lodging subsidies. Contracting out, or purchase of service contracting, has a long history in the personal social services but it has been used primarily in relation to the voluntary sector (Webb and Wistow, 1987, p. 89). So far, direct privatisation has not affected the social services to the same extent as the NHS. But the Local Government Act 1988 gave the Secretary of State for the Environment powers to add to the list of services which must be contracted out.

Some policy analysts have taken the view that the expansion of the private sector at the expense of the public sector is simply an extension of welfare pluralism, leading to increased choice and efficiency, and in any case, a reduced role in the provision of services could be balanced by an increased regulatory role (Day and Klein, 1987). The question of the extent to which the private sector promotes choice has already been discussed. In addition, marketisation may be seen as one among many examples of the New Right's antagonism towards the decommodifying aspects of the welfare state. It is intended to challenge the, albeit-limited, extent to which the social services intrude on market values and threaten their reproduction by promoting citizenship rights and needs-based priorities. It is this ideological driving force behind the expansion of the market, and the simplistic assumptions it is based on concerning the effectiveness of the market, that proponents of regulation tend to overlook. Regulation hinders the efficient operation of the market and this might endanger the primary goal of expanding private provision.

Thirdly, the Government is pursuing the twin-track policy of *decentralising* administration and operations, while *centralising* control over resources. This is one manifestation of the general neo-liberal strategy of rolling back the frontiers of the state while centralising state control (Gamble, 1987). The process of centralising control over social services resources began early in the life of the first Thatcher administration with the introduction of the block grant and, within it, detailed GREA assessments for the different elements of the personal social services (Walker, 1985, p. 27), but responsibility for the operation of social services within centrally determined budgets remains with local authorities. A similar policy has been implemented with regard to housing benefit and the health service. In the NHS the centralisation of control over management and budgets has concentrated on efficient financial management, with the issue of the effectiveness of the treatment and care provided taking second place. In theory the decentralisaiton of operations offers the prospect of greater user involvement. But this is unlikely to be realised unless resources and responsibility are also devolved.

The cumulative impact of these three sets of policy developments is a strategy aimed at further residualising the role of local authorities providing community care. This was the process envisaged by the chief architects of the present community care policy, Patrick Jenkin and Norman Fowler, and echoed by senior DHSS officials in public statements. For example, in 1980, the head of the Social Work Service observed, 'I do not (therefore) have difficulty in accepting the role of the State as residual – the voluntary sector must to some extent return to providing and for services which we have come to expect from the state' (Utting, 1980).

Although some aspects of these policies were to be found under former governments, for example the 1977 Good Neighbour Scheme was the forerunner of the 1980s initiatives, a concerted strategy of this sort has not been identified previously. Of course in relation to the totality of care, both formal and informal, the social services have never been anything other than residual. The essence of the Government's approach towards community care, however, is that it is attempting, with some success, to reduce the role of local authorities as providers within the formal sector. Furthermore, it is intended to fill this artificially-created care gap with a mixture of private, voluntary and informal care. The likely impact of this policy is considered in the next section.

3 The future of community care

In mid-1988 the future of community care policy hung in the balance. The Griffiths Report awaited an official response. On 25 July the DHSS was split into two departments, the Prime Minister's review of the NHS overshadowing social services issues. However, with spending on private residential care growing so rapidly action is likely to be taken in the near future. It is helpful to consider the short- to medium-term future of community care policy by looking at the main recommendations of the Griffiths Report and their potential impact.

The Griffiths agenda for action

The Griffiths review was designed to be an overview of the management of community care policy, along the lines of the review of the management structure of the NHS, also conducted by Griffiths, in 1983. His remit excluded the content of policy, at least that was the way it was interpreted, and the level of funding (Griffiths, 1988, p. iii).

The debate following the publication of the report focused on the lead role it assigns to local authorities and various commentators have conjectured that the report's release on the day after the Budget signalled the Government's displeasure with this central recommendation. In fact, rather than swimming against the tide of government policy, Griffiths's proposals chime very closely with the strategy outlined above. However, this is not to underestimate the political problem Griffiths posed for the Government in appearing to increase local authority powers. Moreover, the report is critical of government policy, not only in echoing the conclusions of the House of Commons Social Services Committee and the Audit Commission, but also in pinpointing the Government's culpability in three crucial respects. There is the conflict between social security board and lodging subsidies and social services assessments according to need with the result that many elderly people end up in residential care when they do not need to do so (Griffiths, 1988, p. v). Secondly, the Government's block grant policies have reduced the 'support for services such as community care' (Griffiths, 1988, p. 10). Thirdly, there is the failure to set clear and consistent policy objectives at the centre which is 'inconsistent with any claim that there are serious national policy objectives to be achieved' (Griffiths, 1988, p. viii). This latter criticism was reinforced by a report from the House of Commons Public Accounts Committee (1988).

At the heart of the Griffiths Report is the role assigned to local authorities. While there should be a Minister of State to oversee national community care policy, 'I firmly believe that the major responsibility for community care rests best where it now lies: with local government' (Griffiths, 1988, p. 11). The report underlines the centrality of this recommendation: 'This is a key statement. The role of the public sector is essentially to ensure that care is provided'. On the face of it, therefore, this is completely at odds with government policy towards local authorities and particularly the residualisation of their role. But on closer scrutiny there is no paradox: 'How it is provided is an important, but secondary consideration' (Griffiths, 1988, p. vii). This latter statement represents main-stream government policy with clear echoes of Norman Fowler's 1984 speech in Buxton.

Thus, the role envisaged for local authorities would be to *manage* care not to provide it. They would become 'managing agents', overseeing the further residualisation of public sector provision while encouraging the expansion of the private and voluntary sectors. What Griffiths proposes, in effect, is fur-ther privatisation: 'The onus in all cases should be on the social services authorities to show that the private sector is being fully stimulated and encouraged and that competitive tenders or other means of testing the market, are being taken' (Griffiths, 1988, p. vii). Resources would be conditional on the achievement of private and voluntary sector growth and other targets. This contradicts the notion of local authorities acting as free managing agents as well as Griffiths's own critical comments on the damaging impact of privatisation in the field of residential care.

What would be the implications of the adoption of this central item on the Griffiths agenda? For the reasons outlined already the answer to this question also reveals the likely future for community care if present policies continue. First of all there are the well known dangers for users associated with residualised public services: stigma, a reduction in choice as services are run-down, a concentration of the rump of most severely dis-abled and deprived in the public sector, the ghettoisation of special needs, such as those of racial minorities, as the private sector selects the more economically attractive users. Twen-ty years ago Titmuss (1968, p. 143) warned of these dangers: 'Separate state systems for the poor, operating in the context of powerful private welfare markets, tend to become poor standard systems.'

Secondly, there is the difficult position of staff left in the public sector. For example, the unenviable role of care manager social workers having to encourage the growth of the private and voluntary sectors while their colleagues in the residential and domiciliary services experience the falling morale associated with residualisation. For local authority managers, too, many of whom seem to relish the increased power over resources that

Griffiths appears to promise, their position would be heavily circumscribed: targeted grants, expectation of charges for services, tendering and contracting out to the private and voluntary sectors, ministerial veto and so on.

Thirdly, there is the problem of how to ensure effective accountability to users, not to mention participation, in the sort of dual system of welfare envisaged by Griffiths. Thus the separation of control over resources from implementation is likely further to blur lines of accountability and communication and lead to confusion about who is responsible for policy. Can the commercial sector be relied upon to promote user participation? If not will public sector managers have the power to impose such non-commercial criteria on the private sector?

Fourthly, in the drive for cost-efficiency the quality of care might suffer. The experience of competitive tendering in other local authority services has not been a happy one, with private contractors winning tenders with unrealistic performance claims and loss-leader prices (Harris, 1988, p. 15).

As a result, the quality of services has declined and the new private sector providers have become more remote from and less accountable to users. Allied to this concern is the proposal in the Griffiths Report (1988, p. ix) that elderly people might be helped by a multipurpose auxiliary force or school leavers and YTS trainees. However, this proposal misconstrues the nature of the care needs of disabled elderly people. Many of their needs may be practical, but semi-skilled auxiliaries with a low level of commitment to care might reinforce dependency rather than assist independence.

Fifthly, if enacted, the Griffiths recommendations are not likely to overcome entirely the acute problem faced by local authorities of trying to plan service development in the face of the uncontrolled expansion of the private sector. Effective coordination and planning relies on social services departments having power over the private sector. The paradox of how service development can be managed and controlled while leaving the private sector with sufficient flexibility to be economically viable was unresolved in the Griffiths Report. There are a range of other proposals made by Griffiths: some desirable, such as the reinstatement of central monitoring of local authority provision abandoned in 1979 and some, such as the proposal that social

workers should administer the community care grant element
of the social fund, very undesirable (see Allen, 1988).

An alternative agenda for reflection

The future which the Griffiths Report has given further impetus to
is an increasingly residual role for the public sector in the provision
of community care and an extension of the dual system of welfare
already well entrenched after more than a decade of Conservative
government. Unfortunately, the managerial review that Griffiths
conducted put the cart before the horse. In other words there was
no clear statement about the philosophy that should underpin
community care policy, ministers being asked to provide this.
However, without first establishing the goals of policy it is difficult
to evaluate the managerial arrangements designed to achieve
them. What steps are required before a constructive debate can
take place about the organisational form of community care?

   First of all it is essential to establish the philosophy that will
underpin community care policy, not only at the level of concepts,
such as normalisation, but also in terms of the concrete assistance
that individuals in need of care and their families may reasonably
expect. There is a risk that, in the absence of a clear statement of
the goals of policy, it will be assumed that the present bases of community care are acceptable. The failure to reassess the assumptions
underlying community care policy are a fundamental weakness of
the Griffiths Report. Thus the report emphasised the importance
of the informal sector as the primary source of care and argued
that the public sector's first duty is to support and strengthen
these networks of carers (Griffiths Report, 1988, p. 5). But this
position represents a very limited conception of community care
and an apparent lack of appreciation of the 'meaning' of care for
those involved, including for example, the physical, psychological,
economic and social costs it may entail for mainly female carers. If
policy automatically assumes that supporting informal care is necessarily the primary goal these costs will continue to fall on women.
Research shows that family care for elderly people can be the best
and the worst form of care and, therefore, policies which assume
its primacy may impose very destructive relationships on elderly

people and their carers (Qureshi and Walker, 1989). So the Griffiths approach would simply sustain the existing system of care which relies overwhelmingly on female kin with social care operating on a casualty basis when informal relationships breakdown.

An alternative policy aimed at sharing care more effectively would beware of placing unreasonable expectations on the informal sector and attempt to redress the inequality in caring between the sexes. A start could be made in this direction by thinking in terms of social support networks geared towards sharing care between female kin and the state. Such support networks comprise both formal and informal helpers, professional as well as non-professional personnel, and should be created to ensure that care is shared rather than waiting for the informal caring relationship to breakdown (Walker, 1987b). Of course this implies a substantially more costly service than that provided currently and unless there is a commitment of resources no amount of discussions about the philosophy of community care will be worthwhile.

Secondly, it is important to guard against uncritical acceptance of changes in the welfare mix. As we have seen above, on the one hand a policy of privatisation has been pursued under the guise of creating a more pluralistic system and, on the other, reductions in the level of formal services have major implications for the informal sector. One of the main concerns of the Griffiths review was the monopolistic power of the public sector of residential and nursing homes (Griffiths, 1988, p. 20), despite the fact that the public sector is no longer a monopoly provider in many areas of the country. But, in addition, this concern is based on two false assumptions.

It is assumed both that monopolies only operate in the public sector and that private provision can adequately substitute for public provision. However, as far as, for example, an elderly resident in a private or public home is concerned her provider *is* the monopoly power because shopping around for an alternative is not a realistic proposition. Having a range of alternatives to the public sector will not make the consumer sovereign if she cannot exercise effective choice. But ensuring that users have a *right* to services of a certain level and quality would begin to redress the power imbalance in service provision, which brings me to the second assumption. The motivations of a for-profit private producer are quite different from those of a public sector provider. Although both may provide opportunities to exploit vulnerable people it is only in the public sector that a direct line of enforceable public accountability exists and, moreover, it is only the public sector that can provide rights to services (Walker, 1988).

This raises the issue, thirdly, of professional power. A new role for social services departments in community-based social support networks implies changes in professional autonomy and orientation and, therefore, in the training of professionals. This means challenging, to some extent, the traditional basis of professional status and providing for the input of informed user knowledge and preferences. This means finding ways for the community members themselves to influence community care policy – in short, power sharing. The role of local authorities, as Griffiths recognised, is central to the provision of a local service, but he avoided the question of user participation.

Finally, the major lesson from the post-war history of community care policy in this country is the failure to plan the the development of community services and the run-down of the residential as well as the hospital sectors. The opportunity offered by the Griffiths Report is to put strategic planning, at both local and central levels, back on the agenda. This would necessarily entail assessments of priorities in social services policy and their outcomes.

Conclusion

Looking back over the post-war period it is clear that the precarious political consensus on community care held together because of the remarkable gulf between rhetoric and action and the interest of the most powerful groups involved in sustaining it. The consensus began to breakdown in the mid-1970s under economic pressures, but there was still a commitment to publicly-provided domiciliary services. The real challenge to the consensus came in the early 1980s when the Government set about a radical shift in policy, towards an increasing use of private and informal care and the residualisation of the social services. The publication of the Griffiths Report might have marked a watershed in raising public consciousness about community care and, therefore, led towards the development of a policy that reflects the needs of severely disabled people and their families. Unfortunately, it looks as if this particular opportunity has been missed and it will represent only another milestone in the decline of public provision of decent social services.

9

Private and Voluntary Welfare

MARTIN KNAPP

'Conservatives reject Labour's contention that the state
can and should do everything . . . . we shall promote closer
partnership between the state and the private sectors in
the exchange of facilities and of ideas in the interests of
all patients. We also welcome the vital contribution made
by voluntary organisations in the social services. We shall
continue to give them strong support. The Conservative
Government has already made many radical changes in
law and taxation which have greatly improved the way
charities and voluntary bodies are financed . . . .. We shall
continue to support our highly successful "Opportunities
for Volunteering" scheme. In the next Parliament, we
shall develop other new ways to encourage more private
giving.' (*The Conservative Manifesto 1983.*)

Forgotten dimensions

To the vast majority of the British population the term *welfare*
is synonymous with state provision. Mention health care and
most people think immediately of the NHS; social care and
social services departments are seen as one and the same;
education is the local comprehensive. If you quizzed members of the population about *privatisation* they would most
likely respond, perhaps in approving or disapproving tones,
with tales of quick profits on British Telecom shares or the
sale of council houses. Even after ten years of Mrs Thatcher's

governments, welfare is still seen as something the state provides and privatisation is seen as a return to market principles. These popular views are not so much wrong as over-simplistic, for most social services are still directly produced by the public sector and an important ideological strand to Thatcherism is a belief in the desirability of market allocations. In reality, of course, there is a fascinating variety of organisational and economic arrangements for the delivery, funding and regulation of welfare.

The purpose of this chapter is to describe and discuss these various arrangements for producing or delivering social policy services, their reliance on a diversity of resources including both cash and the (uncosted) inputs of time and care from volunteers and relatives, and their regulation. These arrangements – collectively labelled *the mixed economy of welfare* – are in fact too numerous and too various to be comprehensively reviewed in a chapter of this length, but the variety does lend itself to a degree of reduction and categorisation, which is the subject of the next section. The structure offered for describing the mixed economy is, however, merely a parameterisation useful for didactic purposes, and it should not distract from the almost infinite variability of welfare policy arrangements and ideologies. Subsequent sections then pull out some of the salient and controversial policy topics arising from today's mixed economy in the context of policy trends in the 1970s, illustrating each where appropriate.

The first of these topics is the long-established but recently extended policy of *charging* consumers to public services, which we discuss and illustrate by focussing on pricing in the NHS. The chapter then turns to *contracting out*, with examples drawn from a number of social policy areas, and finally confronts the *market allocation* of welfare services: the quintessence of privatisation.

The mixed economy of welfare

The mixed economy of welfare is becoming increasingly complex. The number and variety of producers grow, the funding sources multiply and different regulatory styles proliferate. Privatisation, in fact, can be taken to mean any relaxing of the public sector's

Table 9.1 *Some formal differences between public, voluntary and private social agencies*

	Public agency	*Voluntary agency*	*Private agency*
Philosphy	Justice	Charity	Profit
Represents	Majority	Minority	Owners and managers
Legal basis of service	Right	Gratuity	Fee for service
Primary source of funds	Taxes	Contributions, fees, payments and grants	Payments from customers or third parties
Determination of function	Prescribed by law	Selected by group	Chosen by owners/managers
Source of policy-making authority	Legislative body	Charter and bylaws authorising board of directors	Owners or corporate board of directors
Accountability	To the electorate via a legislative body	To constituency via board of directors and to funders	To owners
Scope	Comprehensive	Limited by location and ideology	Limited to those who can pay
Administrative structure	Large, bureaucratic	Small, bureaucratic	Bureaucratic – may be a franchise operation or part of a national company

Source: Slightly adapted from Kramer (1987).

dominance or control of any one of the three dimensions of production, funding and regulation and, equivalently, greater responsibility for voluntary organisations, private (commercial) enterprises and informal providers such as relatives or neighbours.

We can distinguish four basic *production* or *supply* sectors: public, voluntary (non-profit), private (for-profit) and informal provision. Their definitions are not without controversy and the margins between them are blurred. Public providers include central government (the Home Office provides prison accommodation, the Department of Health manages youth treatment centres, their maintenance is a central government duty), the various tiers of local government with responsibility for producing *inter alia*, education, social care and housing services, the NHS and numerous non-departmental public bodies (formerly quangos) such as the Manpower Services Commission and the Housing Corporation. The private and voluntary sectors are constitutionally separate from government. So too, is the informal sector but this has no formal constitution or set of rules. The primary difference between private and voluntary organisations is the *non-distribution constraint* characterising the latter: a voluntary organisation 'is barred from distributing its net earnings, if any, to individuals who exercise control over it, such as members, officers, directors, or trustees' (Hansmann, 1980, p.838). By no means all voluntary organisations are charities; 'political' activities preclude charitable status (see Brenton, 1985, for a fuller discussion of these and related issues). Some private agencies disguise themselves as voluntary, some voluntary agencies behave in a manner fully consistent with maximisation of either profits or managers' salaries, and a growing number of public agencies are developing direct labour organisations promoting internal markets and acquiring many of the trappings – but without the benefits – of a commercial enterprise. Not surprisingly there is some debate, indeed controversy, about the precise location of the boundaries between the sectors. The essential differences between the sectors can be caricatured by Table 9.1, adapted from Kramer (1987).

The *funding* or *demand* dimension of the mixed economy describes the source of revenue: who pays for a service, either as consumer, tax payer or donor? Funds get channelled through different stages. For example, the board and lodging payments which help to sustain many private old people's homes are

clearly linked to specific residents and their needs, yet the
funds come originally from social security coffers and so from
tax and national insurance revenues. They could thus be described
either as public funding or as (compensated) individual payments
for services, recognising the growing emphasis on choice and
consumerism. To impose some order on the funding dimension
we can distinguish six varieties of demand:

- *Coerced collective demand*, where the public sector acts as
  purchaser on behalf of citizens, mandated by democratic
  or electoral processes. Funding comes predominantly from
  coercive taxation.

- *Uncoerced or voluntary collective demand*, where voluntary
  organisations use voluntarily donated funds to purchase services. The choice as to precisely what goods or services
  to purchase, and for precisely whom, is controlled by the
  organisation and not (directly) by individual donors.

- *Corporate demand*, which is demand or funding or support
  in kind from private sector corporations or firms.

- *Uncompensated individual consumption*, which is payment for
  goods or services consumed by the payer, but not subsidised
  from social security or other transfer payments.

- *Compensated individual consumption*, which is also payment
  for consumption by the payer, but now subsidised from transfer
  payments such as social security, housing benefit or state
  pension.

- *Individual donation*, which is payment for goods and services
  to be consumed by someone else, payments being made directly
  to suppliers and not to voluntary organisations as intermediary
  bodies (the latter being uncoerced collective demand).

In each case the term 'payment' is used as a shorthand for
the transfer of money, goods or time. If it is the last of

Table 9.2   *The mixed economy of welfare: service configurations*

Form of funding or demand	Form of production or supply			
	Public	Voluntary	Private	Informal
Coerced collective	NHS hospital stays	Contracted-out day care	Contracted-out school cleaning	Social security payments to encourage family care of disabled
Uncoerced collective	Registration fees paid by voluntary residential homes	Federated fund-raising	Charities' purchase of goods and services	Foster family placements by Barnardo's
Corporate	Companies' purchase of public training programmes	Corporate donations to charities	Private nursing home purchases of food, etc.	Cottage industries
Uncompensated individual consumption	Prescription charges, dental fees	Pre-school nursery fees	Purchases of aspirin, student textbooks, private medicine – market allocations	Private child-minders and babysitters
Compensated individual consumption	Public residential home fees backed by pensions	Board and lodging payments to voluntary homes	House mortgages with tax relief	Purchases from community care grants
Individual donation (for consumption by others)	Donations of clothes and toys to social services departments	Oxfam, Live Aid, etc. donations. Eleemosynary charities	Volunteering in private children's homes	Intra-family transfers of resources

these then we have *volunteering*. In principle, neither individual consumption nor donation is coerced although there may be cases where individuals feel morally bound to contribute or assist.

It is crucial to maintain a clear distinction between the production and funding dimensions when describing and analysing the mixed economy. For example, policy assumptions behind supply-side subsidies to the voluntary sector – such as tax exemptions, grants or purchase of service contracts – are very different from the assumptions behind demand-side subsidies to consumers of voluntary sector services, such as vouchers, food stamps or social security allowances. We will need to examine these assumptions, and particularly describe their practical implications, later in this chapter.

If we cross-classify the four sectors of production against the six forms of funding we have a simple and informative representation of a pluralist welfare system. This 24-celled matrix is obviously only a highly simplified description of the myriad inter-relationships between demand and supply (between funding and production), but it has the signal virtues of describing the mixed economy and highlighting policy options (as in Table 9.2). Employing this representation of the mixed economy we can define *privatisation* as any move from the first row downwards (a reduction in direct or total public expenditure) or from the first column to the right (delegation of production to non-public agencies or to individuals). In addition, there is a third form of privatisation which can be superimposed onto the matrix. This is *deregulation*: any relaxing of public control over either production or funding. For example, the deregulation of bus services in many areas had nothing to do with changes in public subsidies or provision, but certainly reduced the degree of public sector intervention in the market place.The same would apply to relaxing of rent controls in the private rented housing sector.

It is unnecessary to comment at length on Table 9.2. What must be pointed out – and readers are invited to offer their own explanations – is that every cell of the matrix can be filled. That is, the British welfare state contains an almost bewildering array of transaction types between the funding, demand or patronage side of the economy and the provision or supply side. What is more, it is most unlikely that any of the cells will be empty at the end of the century; the British mixed economy of welfare is inherently very mixed! Of course, the balance between the cells is far from static – the policies cited in Table 9.2 are effecting fundamental changes in some service areas.

Consumer charges

One of the contributing factors to Labour's defeat in the 1979 election was its inability to deal (to the electorate's satisfaction) with the economic problems that had been besetting Britain since the oil crisis of 1974. Keynesian attempts to spend the country out of recession were, Labour's opponents argued, merely overheating the economy, pushing inflation well above 20 per cent a year. Mrs Thatcher was propelled into Downing Street armed with what, in hindsight, was a fairly unsophisticated strain of monetarism. Central to her economic strategy at that time, as now, was the belief that public spending crowded out private sector investment and stifled economic growth. There was an urgent need, her Government maintained, to rein in public expenditure, and a relatively easy and immediate way to do so, albeit by small amounts, was to increase charges for the consumers of public services.

One of the earliest social policy consequences of the change in government, then, was the extension of consumer charges. Since 1979 we have seen year on year increases in the real value of drug prescription and dental treatment charges, reduced subsidies for school meals, increases in home help charges, falls in the real value of student grants and a host of other changes. In those first years of Conservative government many social policy researchers turned their attention to the analysis of charging and to price and non-price rationing generally (for example, see Judge, 1980; Judge and Matthews, 1980; Walker, 1982; Foster, 1983). In more recent years the analytical and political responses to consumer charges have been muted, not out of apathy or altered preferences but simply because critics of the kind of privatisation that characterises the Thatcher years have bigger fish to fry. Anyway, increases in consumer charges do not address one of the other tenets of Thatcherism that many public bureaucracies are inherently inefficient and need to be replaced by private or voluntary agencies. It is not enough merely to trim them by persuading consumers to meet a higher proportion of costs.

Health service charges

Parker's (1976) review of consumer charges distinguished five linked objectives for such a policy: to raise revenue, to reduce demand, to shift priorities, to check abuse and improve regulation, and to act as symbols. Each of these objectives has some relevance to charging policies in the NHS, though one suspects that recent price increases have revenue-raising as their primary purpose. The same would apply to local authority policies which have raised charges for meals services, home help and some day care. The problem that such an objective poses is that a large number of health and social care clients are exempted from charges on the grounds of low income or pensionable status, and many of the others respond to price increases by postponing or reducing consumption to the detriment of their and the nation's health. The higher the price elasticity of demand the greater this reduction. Empirical estimates of this elasticity for Britain are very tentative, but suggest that a 10 per cent increase in prescription charges will reduce demand for prescriptions by between 1 and 2 per cent (Birch, 1986). When we notice that prescription charges increased by over 550 per cent in real terms between 1979 and 1986, the impact on the social efficiency of the NHS would, by these figures, have been enormous. Over the same period the maximum charge for dental treatment doubled in real terms (King's Fund Institute, 1988).

A further point to note about the revenue raising objective of consumer charges is that administrative costs will eat into revenue receipts thus reducing, perhaps considerably, the net impact on public expenditure. On these grounds the inflation of existing charges or the restriction of exemptions are more attractive options than the introduction oof new charges for, say, the 'hotel' component of in-patient hospital stays. For example, charges introduced for overseas users of the health service were expected to raise the modest sum of £6 million per annum, but the NHS in fact netted only £1.5 million after direct administrative outlays had been deducted.

We can therefore see that a form of privatisation as modest in its intentions (when compared with other forms) as the inflation of charges to public service users can damage both efficiency and distributional objectives of the NHS. It may be a laudable aim to expect those who can afford to pay for services to contribute to their costs, but the instruments of policy to date have been too blunt, and it is unlikely that any sharper instrument could be employed at an affordable administrative cost.

Contracting-out

There are four varieties of contracting-out, although each raises similar issues of ideology and practice. The most specific contracts are those drawn up after *competitive tendering* for, say, hospital catering, refuse collection, vehicle maintenance or school cleaning. The tasks to be undertaken by the contractor are clearly identified at the outset, quantity and quality requirements may be laid out and penalty clauses will be agreed. Public agencies do not always award contracts to the lowest bidder and, with experience, have become more adept at negotiation and contract supervision (Hartley and Huby, 1985). The Local Government Act, 1988, extended the range of services to be put out to competitive tender, so local authorities will have to extend their newly acquired skills. But skills developed in relation to the competitive tendering for services with such a readily monitored output as cleaning or catering will be of only limited relevance to other forms and areas of contracting-out. *Vendor reimbursement* is a common form of contracting in welfare contexts. It is payment of an agreed price per unit of service: a local authority may contract to place children in homes run by the National Children's Home at a fee agreed on behalf of all authorities by the London Borough of Islington. Less specific is contracting with *delegate agencies* which assume total responsibility for meeting the needs of a particular client group – the deaf, people with AIDS, children abused by their parents – in return for a lump sum payment to cover all or part of the contractor's costs. Finally, there are smaller *grants* paid to voluntary or private agencies to enable them to provide services which either substitute for or complement statutory provision (see Judge, 1982, on contracting types). With delegate agencies and smaller grants the contractual link between public agency and contractor is rarely very specific and quality is most likely to be monitored informally and irregularly.

There is no shortage of ideological foundation to support policies of contracting-out: there are many who maintain that non-public agencies which have to compete for contracts will be more efficient in production and more responsive to the demands of consumers. But there is only limited evidence to bolster these contentions. Consider the most common rationales for contracting-out (see Knapp, Robertson and Thomason, 1989, for a fuller account).

Choice

A common and potentially strong argument for contracting-out is that it increases the available choices to consumers. This can be seen in the health and social care fields. Services may be distinguished by religion (the Jewish Welfare Board, Salvation Army, Methodist Homes for the Elderly, to name but a few); by culture or ethnicity (West Indian Concern, the Community Health Group for Ethnic Minorities); by ideology (compare the Royal Masonic Hospital and the Socialist Health Association); by industry or employment (Railcare, the Bank Clerks' Orphans' Fund, the Sailors' Children's Society, the Coal Industry Social Welfare Organisation); or simply by treatment preference (the British Acupuncture Association, the National Childbirth Trust, Exit, and private or voluntary hospital treatment financed by insurance companies, which are themselves mostly voluntary bodies). In many cases, simply by not being a statutory agency, a voluntary or private body will be attractive to those in need. State health and social care services sometimes carry a stigma for the middle classes, many of whom may prefer the Marriage Guidance Council to the social work department, the child-minder to the local authority nursery, and the Brook Advisory Clinic to the NHS family planning clinic. James (1987) found the voluntary schools sector to be bigger in countries with a more heterogeneous population.

But what happens when governments contract out in order to promote choice? We must remember that governments often took responsibility in the first place because they were not happy to leave the service to market forces. In social policy contexts, the government takes responsibility partly because the users of services – school pupils, hospital patients, old people's home residents – might not be able to act with sufficient competence or power as consumers. They often cannot make their views known and cannot easily move to another supplier. So, on the one hand, the government wants to promote choice, but on the other hand it must recognise that the consumer may find it difficult to exercise choice. It must regulate the quality of service. The problem is that there is now enough evidence to suggest that government regulation of private and voluntary producers of services can greatly interfere with their patterns of working. In particular, the government will require that they meet certain standards. In the extreme this makes the non-public producers more and more alike, and more and more similar to the government's chosen style, quality or orientation of service. It is also likely to encourage faithful adherence to those practices which are readily subjected to monitoring to the neglect of other objectives or activities. In other words, government regulation of quality can *reduce* choice and variety. The paradox is clear. Governments sometimes contract-out in order to promote consumer choice. Promoting choice should, in principle, raise the efficiency of service systems, since consumers should, in principle, be more contented with the service they receive. But governments have to regulate quality and the regulation process itself can create inappropriate or at least inadequate incentives, and can have the effect of *narrowing* choice.

Innovation

It is often claimed that non-public agencies are more likely to experiment and innovate and therefore raise the efficiency of systems of services by reducing costs, improving quality, or improving the welfare of consumers. There are plenty of examples of new ideas which have been pioneered by voluntary organisations or the private sector. But the policy question is whether these sectors are *more* innovative than the public sector. It seems most likely that a *multiplicity* of service providers – in whatever sectors – offers the best chance of innovation and accompanying efficiency gains.

Can contracting-out encourage innovation? In principle it is easy to see how, say, a local authority can finance new or innovative services offered by non-public agencies. But contracting-out may or may not create an environment conducive to further, unplanned or spontaneous innovation. It can leave voluntary and private agencies either with very *specific* tasks which are not at all new, or it can give the public agency such control over the voluntary or private sectors – through its accountability and regulation requirements – that they merely copy the public style of service. Alternatively, it could mean that organisations face financial insecurity. Many public contacts are only *short term* and in these circumstances the non-public contractor may be afraid to experiment. They cannot afford to take the risk of failure. *Long-term* government funding, on the other hand, may encourage complacency.

Thus, contracting-out *can* encourage innovation – and that includes innovations which improve efficiency, a particular and legitimate concern of governments during the 1980s – but this is not inevitable and there are dangers that contracting-out *reduces* innovation.

Cost-effectiveness

The final justification for contracting-out considered here (and there are others that have been neglected, such as flexibility, participation and advocacy) is that public agencies believe that private and voluntary producers are more 'cost-effective' – they are more efficient in the narrower technical sense of productive efficiency. It is thus often argued either that private and voluntary agencies can produce services of identical quality at lower cost, or they can improve quality for the same cost, or they can simultaneously lower cost and raise quality. These are all *beliefs* about the relative efficiency of public, voluntary and private sector producers. They stem from basic assumptions such as a less bureaucratic and slimmer administration, a supply of free or cheaper labour for voluntary organisations, fewer constraints from trade unions, and the incentives offered to managers in the private sector to raise profits.

What is the evidence? There is a growing volume of evidence from schools, old people's homes, nursing homes, hospitals, universities, and from a number of countries. In a moment we will consider residential child care. It is important to notice that some of the apparent cost-effectiveness differences between sectors are due to the fact that they are producing slightly different services or serving different groups of people. For example, some studies in the USA and the Netherlands suggest that private or voluntary schools get better examination results than public schools. But most of this difference is due to the fact that non-public schools take children who are better qualified at the time they enter and have better facilities at home and better parental support. Another example is provided by the observation that voluntary old people's homes in England are cheaper than local authority homes, but they also provide services for people who are less dependent (Knapp, Montserrat, Darton and Fenyo, 1987). So before we can say whether one sector is more efficient than another we must be clear that we are comparing like with like. When studies *have* made valid comparisons, they have not produced clear support or rejection of the cost-effectiveness assumption for contracting-out. In some areas of work the private or voluntary sector has been shown to be more cost-effective than the public; in other cases less cost-effective. One generalisation *does* look possible. Most of the evidence suggests that private producers are more cost-effective than voluntary. But before policy makers rush off to contract-out to the private sector it must be said that when production processes are complex and when effects or outcomes are hard to measure and observable only over a long period of time – and these conditions apply almost tautologically in welfare contexts – the private sector represents a bigger risk than the voluntary. The private sector may want to cut corners in order to increase its profits, to the obvious detriment of clients. One very interesting study looked at private and voluntary nursing homes in Wisconsin (USA). Weisbrod and Schlesinger (1986) found that voluntary establishments were *less* likely to comply with state regulations regarding numbers of staff, facilities, and so on, but were also *less* likely to have complaints from residents. In terms of the well-being of residents, the private nursing homes appeared not to be performing as well as the voluntary.

Most empirical research shows that efficiency differences are bigger *within* sectors than between them. If a government department's only objective is to improve efficiency it could have a greater impact if it put its *own* house in order rather than engage in contracting-out. Of course, this could only be a short-term option and in the longer term contracting-out may well be deserving of encouragement. Indeed, many of the efficiency improvements that have undoubtedly been achieved in the British public sector in

Table 9.3 *Total public sector support for voluntary organisations 1983–6*

	£m
Central government departments	268
Non-departmental public bodies	1,574
Local authorities	318
Health authorities	25
(Total direct support	2,185)
Tax exemptions	795
Support 'in kind' – local authorities	159
– health authorities	12
(Total indirect support	966)
Total public sector support	3,151

Source: Knapp, Robertson and Thomason (1989).

Table 9.4 *Growth in public sector support for voluntary organisations*

	76–77	79–80	80–81	81–82	82–83	83–84	84–85	85–86
Central government								
Direct support (£m)[1]	93	167	175	181	182	202	238	268
Annual growth (%)		21.3	5.1	3.3	0.8	10.6	17.7	12.8
Support as proportion of total central government expenditure (%)	0.2	0.4	0.4	0.4	0.4	0.4	0.5	0.6
NDPBs[2]								
Direct support[1]					1,020	1,607	1,566	1,574
Annual growth (%)						57.5	−2.6	0.4
Local authorities								
Direct support (£m)[1]						392	454	318
Annual growth (%)							15.8	−30.0
Health authorities								
Direct support (£m)[1]							12	25
Annual growth (%)								100.5

1. At 1985 or 1985–86 prices.
2. Non-departmental public bodies (quangos)

Source: Knapp, Robertson and Thomason (1989), extracted from Charities Aid Foundation annual publications.

recent years have been possible because successful practices have been copied from the private or voluntary sectors or because the threat or reality of competition has precipitated change.

There are *indirect costs* of contracting to be carried by the public sector. It must advertise for tenders, draw up and enforce contracts, and monitor quality. Some private and voluntary services need *specialist* inputs from the public sector. Children placed in a voluntary home for handicapped persons, for example, still need to be visited by their local authority social workers. At the same time, contracting-out raises costs in the *non*-public sectors. It can make them more bureaucratic because of the burden of contract compliance. It has also been observed in the US that salary bills increase. This is partly because contracting gives them the *ability* or *opportunity* to pay higher wages, partly because the government may demand they pay higher wages as a condition of contracting, and partly because trade unions establish themselves and campaign for better terms of employment (James and Rose-Ackerman, 1986). In addition, delays in payment by government – or only partial recompense of full costs – can leave non-public producers charging higher fees simply to cover their risks.

Consider now some examples of contracting-out.

Public funding of voluntary organisations

I totally reject the approach – still promoted in some quarters – which argues that the State should seek to take over all responsibility for the financing and the provision of care – that the existence of voluntary activity is somehow a cause for shame. To take that view would be to turn our backs on a wealth of willing voluntary supporters and would be to go against the wishes of many of those actually in need of care. We would fail to draw on those immense resources which are readily available in the community. A service of that kind would cut off a major source of new ideas and practices, as well as the chance to compare performance and to exchange opinions, which comes from the fact that there are several different potential providers of support. It would reduce the opportunities now open to so many tens of thousands of people to give something back to their own local community by participating in social support (Norman Fowler, then Secretary of State for Social Services, in a speech to the Joint Social Services Annual Conference, Buxton, 1984).

At a time when public expenditure was falling or static, the Thatcher Governments pushed more and more resources into the voluntary sector. Support comes in many forms – the varieties of contracting noted earlier plus local and central tax exemptions, income tax deductibles for covenants and donations, and transfers in kind – and from all parts of the public sector. This support is aggregated in Table 9.3. Hidden aid to voluntary organisations includes free premises and professional support, training programmes, photocopying and so on and can be substantial. Leat, Tester and Unell (1986) estimated that it could amount to as much as 50 per cent of total grant aid from a local authority. In addition, there are tax exemptions worth an estimated £795 million (Ashworth, 1985). Overall, public sector support to the voluntary sector amounted to about £3.2 billion in 1985–6, equivalent to around 7 per cent of total central government expenditure on goods and services (Knapp *et al.*, 1989a). This *excludes* public sector support through the demand side, such as third-party reimbursements (for example, board and lodging allowances) and other social security payments, vouchers and service credits.

Available figures do not allow the comprehensive plotting of trends in public support over time, but there is little doubt that there have been year on year increases from most government sources (see Table 9.4). Furthermore, direct grants to voluntary bodies have doubled as a proportion of central government expenditures over a ten year period, and the Thatcher administration has also sought to encourage *private* philanthropy.

Residential child care
A small proportion of the children in the care of local authority social services departments – an average of around 4 per cent in England and Wales – are living in residential homes run by voluntary organisations or the private sector. Although voluntary home charges are some 25 per cent lower than local authority costs and private sector fees are lower still, and although these differences appear to reflect *cost-effectiveness* differences (Knapp, 1986), social services departments place children in voluntary and private homes for a host of reasons not directly related to cost. The non-public sectors often offer a specialised service not available within a local authority's own provision; they are accredited with the ability to respond more flexibly and speedily to individual needs and other

circumstances; they offer a degree of choice; they are believed (not always based on evidence) to offer a superior standard of care; and they are used because they have always been used. Traditional patterns of care are very influential.

These reasons for placing some children in homes run by voluntary or private organisations are important determinants of practice, but costs have played an increasingly important part over the last few years. Analysis of data on all English local authorities found, on average, that a 10 per cent increase in the relative cost of voluntary sector fees to public sector costs will reduce a local authority's residential home placements in the voluntary sector by about 6 per cent (Knapp, *et al.* 1989b, ch. 9).

However, in this area of residential child care, contracting-out is on the wane. Falling numbers of children in local authority care since 1980 and a growing preference for foster rather than residential placements have brought about home closures in all three sectors. Most local authorities have preferred to keep their own homes full than contract-out, and the voluntary and private residential care sectors, over 90 pr cent of whose placements are sponsored by public agencies, have declined. At the same time, the cost-effectiveness advantage enjoyed by the non-public sectors is being eroded as local authorities get more cost-conscious, bargaining over fees, and as voluntary and private homes offer conditions of employment which more closely mirror those in the public sector.

Competitive tendering in the NHS

In 1984, Kenneth Clark, then junior Minister of Health, set out the Government's policy 'that the NHS should contract out all services where this can be shown to be cost-effective and operationally sound' (Hansard, col. 589). But despite the prominence given in 1979 to the contracting-out of NHS domestic services – catering, laundry and cleaning – and a series of letters and circulars in the early 1980s, by 1987 only about half of these services had been put out to competitive tender and about 80 per cent of the contracts had been won by in-house bids from health service employees (Key, 1987). This 'scoresheet' of contracts awarded, as Key argues, is not an adequate appraisal of this policy, but to date nothing else is available. What is needed is a careful reckoning of the expenditure savings generated (is competitive tendering keeping

NHS costs down? what are the administrative costs of supervising contracts?), the impact on employees and employment levels generally (what redundancy costs are involved?) and the effects on quality of service (are media stories of dirty hospitals and inedible meals accurate and generalisable?). But what is *not* needed is any more unthinking, blinkered knee-jerk reactions against either competitive tendering or the *status quo*. To date the debate on NHS contracting out has generated a lot more heat than light.

Occupational sick pay
The Conservative governments of the 1980s sought to improve the target efficiency of social security through selective rather than universal benefits and to cut spending by transferring responsibilities. 'The basic principle [is] that social security is not a function of the state alone. It is a partnership between the individual and the state – a system built on twin pillars' (DHSS, 1985, p.1).

Proposals were made to devolve responsibility for retirement pensions, maternity benefit and occupational sick pay (OSP) to other agencies. In the case of OSP, earnings-related supplements were abolished in 1980 – with consequent public expenditure savings of perhaps £185 million per year (Confederation of British Industry, 1980) – and Statutory Sick Pay (SSP) was introduced in 1983. Employers are compelled to provide sick pay for the first 28 weeks of sickness and payments are refunded in full by reduced taxation and national insurance contributions. Because SSP is taxable the government anticipated significant savings in public spending (House of Commons Committee of Public Accounts, 1985). The actual gains proved to be rather small (Disney, 1987). The costs of administering the benefit now fall to employers, but the financial gains to the government are due less to this transfer of responsibility than to the introduction of taxable sickness benefits. Such financial gains as there have been would be wrongly attributed to the contracting out of responsibilities, for they could probably have been achieved within the previous, national insurance, arrangements (Bolderson, 1985). Occupational sick pay organised in this way was, however, found to command wide acceptance (Taylor-Gooby and Lakeman, 1988), and Disney and Webb (1988) found that, whereas in 1974 'occupations with higher than average rates of sickness had lower than average rates of occupational sick pay coverage, (this) relationship had disappeared by 1984'. The extension of market principles had apparently helped remove market failure.

Private prisons

In 1986 the House of Commons Home Affairs Select Committee made public its interest in the small number of privately-run prisons in the USA. MPs, Home Office officials, Prison Officers' Association members, and journalists were despatched to Louisiana and Tennessee. Few recalled Britain's own private prisons in medieval times. 'Jurisdictional franchises' were granted to landowners. Costs were met not from taxation but from fees charged to inmates, and higher fees guaranteed more comfortable incarceration (Harding, 1985). The US private prisons have not gone quite so far, nor is there any serious suggestion in Britain that market allocations could be appropriate. Contracting out, however, is on the policy agenda.

Today's debate centres on a number of supposed advantages of contracting out imprisonment: it would remove the burden of funding the construction of new prisons (well over £25 million per prison); it would simultaneously increase the number of prison places and so reduce overcrowding; it would improve the regime and standards of accommodation, food and discipline (as is argued to have occurred in the US); it would be more flexible and responsive to changing penal needs; it would side-step the 'bureaucratic inefficiency and systematic inertia' of the Prison Department; it would get around awkward and militant unions; and it would be cheaper to run because the private sector is inherently more efficient. At worst, supporters of privatisation argue, the private sector should be allowed to construct new prisons for the Home Office to staff and manage, for building costs and delays are argued to be rather smaller for private contracts than those associated with the beleaguered Property Services Agency.

The counter-arguments will be familiar to veterans of previous privatisation debates – fears of corruption, poorer quality services with poor outcomes, loss of public sector control over the provision of a service which is so inherently sensitive yet hidden from public accountability, and moral indignation that prisons simply should not be run for profit. There has been very little investigation of the supposed operating cost advantages – claimed to be as much as 20 per cent of state prison costs – and there are concerns that these could be achieved only by having lower staffing levels (Matthews, 1987). Anyway, the opposition points out, the assumptions upon which the privatisation case is built – our prison system is grossly overcrowded, therefore new prisons are needed and these are more efficiently located outside the public sector – fails to tackle the root of the problem: too many people are remanded and sentenced to Britain's prisons. Indeed, a privatisation policy may exacerbate it.

Market allocations

Introducing or raising consumer charges for public sector services, or funding contracted-out production from tax revenues, are undoubtedly pervasive and controversial facets of Conservative government welfare policies of the 1980s and early 1990s. But they are not enough to satisfy the majority of Tory backbenchers, nor are they the sum of Mrs Thatcher's approach to welfare. Free market forces lie at the heart of her economic policy and are believed to have a role to play in Britain's social policy. Adam Smith's description of the 'invisible hand' of the market goading the economy along to an efficient allocation of resources continues to have much appeal. The price mechanism is believed to efficiently match the demands of consumers with the supplies of producers, allowing actors on both sides of the exchange relationship to make their wants known. Subject to the removal of inequalities of access and opportunity, the market mechanism is argued to allow the full expression of choice, so promoting freedom and autonomy (Friedman and Friedman, 1980; Hayek, 1960).

For a market economy to fully achieve an efficient and just allocation of resources, a number of stringent conditions must be met. There are no circumstances in which all such conditions are simultaneously satisfied: consumers have insufficient information; 'externalities' or side-effects of consumption or production are not taken into account in setting prices; monopoly power is acquired by suppliers of certain goods and services, or trade unions wield monopsony power as suppliers of labour; and income, need and opportunity are far from equitably distributed. 'Residualisation' of the poor may be the price of freedom of choice for the rich. These drawbacks are recognised by most observers of Britain's welfare

services, and what is at issue is the *degree* to which market forces
may fail to achieve the desired end-states. Discussions of market
allocation mechanisms of welfare services often fall into the trap
of comparing the reality of one system with an idealisation of
the alternative. Tory reformers 'wishing to administer a brisk
restorative to the welfare state with a purging dose of market
principles' (Taylor-Gooby and Lakeman, 1988, p. 23) frequently
and mistakenly set today's public sector inadequacies against the
unattainable perfection of a properly functioning market complete
with equality of opportunity or access. Sentimental socialists are
wont to ignore many of the inherent problems of a universalist,
need-based system when opposing the onward march of the
market. These are caricatures but they are really not so far
from the positions adopted on many welfare reforms.

Health care

In the 1970s a major concern of the Labour governments was
the continued existence of NHS 'pay beds': private in-patients
treated in NHS hospitals by NHS staff. These had been built
into the original plans of the 1940s to attract consultants into the
new service and to discourage a parallel private system. Labour's
commitment to phase out pay beds was intended to prevent queue
jumping (lengthening waiting times for NHS patients) and to limit
the private practice activities of consultants. But this concern and
commitment had no discernible effect: the number of private
in-patients treated in public hospitals remained steady at around
100,000 a year from 1974 to 1979. By contrast, the number dropped
below 70,000 after seven years of Conservative administration.
This gave little cause for socialist celebration, for over the same
period spending on private health care more than trebled, the
number of persons covered by private medical insurance almost
doubled, and more than 50 new private hospitals were opened.
(It should be noted that almost all health insurance coverage
is provided by three voluntary sector agencies: British United
Provident Association, Private Patient's Plan and Western Provident Association. Many of the hospitals and registered nursing
homes labelled as private are also in fact voluntary agencies in
so far as they satisfy the non-distribution constraint.) The growth
in private medical insurance subscribers slowed after 1981, but

many of the long-term funding options suggested for health care include a substantial shift from public to private finance. Simply giving private policy holders the power to opt out of some of their national insurance contributions would greatly alter the system of provision (Brittan, 1988; Redwood, 1988).

Demographic trends and other pressures are clearly putting a major strain on the NHS. In these circumstances, the Thatcher Government elected in 1987 seriously considered sources of private funding to supplement tax and national insurance revenues. Extended consumer charges have been one response, as we saw earlier, and contracting out may help to cut spending levels, but many groups and individuals actively canvassed the introduction of market forces. The difficulty that all advocates of market forces for health care must face, however, is the almost unparalleled imbalance between, on the one hand, the powerful suppliers of medical care – the medical profession with its (thankfully) highly specialised technical knowledge of both health care needs and ways to meet them, and its oft-criticised but rarely dented restrictive practices – and, on the other, the consumer, tautologically below par at the point of demand but, even in the best of health, ignorant of the mysteries of medical treatment and unskilled through infrequency of contact in the ways of negotiation. Supplier-induced demand, in which health care professionals recommend and provide more health care than is actually needed (as defined by reference to society's criteria of equity and efficiency in meeting need), is a problem in the NHS, but the incentives for abuse in a free market look to be greater. Furthermore, patients have an incentive to collude with their doctors to get more and better medical treatment because of third-party payments by insurance companies. The opportunity for such collusion obviously also arises in today's NHS, but the centrally regulated service is supposed to help minimise this form of abuse.

One response to the cost inflation that supplier-induced demand and third party payments wrought on the US health care system has been the development of *health maintenance organisations* (HMOs). Individuals make annual lump sum payments to groups of doctors in return for comprehensive health care. The doctors have an incentive to contain costs if the HMO is in the private (for-profit) sector, and members of the HMO have an incentive to do likewise if it is non-profit (any surplus is ploughed back into the organisation). A number of people have considered the relevance of the HMO in Britain, but while it offers a solution to the inappropriate incentives inherent in a market system such as operates in the USA, does it really solve the problems facing the NHS? And if market forces have a part to play, might it not be worth testing their efficacy in *internal* NHS markets? (Bosanquet, 1986).

Table 9.5   *Residential accommodation for elderly and younger physically handicapped people in England and Wales 1977–85*

	Type of home			All homes
	Local authority	Voluntary	Private	
Number of homes				
1977	2,799	1,065	1,920	5,784
1981	2,861	1,161	2,609	6,631
1985	2,880	1,144	5,602	9,626
% change				
1977–81	2.2	9.0	35.9	14.6
1981–85	0.7	−1.5	114.7	45.2
Number of residents				
1977	11,4811	30,046	24,578	169,435
1981	11,5833	33,047	34,830	183,710
1985	11,3853	32,057	72,333	218,243
% change				
1971–81	0.9	10.0	41.7	8.4
1981–85	−1.7	−3.0	107.7	18.8

Sources: Department of Health and Social Security statistical collections.

Residential care for elderly people

Long-term institutional care for elderly people in the UK is provided in hospitals, nursing homes and residential care homes. The distinction between the second and third kinds of facilities remains, although legal restrictions on combining residential and nursing home facilities (outside the public sector) were removed in 1984. In the same year the first comprehensive code of practice was published to guide residential care in the non-public sectors (Centre for Policy on Ageing, 1984).

We focus on these *residential care* services here, but the large and growing private and voluntary nursing home and hospital sectors have equivalent policy importance.

Together the public, voluntary and private sectors manage some 10,000 residential homes, accommodating not far short of a quarter of a million persons (see Table 9.5). The residential care sector grew rapidly after 1981, due almost entirely to the dramatic increase in the private sector which more than doubled in size in just four years. The voluntary and public sectors have barely changed. Accordingly, the market share of the private sector grew from 14 to 33 per cent between 1979 and 1985.

Over the course of the 1980s the ageing population and fiscal trends did not allow local authorities to expand their provision in line with need. Excess demand built up rapidly. The *nature* of demand may also have changed – more elderly people have a preference and the wherewithal (through occupational pension schemes, generally higher standards of living and – crucially – a liberalisation of social security payments) to seek non-public accommodation. On the supply side, constraints on the voluntary sector allowed the private sector to reap the rewards of these changes. We have probably been seeing a *labour supply* constraint – volunteer or low-paid staff will have found other voluntary activities to be more attractive than residential care of the elderly (a long-standing problem for this sector) and those seeking a career in this service area may have been attracted by local authority rates of pay. Of far more importance has been the *capital* constraint. Voluntary bodies have always responded less rapidly than the private sector to sudden increases in demand. Although they are non-profit-distributing and, if registered as charities, not taxed on retained earnings, few voluntary bodies manage to build up size-able funds for new investment. In borrowing they enjoy no tax or other significant advantages over the private sector. Furthermore, the returns on equity capital – which of course are only available in the private sector – have proved very attractive, particularly as the waiting time and the risks involved are both very slight.

By the middle of the decade, approximately 12 per cent of residents in voluntary homes were sponsored by local authorities (through contracting-out – vendor reimbursement – arrangements), and a further 37 per cent received supplementary benefit (social security payments). Around 36 per cent of private home residents received supplementary benefit (Ernst and Whinney, 1986). Social security subsidies, unlike local authority contracting, operate on the demand side of the market and essentially introduce 'fourth party' payments: the elderly person consumes the service, the voluntary or private home supplies, the local authority social services department regulates the home and the local social security office assesses the resident's claim for support. Devising suitable incentive-based regulations in such a system is particularly problematic, and is at the heart of the Audit Commission (1986) and Griffiths (1988) reports, as we saw in Chapters 1 and 8.

What is interesting about this second example of a return to what is essentially a market allocation system, and a fairly successful return if that is what appeals, is that it happened more by accident than design. Spending on board and lodging payments had been creeping up. Day and Klein take up the story:

> In 1983 the DHSS decided to halt this spending creep. And, in what must be one of the neatest case studies of perverse policy outcomes, it introduced a new system. Each local social security office was asked to set limits reflecting the highest reasonable charge for suitable accommodation in the area. Most social security offices knew little about the structure of charges; there was some frantic ringing around; figures were, often somewhat arbitrarily, invented. The result was a leap in the level of allowable payments, with large variations between different offices. While before the 1983 policy change, most offices had worked to a ceiling of about £65 a week for people in residential and nursing homes – the same limit as that for ordinary board and lodging allowances – the new local limits ranged up to £215 a week for residential homes and £290 for nursing homes. Not surprisingly, the owners of homes put up their charges in line with the limits: the maximum quickly became the average (1987, p.19).

The DHSS soon regained control over payments, but an enormous and irreversible cost explosion had occurred, and the 1983 changes had drawn attention to the social security entitlements for many elderly people. Private residential homes opened quickly to meet the new demand, but it is by no means clear that this greatly expanded market has significantly extended opportunities for exercising consumer choice to all (potential) residents. It has certainly offered the choice of private or voluntary sector care to a number of elderly people who would never previously have contemplated such a domicile, but the outcome may not be ideal either for residents or for public spending. Many people remain unconvinced by Bradshaw and Gibbs' (1988) findings that only a small proportion of recently admitted residents of private and voluntary homes were inappropriately sucked into residential care. (To be fair, many local authority home residents are similarly inappropriately placed.) Even if these misgivings about choice and appropriateness of placement prove unfounded, there remain the huge problems of quality assurance and public accountability. This is a market that cannot be left unfettered.

Housing

The final example of the extension of market principles under Mrs Thatcher's stewardship is also the most dramatic. Between 1979–80 and 1984–5, total public spending on housing was halved, with the biggest decrease being in central government subsidies to local authority housing (Robinson, 1986). Rent subsidies for public sector tenants fell by 80 per cent in real terms over this five year period, new public housing starts fell, sales of council houses rocketed and private sector rent controls were eased (Flynn, 1988, offers a useful review). Yet housing provides students of social policy with one of their best examples of market failure. Housing is expensive and incomes are unevenly distributed, generating marked housing *inequities,* and huge subsidies are paid through mortgage interest tax relief to those who least need them. At the same time, market *inefficiencies* stem from imperfections in the capital market (excessive caution on the part of lenders), consumer ignorance and the difficulties of getting accurate and unbiased information from estate agents, externality problems (the state of my house effects the value of my neighbour's house), and inelasticities of supply so that shortages of housing are more likely to push up costs than stimulate new building (Le Grand and Robinson, 1984, ch. 4). So a sector which is already beset with distributional problems has been further polarised, and the marked inefficiencies in the market have not been tackled. But the political pay-offs for the Conservative administrations have been tremendous, for the market failures work to the benefit of the majority: the owner-occupiers (accounting for two-thirds of the housing stock) with their £5 billion worth of tax allowances on mortgage interest payments.

> Local authority tenants are a residual, marginalised and stig-matised minority, whereas owner occupiers (whatever the condition of their property and their own resources) are economically advantaged and ideologically privileged. It is therefore highly unlikely for there to be much effective oppo-sition to recent policies of privatisation, or conversely, support for increased expenditure on public housing and removal of tax subsidies for home owners (Flynn, 1988, p.307).

Even when markets fail famously there may be no incentive for change.

Conclusion

Mrs Thatcher's governments of the 1980s brought about bigger changes to the mixed economy of welfare than had been since the 1940s. Many of those changes have been examined in the wide-ranging contributions to this book. A general theme and con-clusion has been throughout that private and voluntary providers or producers of services have acquired larger, and in some cases now the *largest*, market shares. Private and non-state (uncoerced) collective sources of finance account for higher proportions of total spending on welfare services. Dyed in the wool socialists would do well to recognise the undoubted successes within this huge social experiment. Blue-rinse Conservatives should acknowledge and seek to correct the failings. The prospects for Britain in the 1990s would be rosiest if research replaced rhetoric, and honest pragmatism replaced posturing.

Select Bibliography

1 Personal Social Services

Anderson, M.J. (ed) (1986) *The Unfinished Agenda: Essays in Honour of Arthur Seldon,* London, Institute of Economic Affairs.

Audit Commission (1985) *Managing Social Services for the Elderly More Effectively,* London, HMSO.

Audit Commission (1986) *Managing Social Work More Effectively: A Pilot Study Report,* London, HMSO.

Audit Commission (1986) *Making A Reality of Community Care,* London, HMSO.

Balloch, S. *et al.* (1985) *Caring for Unemployed People,* London, AMA.

Becker, S. and MacPherson, S. (1986) *Poor Clients,* Benefits Research Unit, University of Nottingham.

Beveridge, W.H. (1942) *Social Insurance and Allied Services,* Cmnd 6404, London, HMSO.

Bosanquet, N. (1983) *After the New Right,* London, Heinemann.

Central Statistical Office (1988) *Social Trends 18,* London, HMSO.

Conservative Party (1949) *The Right Road For Britain,* London, Conservative Central Office.

Conservative Party (1979) *The Conservative Manifesto 1979,* London, Conservative Central Office.

Conservative Party (1987) *The Conservative Manifesto 1987,* London, Conservative Central Office.

Cowling, M. (ed) (1978) *Conservative Essays,* London, Cassell.

DHSS (1985) *Reform of Social Security,* Cmnd nos 9517-9519, London, HMSO.

DHSS (1986) *Neighbourhood Nursing: A Focus for Care.*

DHSS (1987) *Promoting Better Health,* Cmnd 249, London, HMSO.

Fimister, G. (1986) *Welfare Rights Work in Social Services* Macmillan.

Firth, J. *et al.* *(1987) Report of the Joint Central and Local Govt. Working Party on Public Support for Residential Care,* London.

Fowler, N. (1984) *The Enabling Role of Social Services Departments,* speech to the Joint Social Services Annual Conference, Buxton, 27 September 1984. (London, DHSS)

Fowler, N. (1986) *Speech to the National Young Conservative Conference*, Blackpool, February.
Fowler, N. (1986) *Speech to the Joint Social Services Conference* Cardiff, 19 September, on the theme of 'community care'
Gamble, A. (1974) *The Conservative Nation* Routledge Kegan Paul.
Gilbert, N. (1983) *Capitalism and the Welfare State: Dilemmas of Social Benevolence,* Yale University Press.
Griffiths, R. (1988) *Community Care: Agenda for Action*, London, HMSO.
Gummer, J.S. (1973) 'A Conservative approach to the social services', *Political Quarterly*, December.
Harris, R. and Seldon, A. (1979) *Over-ruled on Welfare*, London, Institute of Economic Affairs.
House of Commons (1984–5) Social Services Committee, *Community Care* paper 13, 3 vols, London, HMSO.
House of Commons (1984–5) Social Services Committee, *Misuse of Drugs*, paper 208, London, HMSO.
House of Commons (1986–7) Social Services Committee, *Problems Associated with AIDS*, paper 182, 3 vols, London, HMSO.
Judge, K. and Mathews, K. (1980) *Charging for Social Care: A Study of Consumer Charges and the PSS,* London, Allen and Unwin.
Le Grand, J. (1982) *The Strategy of Equality,* London, Allen and Unwin.
Le Grand, J. and Robinson, R. (1984) *Privatisation and the Welfare State*, London, Allen and Unwin.
Loney, M. (1987) *The State or the Market: Politics and Welfare in Contemporary Britain,* London, Sage.
Macmillan, H. (1938) *The Middle Way*, London, Macmillan.
McCarthy, M. (1986) *Campaigning For The Poor*, London, Croom Helm.
McCarthy, M. (1986) *Cycle of Desperation: Hard Drugs, Social Work Today* Supplement 17 February.
McCarthy, M. (1987) '*The Economy, Social Services and Taxation, Social Work Today*, 23 November.
McCarthy, M (1987) '*Community Care For People with a Mental Handicap*', Paper to Price Waterhouse Conference 'Care in the Community: Partnership with the Mentally Handicapped', London 9 June 1987.
Moore, J. (1987) *Speech on the Future of the Welfare State to a Conservative Political Centre Conference,* 26 September, London.
Parker, R.A. (1976) 'Charging for the social services', *Journal of Social Policy* vol. 5, pt. 4, October.
Pym, F. (1985) *The Politics of Consent*, London, Sphere.
Ridley, J. and McCarthy, M. (1986) *Unemployment and the Personal Social Services,* Birmingham, BASW.
Scruton, R. (1980) *The Meaning of Conservatism*, Harmondsworth, Pelican.
Seebohm, L. *et al.* (1968) *Report of the Committee on Local Authority and Allied Personal Social Services,* Cmnd. 3703, London, HMSO.
Tawney, R.H. (1952) *Equality,* London, Unwin Books.

Taylor-Gooby, P. (1985) *Public Opinion, Ideology and State Welfare,* London, Routledge.
Townsend, P. (1974) 'The social underdevelopment of Britain', *New Statesman,* 1 March.
Treasury, H.M. (1984) *The Next Ten Years: Public Expenditure and Taxation into the 1990s,* Cmnd 9189, London, HMSO.
Wagner, L. *et al.* (1988) *Residential Care: A Positive Choice,* London, HMSO.
Walker, A. (1985) *The Care Gap* Local Government Information Unit.
Wilding, P. (ed.) (1986) *In Defence of the Welfare State,* Manchester University Press.
Wilensky. H.L. (1975) *The Welfare State and Equality,* Berkeley, California, University of California Press.

2 Health

Abel-Smith, B. (1988) 'A new regime', *New Society,* 29 April, pp. 16–18.
Acheson, D. (1986) 'Aids: a challenge for public health', *The Lancet,* 2 March, pp.662–6.
Adam Smith Institute (1988) *The Health of Nations,* Box 316, London 5WIP 3DI
Allsop, J. and May, A. (1986) *The Emperor's New Clothes: Family Practitioner Committees in the 1980s,* King's Fund Centre, 113 Albert Street, London NW1.
Agriculture Committee, House of Commons (1987) *The Effect of Pesticides on Human Health,* second special report, session 1986–7, vol. I, London, HMSO.
Audit Commission for England and Wales (1986) *Making a Reality of Community Care,* London, HMSO.
Bachrach, P. and Baratz, M. (1971) *Power and Poverty: Theory and Practice,* London, OUP.
Barnard, K. and Wood, J. (1985) *Family Practitioner Committees 1-7 A Guide For Members,* Bristol, National Health Service Training Authority.
Birch, S. (1986) 'Increasing patient charges in the NHS: a method of privatising primary care', *Journal of Social Policy,* vol. 15 no. 2, pp.163–84.
Birch, S. and Maynard, A. (1986) *The RAWP Review,* Discussion Paper, Centre for Health Economics, University of York.
Bosanquet, N. (1985) *Public Expenditure on the NHS: Recent Trends and the Outlook.* London, Institute of Health Services Management.
Carr-Hill, R. (1987) 'The Inequalities in Health Debate: a critical review of the issues', *Journal of Social Policy,* vol. 16, no. 4, pp.509–42.
Carrier, J. (1978) 'Positive Discrimination in the Allocation of NHS Resources', in M. Brown and S. Baldwin (eds) *The Yearbook of Social Policy in Britain 1977,* London, Routledge.

256   *Select Bibliography*

Centre for Policy Studies (1988) *Britain's Biggest Enterprise: ideas for radical reform of the NHS,* 6 Wilfred Street, London SW1 EPL.
Central Statistical Office (1988) *Social Trends,* 18, London, HMSO.
Crossman, R.H.S. (1972) *A Politician's View of Health Service Planning,* University of Glasgow.
DHSS (1976) *Priorities for Health and Personal Social Services in England,* a consultative document, London, HMSO.
DHSS (1976) *Sharing Resources for Health in England,* report of the resource allocation working party, London, HMSO.
DHSS (1979) *Patients First,* a consultative paper, London, HMSO.
DHSS (1980) *Inequalities in Health,* report of a research working group (Chair: Sir Douglas Black) London, DHSS.
DHSS (1981) *Care in Action,* a handbook of policies and priorities for the health and personal social services in England, London, HMSO.
DHSS (1983) *NHS Management Inquiry Report* London, HMSO.
DHSS (1983–5) *Reports of the Steering Group on Health Services Information* (Chair: Mrs E. Korner, London, HMSO).
DHSS (1986) *Neighbourhood Nursing – A Focus for Care* (Chair: Mrs Julia Cumberlege) London, HMSO.
DHSS (1986a) *Primary Health Care: An Agenda for Discussion,* Cmnd, 9771, London, HMSO.
DHSS (1987) *Promoting Better Health,* the Government's programme for improving primary health care, Cmnd 249, London, HMSO.
DHSS (1988) *Public Health in England.* The report of the Committee of inquiry into the development of the public health function, Cmnd 289, London, HMSO.
Doll, R. (1988) 'Major epidemics of the twentieth century from coronary thrombosis to AIDS', *Social Trends,* 18, pp.13–21.
Elcock, H. and Haywood, S. (1980) *The Buck Stops Where?: Accountability and Control in the NHS,* University of Hull, Institute of Health Studies.
Gretton, J., and Harrison, A. (1987) 'How far have the frontiers of the state been rolled back between 1979–1987? *Public Money,* December.
Griffiths, R. (1988) *Community Care: Agenda for Action,* A report to the Secretary of State for Social Services, London, HMSO.
Hunter, D.J. (1982) *Coping with Uncertainty,* Policy and Politics in the NHS Research Studies Press, Leicester, John Wiley.
Hunter, D.J. and Wistow, G. (1987) *Community Care in Britain:* London, King Edwards Hospital Fund for London.
Jennet, B. (1984) *High Technology Medicine: Benefits and Burdens,* Oxford, Nuffield Provincial Hospital Trust.
Laing, W. (1985) *Private Health Care,* London, Office of Health Economics.
Le Grand, J. (1982) *The Strategy of Equality,* London, Allen and Unwin.
McKeown, T. (1979) *The Role of Medicine,* Oxford, Basil Blackwell.
Macnichol, J. (1987) 'In pursuit of the under-class', *Journal of Social Policy,* Vol. 16, No.3, pp.293–318.

Maynard, A. (1987) 'Logic in Medicine: an economic perspective', *British Medical Journal,* 295, pp.1537–41.

Mays, N. and Bevan, G. (1987) *Resource Allocation in the Health Service,* a review of the methods of the resource allocation working party. Occasional papers on Social Administration, London, Bedford Square Press.

National Audit Office (1986) *Value for Money Developments in the NHS,* Report by the Controller and Auditor General, London, HMSO.

NHS Management Board (1986) *Review of the Resource Allocation Working Party Formula,* Report, London.

Office of Health Economics (1987) *Compendium of Statistics,* 6th edn, (London, OHE.

Owen, D. (1976) *In Sickness and in Health: The Politics of Medicine,* London, Quartet.

Powell, E. (1966) *A New Look at Medicine and Politics,* London, Pitman.

Radical Statistics Group (1987) *Facing the Figures: What's Really Happening in the NHS?,* BSSR, 25 Horsell Road, London, N5 1XL.

Robinson, R. and Judge, K. (1987) *Public Expenditure and the NHS,* trends and prospects, London,Kings Fund Institute for Health Policy Analysis.

Royal Commission on the National Health Service (1979) Report (Chair Sir Alec Merrison) Cmnd 7615, London, HMSO.

Social Services Committee House of Commons (1986) *Public Expenditure on the Social Services,* Fourth report session – 1985–6, vol. I, London, HMSO.

Social Services Committee House of Commons (1988) *Resourcing the NHS: Short Term Issues,* First Report, vol. I, London, HMSO.

Taylor-Gooby, P. (1987) *'Citizenship and Welfare'* in R. Jowell, S. Witherspoon and L. Brooks (eds) *British Social Attitudes 1987,* Aldershot, Gower.

Therborn, G. and Roebrock, J. (1986) 'The irreversible welfare state' *International Journal of Health Services,* 16, pp.319–36.

Thwaites, B. (1987) *The NHS: the end of the rainbow,* Institute of Health Policy Studies, University of Southampton.

Townsend, P., and Davidson, N. (1982) *Inequalities in Health,* Harmondsworth, Penguin.

Webb, A. and Wistow, G. (1982) *Whither State Welfare?* London, Royal Institute of Public Administration.

Wells, N. (1987) 'Changing patterns of disease' in G. Teeling Smith (ed.) *Health Economics: Prospects for the Future,* London, Croom Helm.

3 Housing

Association of Metropolitan Authorities (1986) *Housing Facts,* London.

258   *Select Bibliography*

Association of Metropolitan Authorities (1987) *A New Deal for Home-owners and Tenants,* London.
Association of Metropolitan Authorities (1987) *Greater London House Condition Survey,* London.
Bramley, G. and Paice, D. (1987) *Housing Needs in Non-Metropolitan Areas* School for Advanced Urban Studies, University of Bristol.
Conway, J. and Kemp, P. (1985) *Bed and Breakfast: Slum Housing of the 1980s,* London, SHAC.
Department of Environment (1986) *Housing and Construction Statistics 1976-86* London, HMSO.
Department of Environment, *Quarterly Housebuilding Statistics,* London, HMSO.
Department of Environment (1976, 1981) *English House Condition Surveys,* London, HMSO.
Department of Environment (1985) *Inquiry into the Condition of Local Authority Housing Stock,* London, HMSO.
GLC (1981–5) *Temporary Accommodation: Counting the Cost,* Housing Research and Policy Report 4, London.
House of Commons (1983) Written Answers, 25 November.
House of Commons (1985) Written Answers, 8 January.
House of Commons (1986) Written Answers, 12 May.
House of Commons (1987) Written Answers, 16 January.
Kelly, I. (1986) *Heading For Rubble,* London, CHAS.
Kemp, P. and Raynsford, N. (eds) (1984) *Housing Benefit: The Evidence,* London, Housing Centre Trust.
Kemp, P. (1988) *The Future of Private Renting,* University of Salford.
London Housing Research Unit (1987) *Survey of London Boroughs.*
McCarthy, M.A. (1986) 'On the brink of homelessness', *Social Work Today,* 20 January.
National Federation of Housing Associations (1985) *Inquiry into British Housing: the Evidence,* London.
National Federation of Housing Associations (1988) *A Profile of New Tenancies: the 1988 NFHA Census of New Lettings,* London.
Social Trends 17 (1987) London, HMSO.
Social Trends 18 (1988) London, HMSO.

4   Social Security

Berthoud R. (1985) *The Examination of Social Security,* London, Policy Studies Institute.
Booth A. and Smith R. (1985) 'The irony of the iron fist: social security and the coal dispute 1984–85', *Journal of Law and Society,* vol. 12, no.3.
Brown J. (1987) *The Future of Family Income Support,* London, Policy Studies Institute.
Burton J. (1988) '*File on Four*', *op.cit.*

Cohen R. and Davies R. 'The background' in R. Cohen and M. Tarpey (eds) *Single Payments: The Disappearing Safety Net*, London, CPAG.

Conservative Party (1974) *Campaign Guide*, London, Conservative Central Office, quoted in A. Deacon & J. Bradshaw, *op. cit.*

Conservative Party (1979) *The Conservative Manifesto 1979*, London, Conservative Central Office.

Conservative Party (1987) *The Conservative Manifesto 1987*, London, Conservative Central Office.

Daily Express (1987) 23 March.

Deacon A. and Bradshaw J. (1983) *Reserved for the Poor*, Oxford, Basil Blackwell and Martin Robertson.

Deakin N. (1987) *The Politics of Welfare*, London University.

Dean M. (1980) *Guardian*, 30 January.

Department of Employment (1988) *Training for Employment*, London, HMSO.

Department of the Environment (1987a) *Housing, the Government's Proposal* Cmnd 212, HMSO, London.

Department of the Environment (1987b) *Deregulation of the Private Sector Consultation Paper on the Implications for Housing Benefit*, London, DOE/DHSS/Welsh Office.

DHSS (1978) *Social Assistance*, London, DHSS.

DHSS (1985) *Reform of Social Security*, vol. 1, Cmnd 9517, London, HMSO.

DHSS (1987) Press Release on Social Security Bill 1987, 23 October, London, DHSS.

Donnison D. (1982) *The Politics of Poverty*, Oxford, Martin Robertson.

'File on Four' (1988) 9 and 10 February, BBC Radio 4.

Financial Times (1988) Editorial, 5 April.

Franey, R (1983) *Poor Law* London CPAG/CHAR.

Glendinning C. and Millar J. (1987) *Women and Poverty in Britain*, Brighton, Wheatsheaf.

Golding P. and S. Middleton (1982) *Images of Welfare*, Oxford, Basil Blackwell and Martin Robertson.

Golding P. (1983) 'Rethinking common sense about social policy' in D. Bull and P. Wilding (eds) *Thatcherism and the Poor*, London, CPAG.

Gordon P. and Newnham A. (1986) *Passport to Benefits*, London, CPAG/Runnymede Trust.

Griffiths R. (1988) *Community Care: Agenda for Action* (Griffiths Report), London, HMSO.

Guardian (1983) 17 February.

Guardian (1988) 25 February.

House of Commons Debates (1979) 12 June, col. 253.

House of Commons Debates (1987a) 25 November, written answers, col. 245.

House of Commons Debates (1987b) 27 November, col. 186.

House of Commons Debates (1987c) 30 November, written answers, col. 464.

House of Commons Debates (1988), 25 March, written answers, cols. 243–4.
Hurstfield J. (1987) 'Parenthood and part-time work: the Swedish approach', *Poverty*, no. 68, London, CPAG.
ILO (1984) *Into the 21st Century: The Development of Social Security*, Geneva.
The Independent (1987) 30 December.
Johnson P. (1985) *The Historical Dimensions of the Welfare State 'Crisis'*, London, Suntory Toyota International Centre for Economics and Related Disciplines/LSE.
Leadbeater C. (1987) 'In the land of the dispossessed', *Marxism Today*, April.
Marshall T.H. (1963) *Citizenship and Social Class*, Cambridge. Cambridge University Press.
McKnight J. (1985) 'The crisis in management' in S. Ward (ed) *DHSS in Crisis*, London, CPAG.
Moore J. (1987) Speech, 26 September, London, Conservative Central Office
Morley R. (1988) 'Charities, single payments and the social Fund' in R. Cohen and M. Tarpey (eds) *op, cit.*
Piachaud D. (1987a) 'The growth of poverty' in A. Walker and C. Walker, *op. cit.*
Piachaud (1987b) 'The Distribution of Income and Work', *Oxford Review of Economic Policy*, vol. 3, no. 3.
Pugh R. (1987) 'Financial Nightmares: legacy of an unsocial fund', *Community Care*, 10 December.
Scott N. (1987) Letter to Chair of SSAC, 25 August, London, DHSS.
Social Services Insight (1987), 18 December.
The Times (1984), 20 January.
The Times (1987), 7 December.
Timmins N. (1988) 'A harsh way to end the "dependency culture"', *The Independent*, 6 April.
Treasury, H.M. (1979) *The Government's Expenditure Plans 1979–80 to 1982–83*, Cmnd 7439, London, HMSO.
Walker C. (1987) 'Reforming social security – despite the claimant' in A. Walker and C. Walker, *op. cit.*
Walker A. and Walker C. (1987), *The Growing Divide*, London, CPAG.
Wicks M. (1987) *A Future for All*, Harmondsworth, Pelican.
Young G. (1987) *Guardian*, 20 November.

5   Employment

CBI (1984) *Attitudes Towards Unemployment*, London, Social Affairs Directorate.
Department of Employment (1987) *Action for Jobs*, London.
Employment Gazette (1987) November.

Goldman Sachs (1987) *The UK Economics Analyst*, London.
House of Commons Debates (1987) 18 November, col. 1074.
Department of Employment (1988) *Training for Employment*, Cmnd 316, London, HMSO.
Jangenes, B. (1986) *The Swedish Approach to Labour Market Policy*.
Lawson, N. (1985) HM Treasury mimeo. London.
Layard, R. (1987) *How To Beat Unemployment*, Oxford University Press.
Layard, R. (1988) *How to Beat Unemployment*, Campaign for Work pamphlet, no. 1, London.
MSC (1984) *Competence and Competition* London, HMSO.
Normington, D., Brodie, H.and O. Munro, J. (1986) *Value for Money in the Community Programme*, report to the Secretary of State for Employment and the Chairman of MSC.
Platt, S. (1984) 'Unemployment and suicidal behaviour: a review of the literature, *Social Science and Medicine*, 19–93–115.
Scott Samuel, A. (1984) 'Unemployment and health', *Lancet*, ii, pp.1464–5.
Smith, R. (1985) 'The physical health effects on the unemployed', *British Medical Journal*, vol. 291.
Unemployment Unit (1986) *Unemployment Bulletin*, no.22, Winter.
Unemployment Unit (1987) *Half Measures*, London.
Unemployment Unit (1987) *Trial By Restart*, London.

6 Education

Centre for Contemporary Cultural Studies (CCCS) (1981) *Unpopular Education*, London, Hutchinson.
Cox, C.B. and Dyson, A.E. (1969) *Fight for Education, A Black Paper*, Critical Quarterly Society.
Cox, C.B. and Dyson, A.E. (1970) *The Crisis in Education*, Black Paper 2, Critical Quarterly Society.
Cox, C.B. and Dyson, A.E. (1971) *Goodbye Mr Short* Black Paper 3, Critical Quarterly Society.
Cox, C.B. & Boyson, R. (1977) *Black Paper 1977*, Critical Quarterly Society.
Cox, C.B and Boyson, R. (1975) *Black Paper 1975, The Fight For Education* London, Dent.
Crosland, A. (1956) *The Future of Socialism*, London, Allen and Unwin.
David, M.E. (1980) *The State, the Family and Education*, London, Routledge.
David, M.E. (1983) 'The New Right, sex, education and social policy' in J. Lewis (ed.) *Women's Welfare, Women's Rights*, London, Croom Helm.
David, M.E. (1985) 'Motherhood and social policy: A matter of education?' *Critical Social Policy*, 12, Spring.

DES (1984) *Report by Her Majesty's Inspectors on the Effects of Local Authority Expenditure Policies on Education Provision in England 1983.*

Finch, J. (1984) 'The deceit of self-help: parental playgroups and working class mothers' *Journal of Social Policy*, vol. 13,pt 1, pp.1–21.

Gough, I. (1979) *The Political Economy of the Welfare State*, London, Macmillan.

Halsey, A.H. (ed.) (1972) *Educational Priority*, vol. 1, London, HMSO.

Knight, C. unpublished dissertation in preparation, *The Conservative Educationalists*, South Bank Polytechnic.

Mishra, R. (1984) *The Welfare State in Crisis*, Brighton, Wheatsheaf.

Spender, D. (ed.)(1981) *Men's Studies Modified*, Oxford, Pergamon.

Taylor Report (1977) *A New Partnership for our Schools*, London, HMSO.

Worsthorne, P. (1983). *The Sunday Times*, 27 February.

7   Criminal Justice

Statutes cited

Criminal Justice Act 1961
Children and Young Persons Act 1969
Criminal Law Act 1977
Criminal Justice Act 1982
Police and Criminal Evidence Act 1984
Sporting Events (Control of Alcohol etc.) Act 1985
Prosecution of Offences Act 1985
Drug Trafficking Offences Act 1986
Public Order Act 1986
Firearms Act 1988

Bibliography

Ashworth A. (1983) *Sentencing and Penal Policy*, London, Weidenfeld and Nicolson.

Aughey, A. and Norton, P. (1984) 'A settled polity: the Conservative view of law and order' in Norton P. (ed.) *Law and Order and British Politics*, Farnborough, Gower.

Baxter, J. and Koffman, L. (eds) (1985) *Police: the Constitution and the Community*, London, Professional Books.

Bottomley, K. and Pease, K. (1986) *Crime and Punishment: Interpreting the Data*, Milton Keynes, Open University Press.

Brody, S. (1976) *The Effectiveness of Sentencing: a Review of the Literature*, Home Office Research and Planning Unit, London, HMSO.

Brogden, M. (1982) *The Police: Autonomy and Consent*, London, Academic Press.

Butler, A.J.P. (1984) *Police Management,* Farnborough, Gower.
Christian, L. (1983) *Policing by Coercion,* London, GLC Police Support Unit.
Clarke R. and Hough, M. (1984) *Crime and Police Effectiveness,* Home Office Research and Planning Unit, London, HMSO.
Conservative Party (1979) *The Conservative Manifesto 1979,* London, Conservative Central Office.
Conservative Party (1987) *The Next Moves Forward,* London, Conservative Central Office.
Council of Europe (1987) *Rubrique Statistique du Bulletin d'Information Penitentiaire No. 8,* Centre de Recherches Sociologiques sur le Droit et les Institutions Penales, Janaury.
Crown Prosecution Service (1986) *Code for Crown Prosecutors,* London, HMSO.
Crown Prosecution Service (1987) *Annual Report 1986–7,* London, HMSO.
Curtis, L. (1986) 'Policing the streets' in Benyon J. and Bourn C. (eds) *The Police: Powers, Procedures and Proprieties,* Oxford, Pergamon.
Draper, H. (1978) *Private Police,* Harmondsworth, Penguin.
Her Majesty's Chief Inspector of Constabulary (1984) *Report for 1983,* HC 528, London, HMSO.
Home Office (1986) *Criminal Justice: A Working Paper,* 2nd ed., London, Home Office.
Home Office (1987) *Statistics on the Operation of Certain Powers under the Police and Criminal Evidence Act 1984, Second quarter 1987,* Home Office Statistical Bulletin, November.
Home Office Circulars: 114/1983 *Manpower, Effectiveness and Efficiency in the Police Service,* 14/1985 *The Cautioning of Offenders.*
Horton, C. and Smith, D. (1988) 'Evaluating police work' in Morgan R. and Smith D. (eds) *Coming to Terms with Policing,* London, Routledge.
Hough, M. and Mayhew, P. (1985) *Taking Account of Crime: key findings from the second British Crime Survey,* Home Office Research Study no. 85, London, HMSO.
House of Commons Committee of Public Accounts (1986), 13th Report, *The Financial Management Initiative,* London, HMSO.
House of Commons Home Affairs Committee (1987a) 3rd report, session 1986–7, *State and Use of Prisons,* London, HMSO.
House of Commons Home Affairs Committee (1987b) 4th report, session 1986–7, *Contract Provision of Prisons,* London, HMSO.
Jones Maclean and Young, J. (1986) *The Islington Crime Survey.*
King, R. and Morgan, R. (1980) *The Future of the Prison System,* Farnborough, Gower.
Kinsey, R. (1985) *Crime and Policing on Merseyside,* Merseyside Metropolitan Council.
Labour Party (1986) *Protecting Our People,* London, Labour Party.
Loveday, B. (1985) *The Role and Effectiveness of the Merseyside Police Authority,* Merseyside County Council.

Lustgarten, L. (1986) *The Governance of the Police,* London, Sweet and Maxwell.

May Committee (1979) *Report of the Committee of Inquiry into the United Kingdom Prison Services,* London, HMSO.

Morgan, R. (1983) 'How resources are used in the prison system' in *A Prison System for the 1980s and Beyond: the Noel Buxton Lectures 1982–3,* London, National Association for the Care and Resettlement of Offenders.

Morgan, R. (1987a) 'The local determinants of policing policy' in Willmott P. (ed.) *Policing and the Community,* London, Policy Studies Institute.

Morgan, R. (1987b) 'Police' in Parkinson M. (ed.) *Reshaping Local Government,* Newbury, Policy Journals.

Morgan, R. and King, R. (1987) 'Profits from prisons' *New Society,* 23 October.

Morgan, R. (1989) '"Policing by consent": legitimating the doctrine' in Morgan, R. and Smith, D. (eds) *Coming to Terms with Policing,* London, Routledge.

National Audit Office (1985) *Programme for the Provision of Prison Places,* London, HMSO.

National Audit Office (1986) *The Financial Management Initiative,* London, HMSO.

O'Higgins, M. (1983) 'Rolling back the welfare state: the rhetoric and reality of public expenditure and social policy under the Conservative government' in Jones, C. and Stevenson, J. (eds) *The Yearbook of Social Policy in Britain,* London, Routledge.

Oxford K. (1986) 'The power to police effectively' in Benyon, J. and Bourn, C. (eds) *The Police: Powers, Procedures and Proprietories,* Oxford, Pergamon.

Prime Minister (1982) *Efficiency and Effectiveness in the Civil Service,* London, HMSO.

Report of the Royal Commission on Criminal Procedure (1981), Cmnd 8092, London, HMSO.

Robinson, R. (1986) 'Restructuring the welfare state: an analysis of public expenditure 1979–80–1984–5', *Journal of Public Policy,* vol. 15, no.1.

Rutherford, A. (1986) *Prisons and the Process of Justice,* Oxford University Press.

Sinclair, I. and Miller, C. (1984) *Measures of Police Effectiveness and Efficiency,* Research and Planning Unit Paper no. 25, London, HMSO.

Spencer, S. (1985) *Called to Account: The Case for Police Accountability,* London, National Council for Civil Liberties.

Stern, V. (1987) *Bricks of Shame: Britain's Prisons,* Harmondsworth, Penguin.

Widdicombe Report (1986) *The Conduct of Local Authority Business,* Cmnd 9797, London, HMSO.

8 Community Care

Abrams, P. (1977) 'Community care: some research problems and priorities', *Policy and Politics*, no.6, pp.125–51.

ADSS (1986) *Who Goes Where?*, London, ADSS.

Allen, I. (ed) (1988) *Social Services Departments as Managing Agencies*, London, Policy Studies Institute.

Audit Commission (1986) *Making a Reality of Community Care*, London, HMSO.

Bradshaw, J. (1988) 'Financing private care for the elderly', Department of Social Policy and Social Work, University of York.

Bradshaw, J. and Gibbs, I. (1988) *Public Support for Private Residential Care*, Aldershot, Avebury.

Committee of Public Accounts (1988) *Community Care Developments*, HC300, London, HMSO.

Day, P. and Klein, R. (1987) 'The Business of Welfare', *New Society*, 19 June, pp.11–13.

DHSS (1976) *Priorities for Health and Personal Social Services in England*, London, HMSO.

DHSS (1977) *The Way Forward*, London, HMSO.

DHSS (1981a) *Care in the Community*, London, DHSS.

DHSS (1981b) *Growing Older*, Cmnd 8173, London, HMSO.

DHSS (1983) *Explanatory Notes on Care in the Community*, London, DHSS.

Edelman, M. (1977) *Political Language*, New York, Academic Press.

Fowler, N. (1984) *Speech to Joint Social Services Annual Conference*, 27 September, London, DHSS.

Gibbs, J. Evans, M. and Rodway, S. (1987) *Report of the Inquiry into Nye Bevan Lodge*, London, Southwark Council.

Gray, A.M. Whelan, A. and Normand, C. (1988) *Care in the Community: A Study of Services and Costs in Six Districts*, University of York, Centre for Health Economics.

Griffiths, Sir R. (1988) *Community Care: Agenda for Action*, London, HMSO.

Herman, H. and Lowe, M. (1986) *No Place Like Home*, London, House of Commons.

Harris, T. (1988) 'All quiet on the government front', *Insight*, 22 April, pp.14–15.

Jenkin, P. (1979) *Speech to Social Services Conference*, Bournemouth, 21 November.

Jenkin, P. (1980) *Speech to the Conference of the Association of Directors of Social Services*, 19 September.

Klein, R. (1983) *The Politics of the National Health Service*, London, Longman.

Larder, D. Day, P. and Klein, R. (1986) *Institutional Care of the Elderly: the Geographical Distribution of the Public/Private Mix in England*, University of Bath.

Le Grand, J. and Robinson, R. (1984) *Privatisation and the Welfare State*, London, Allen and Unwin.

Offe, C. (1984) *Contradictions of the Welfare State*, London, Hutchinson.

Qureshi, A. and Walker, A. (1989) *The Caring Relationship*, London, Macmillan.

House of Commons Social Services Committee (1980) *The Government's White Papers on Public Expenditure: The Social Services*, vol. II, HC 702, London, HMSO.

House of Commons Social Services Committee (1985) *Community Care*, HC 13–1, London, HMSO.

Titmuss, R.M. (1968) *Commitment to Welfare*, London, Allen and Unwin.

Treasury, HM (1979) *The Government's Expenditure Plans 1980–81*, Cmnd 7746, London, HMSO.

Utting, B. (1980) 'Changing ways of caring', *Health and Social Services Journal*, 4 July, p.882.

Wagner, G. (1988) *Residential Care A Positive Choice*, London, HMSO.

Valker, A. (ed.) (1982a) *Public Expenditure and Social Policy*, London, Heinemann.

Valker, A. (ed.) (1982b) *Community Care*, Oxford, Basil Blackwell and Martin Robertson.

Walker, A. (1983) 'A caring community' in H. Glennerster (ed.) *The Future of the Welfare State*, London, Heinemann, pp.157–72.

Walker, A. (1985) *The Care Gap*, London, Local Government Information Service.

Walker, A. (1986) 'More ebbs than flows', *Social Services Insight*, 29 March, pp.16–17.

Walker, A. (1986) 'Community care: fact and fiction' in P. Willmott (ed.) *The Debate About Community: Papers from a Seminar on 'Community in Social Policy*, London, Policy Studies PSI, pp.4–15.

Walker, A. (1987a) 'Community care policy towards people with mental handicaps: matching action to rhetoric', paper presented to Seminar on Care in the Community, Price Waterhouse, June.

Walker, A. (1987b) 'Enlarging the caring capacity of the community: informal support networks and the welfare state', *International Journal of Health Services*, vol. 17, no. 3, pp.369–86.

Webb, A. and Wistow, G. (1982) 'The personal social services: incrementalism, expediency or systematic social planning?' in A. Walker (ed.), (1982(a)) pp.137–164.

Webb, A. and Wistow, G. (1987) *Social Work, Social Care and Social Planning: The Personal Social Services Since Seebohm*, London, Longman.

Wilson, E. (1982) 'Women, the "Community" and the "Family"', in A. Walker (ed.) (1982b) pp.40–55.

9 Private and Voluntary Welfare

Ashworth, Mark (1985) 'Tax and charities', mimeo. London, Charities Aid Foundation.

Audit Commission (1986) *Making a Reality of Community Care,* London, HMSO.

Birch, Stephen (1986) 'Increasing patient charges in the National Health Service: a method of privatising primary care', *Journal of Social Policy,* vol.15, No2, pp.163–84.

Bolderson, Helen (1985) 'The state at one remove: examples of agency arrangements and regulatory powers in social policy', *Policy and Politics,* vol.13, no.1, pp.17–36.

Bosanquet, Nick (1986) 'GPs as firms: creating an internal market for primary care', *Public Money,* vol.5, no.4, pp.45–48

Bradshaw, Jonathon and Gibbs, Ian (1988) *Public Support for Private Residential Care,* Aldershot, Gower.

Brenton, Maria (1985) *The Voluntary Sector in British Social Services,* London, Longman.

Brittan, Leon (1988) *A New Deal for Health Care,* London, Conservative Political Centre.

Confederation of British Industry (1980) Submission on Government proposals set out in Cmnd 7864, London, CBI.

Day, Patricia and Klein, Rudolf (1987) 'Residential care for the elderly: a billion-pound experiment in policy-making, *Public Money,* vol.6, no.4, pp.19–24.

DHSS (1985) *Reform of Social Security* vol.1, Cmnd 9517, London, HMSO.

Disney, Richard (1987) 'Statutory sick pay: an appraisal', *Fiscal Studies,* vol.8, no.2, pp.58–76.

Disney, Richard and Webb, Steven (1988) 'Is there a market failure in occupational sick pay?', mimeograph, University of Kent at Canterbury and Institute for Fiscal Studies.

Ernst and Whinney, Management Consultants (1986) *Survey of Private and Voluntary Residential and Nursing Homes for the Department of Health and Social Security,* London.

Flynn, Rob (1988) 'Political acquiescence, privatisation and residualisation in British housing policy', *Journal of Social Policy,* vol.17, no.3, pp.289–312.

Foster, Peggy (1983), *Access to Welfare,* London, Macmillan.

Friedman, Milton and Friedman, Rose (1980) *Free to Choose,* Harmondsworth, Penguin.

Griffiths, Sir Roy (1988) *Community Care: Agenda for Action,* London, HMSO.

Hansmann, Henry (1980) 'The role of nonprofit enterprise' *Yale Law Journal,* 89, pp.835–901.

Harding, Christopher, Hines, Bill, Ireland, Richard and Rawlings, Philip (1985) *Imprisonment in England and Wales: A Concise History,*

London, Croom Helm.

Hartley, Keith and Huby, Meg (1985) 'Contracting-out in health and local authorities: prospects, progress and pitfalls, *Public Money*, vol.5, no.2, pp.23–6.

Hayek, Friedrich (1960) *The Constitution of Liberty*, London, Routledge.

House of Commons Select Committee of Public Accounts (1985) *Statutory Tenth Report of the Committee*, HC176 (1984–5 session) London, HMSO.

James, Estelle (1987) 'The nonprofit sector in comparative perspective', in Walter W. Powell (ed.) *The Nonprofit Sector*, Yale University Press.

James, Estelle and Rose-Ackerman, Susan (1986) *The Nonprofit Enterprise in Market Economies*, London, Harwood.

Judge, Ken (ed.) (1980) *Pricing the Social Services,* London, Macmillan.

Judge, Ken (1982) 'The public purchase of social care: British confirmation of the American experience', *Policy and Politics*, vol.10, no.4, pp.397–416

Judge, Ken and Matthews, James (1980) *Charging for Social Care*, London, Allen and Unwin.

Key, Tony (1987) 'Contracting out in the NHS, in Anthony Harrison and John Gretton (eds) *Health Care UK 1987*, Policy Journals, London.

King's Fund Institute (1988) *Health and Health Services in Britain, 1948–88*, London.

Knapp, Martin (1986) 'The relative cost-effectiveness of public, voluntary and private providers of residential child care',in Anthony Culyer and Bengt Jonsson (eds) *Public and Private Health Services,* Oxford, Blackwell.

Knapp, Martin, Baines, Barry, Fenyo, Andrew and Robertson, Eileen (1989), *The Costs of Child Welfare*, Aldershot, Gower.

Knapp, Martin, Montserrat, Julia, Darton, Robin and Fenyo, Andrew (1987), 'Cross-sector, cross-country efficiency comparisons: old people's homes in Catalunya and England and Wales, Discussion Paper 513, Personal Social Services Research Unit, University of Kent at Canterbury.

Knapp, Martin, Robertson, Eileen and Thomason, Corinne (1989) 'Public money, voluntary action: whose welfare?', in Helmut Anheier and Wolfgang Seibel (eds) *The Nonprofit Sector: International and Comparative Perspectives,* New York, de Gruyter.

Kramer, Ralph (1987) 'Voluntary agencies and the personal social services', in Walter W. Powell (ed.) *The Nonprofit Sector*, Yale University Press.

Leat, Diana, Tester, Susan and Unell, Judith (1986) *A Price Worth Paying?*, London, Policy Studies Institute.

Le Grand, Julian and Robinson, Ray (1984) *The Economics of Social Problems,* 2nd edn, London, Macmillan.

Matthews, Roger (1987) 'Criminal business', *New Society*, 2 January, pp.14–15.

Parker, Roy A. (1976) 'Charging for the social services', *Journal of Social Policy* vol.5 No.4, pp.359–73.

Redwood, J. (1988) *In Sickness and in Health: Managing Change in the NHS,* London, Centre for Policy Studies.

Robinson, Ray (1986) 'Restructuring the welfare state: an analysis of public expenditure, 1979–80–1984–85', *Journal of Social Policy*, vol.15, no.1, pp.1–21.

Taylor-Gooby, Peter and Lakeman, Susan (1988) 'Back to the future: statutory sick pay, citizenship and social class', *Journal of Social Policy*, vol.17, no.1, pp.23–40

Walker, Alan, (ed.) (1982) *Public Expenditure and Social Policy* London, Heinemann.

Weisbrod, Burton and Schlesinger, Mark (1986) 'Public, private non-profit ownership and the response to asymmetric information', in Susan Rose-Ackerman (ed.), *The Economics of Nonprofit Institutions,* Oxford University Press.

Index